William Richard Harris

The Catholic Church in the Niagara Peninsula

1626-1895

William Richard Harris

The Catholic Church in the Niagara Peninsula
1626-1895

ISBN/EAN: 9783743444034

Manufactured in Europe, USA, Canada, Australia, Japa

Cover: Foto ©ninafisch / pixelio.de

Manufactured and distributed by brebook publishing software (www.brebook.com)

William Richard Harris

The Catholic Church in the Niagara Peninsula

THE

CATHOLIC CHURCH

IN THE

NIAGARA PENINSULA

1626-1895.

DEAN HARRIS

ILLUSTRATED.

TORONTO:

WILLIAM BRIGGS,

WESLEY BUILDINGS.

C. W. COATES, Montreal, Que.   S. F. HUESTIS, Halifax, N.S.

MDCCCXCV.

To

Rev. T. J. Sullivan, P.P.

THOROLD,

WHO FOR THIRTY YEARS HAS BORNE THE BURDEN

OF THE PRIESTHOOD

WITH HONOR TO HIMSELF

AND WITH UNTOLD BENEFIT TO OTHERS,

THIS BOOK

IS AFFECTIONATELY DEDICATED.

*"Gather up the fragments that remain, lest they
be lost."*

(John vi. 12.)

*"Gather up the letters of the past, gather up
the traditions, gather up the pamphlets, gather up
the records that are so essential for the fulness
of our Catholic history; and surely the Catholic
people have no reason to be ashamed, but every
reason to be proud, of their glorious traditions."*

(Extract from the address of Governor John Lee, of Maryland,
before the Catholic Historical Society, Philadelphia, March,
1894.)

PREFACE.

I CAN offer no other apology for the publication of the present work than the desire to rescue from oblivion, if not destruction, the valuable records, traditions and manuscripts touching the Catholic history of the Niagara peninsula. In a few years all of the early pioneers will have disappeared, and with them, if they had not been personally interviewed, much that was caught from their lips and committed to these pages. When I first ventured to treat of the early history of this section of our province, I did not realize the serious nature of the contract I had entered upon. The nearest reference library was in Toronto, and I owe it to the good-will and kindness of Mr. Bain, the courteous librarian, that I was able to complete the first five chapters and continue my researches. Again, owing to a pressure of parochial work and frequent interruptions, I could only devote an occasional hour to the task; and it is not without serious misgivings I venture to publish this contribution to the Catholic history of Ontario.

I regard myself as singularly fortunate in being able to collect, from various sources, no inconsiderable amount of materials which have hitherto had no place in history, and which in a few years would have been entirely lost. In gathering the fragments for this volume I have received valuable assistance and encouragement from O. A. Howland, Esq., M.P.P., Toronto; Mr. Frank H. Severance, the historical writer and editor of the Buffalo *Sunday Express*, whose impartiality and honesty in matters affecting the early history of the Catholic Church in Western New York have won for him the respect and gratitude of his Catholic readers; and General John A. Clark, of Auburn, N.Y., whom I regard as the best living authority on Indian topography. I also acknowledge myself deeply indebted to Mr. David Boyle, the archæologist, without whose invaluable aid Chapter V., treating on the archæology of the Neutrals, could not have been written.

It is scarcely necessary for me to add that this volume required in its compilation patient collection and research, and that over five hundred letters were addressed to various parties for information before it could be satisfactorily completed. I offer it as a contribution to the Catholic literature of our country, with the expression of the hope that abler pens than mine will soon be enlisted in this great and meritorious work.

St. Catharines,
May 15th, 1895.

TABLE OF CONTENTS.

CHAPTER IV.

THE JESUITS AND THE NEUTRALS.

CHAPTER V.

THE FLINT WORKERS.

CHAPTER VI.

FATHER HENNEPIN.

Contents.

CHAPTER VII.

THE PRIEST AND THE EXPLORER.

CHAPTER VIII.

LAMBERVILLE AND THE IROQUOIS MISSION.

CHAPTER IX.

FROM THE OLD REGIME TO THE NEW.

CHAPTER X.

PIONEER PRIESTS.

CONTENTS.

CHAPTER XVII.

THE RELIGIOUS COMMUNITIES OF THE PENINSULA.

CHAPTER XVIII.

DEAN MULLIGAN.

APPENDICES.

LIST OF ILLUSTRATIONS.

List of Illustrations.

AUTHORITIES CONSULTED IN THE PREPARATION OF THIS WORK.

Prehistoric Man (2 vols.)	*Wilson.*
Wanderings Around Lake Superior	*Kohl.*
North Americans of Antiquity	*Bradford.*
Ancient Mounds of the Mississippi Valley	*Squier.*
The North Americans of Antiquity	*Short.*
Antiquity of Western New York	*De Witt Clinton.*
Travels in North America	*Lyell.*
Relations des Jesuites (3 vols.)	——
Journal des Jesuites	——
Manuscrits de Nouvelle France (4 vols.)	——
Irish History and Irish Character	*Goldwin Smith.*
The Irishman in Canada	*Davin.*
The Irish Race	*Thebaud.*
Description de la Louisiane	*Hennepin.*
Moeurs des Sauvages (2 vols.)	*Lafitau.*
History of Ireland	*Mitchel.*
History of Ireland	*MacGeoghegan.*
The Irish in America	*Maguire.*
Life of Honorable W. H. Merritt	*Merritt.*
Shipyard of the "Griffon"	*Remington.*
Historical Papers	*O. H. Marshall.*
Memoirs of Bishop Burke	*O'Brien.*
Life of Governor Simcoe	*Read.*
Irish Settlers in America	*McGee.*
Glengarry in Canada—Sketches	*Macdonell.*
Voyages dans l'Amerique, Sept. (2 vols.)	*Hontan.*
Collection of Manuscripts	*Smith.*
Dominion Archives	*Brymner.*
The Country of the Neutrals	*J. H. Coyne.*
Primitive Man in Ontario	*Boyle.*
Ecclesiastical History of Newfoundland	*Howley.*
Ten Years of Upper Canada	*Mrs. Edgar.*

The Catholic Church in the Niagara Peninsula.

CHAPTER I.

THE MOUND BUILDERS AND COPPER WORKERS.

Indian Burial Mound—Relics of a Forgotten People—Primitive Man—The
Mound Builders—Mounds of Ohio—Prehistoric Skill—Copper Axes
and Spear Heads—Giant Skeletons—The Mysterious Copper Plate—
Ancient Mines of Lake Superior—The Copper Workers—Their Tools
and Implements—The Great Ontonagon Copper Block—Mysterious
Records—Fate of the Mound Builders.

"The Western Hemisphere is only now beginning to be historical, yet it
proves to have been the theatre of human life and of many revolutions of
nations to centuries reaching back towards an antiquity as vague as that which
lies behind Europe's historic dawn."—Wilson's "Prehistoric Man."

ON June 10th, 1887, Mr. David Boyle, the Canadian archæologist, opened on the shores of
Lake Erie, near the present town of Port Colborne,
an *ossuary* or Indian burial mound. A number
of skeletons were exposed, and fragments of pottery,
clay and stone pipes, flint arrow heads, stone axes,
gouges and beads of Wampum were found among the
bones. For more than two hundred years these relics

of a once brave and populous nation lay hidden in this huge grave, whose silent eloquence, stronger than words, told the melancholy story of a vanished people. In a hundred more years, in all probability, all—save a few imperishable stone tomahawks—that the earth contains of the great nation of Attiwandarons will have entirely disappeared, returning to its parent dust. Archæologists and students of prehistoric times almost unanimously agree that before the occupation of this continent by the American Indian, another race of men more populous and civilized possessed the land. The great mounds of the Mississippi Valley, Indiana, Northern Ohio and Wisconsin, the carved pipes, the copper and iron weapons, and delicately wrought ornaments found in these mounds, the fortifications constructed on geometric lines indicating a knowledge of mensuration and engineering, point to an order of civilization much in advance of that of the Indian of history.   These mounds and fortifications tell us that long prior to the obliterated forests and the Indians who roamed through them, there existed another people gifted with many of the characteristics belonging to nations of civilized tendencies. "Before the Indian hunter wandered there or the great river valleys were overshadowed with their ancient forests, nations dwelt in those valleys practising arts and rites which involve many germs of civilization." (Wilson's "Prehistoric Man,"-p. 259.) This ancient people constructed levees to hold in check and utilize the waters of the Wabash and Mississippi for the purposes of agriculture and irrigation. The number of mounds left by them surpasses belief. More than ten thousand tumuli and a thousand enclosures have been found in the State of Ohio alone.

After a careful study of these works it is impossible to resist the conviction that the builders possessed considerable knowledge of the science of defence. Their number and magnitude, and the regular lines on which they were constructed, lead up to the conclusion that the builders were a very numerous and powerful people.

The great mound of Cahokia, a truncated pyramid between East St. Louis and Alton, is ninety feet in height, while its squared sides are 700 and 500 feet, respectively. On the south side of this mound was a terrace 150 x 300 feet, approached by a graded way. Its flattened summit was 200 x 450 feet, and in its construction marvellous ingenuity must have been used. This mound could not have been built without a knowledge of the regular scales of measurement and instruments for determining the angles, squares and circles. Furthermore, if the tablet which was found in a mound in Iowa be genuine, and many good authorities claim it to be so, then the Mound Builders must have possessed an alphabet or held intercourse with a people who did.* They also, it would appear, possessed an accurate system of weights, for from the

* "North Americans of Antiquity," p. 38.

arms of a skeleton found in one of their tumuli were taken bracelets of copper of uniform size, weighing precisely four ounces.

Again, take their defensive earthworks, the most extensive of which is probably that at Fort Hill, Ohio. This stronghold is on the summit of a hill five hundred feet above the bed of the river which flows by its sloping defences. The wall measures more than a mile and a half in length and encloses an area of forty-eight acres in extent, covered a few years ago with gigantic trees. One of them measured twenty-one feet and another twenty-three feet in circumference.

Lyell, in his "Travels in North America," writes that eight hundred concentric circles were counted in one of the trees near this mound, and he is of the opinion that more than a thousand years have passed away since these works were constructed.

The authors of the " Ancient Mounds of the Mississippi Valley," who, acting under instructions of the United States Government, made very accurate and elaborate surveys, tell us that the earthworks of this prehistoric people are not only accurate squares and perfect circles, but are, in many cases, of corresponding dimensions, each square being 1,080 feet a side, and the diameter of each of the larger and smaller circles a fraction over 1,700 and 800 feet. They add that this correspondence could not be the result of an accident, but goes to prove that these ancient people possessed a standard of measurement, means of determining angles, instruments, and a knowledge of their use. The most advanced Indian tribes since the discovery of America showed no such intellectual development as that possessed by these people.

"The most skilful engineer of our own day," writes the author of "Prehistoric Man," "would find it difficult, without the aid of instruments, to lay down an accurate square on the scale of some of those described, enclosing an area four-fifths of a mile in circumference." Circles of moderate dimensions might indeed be constructed, so long as it was possible to describe them by a radius, but with such works measuring 5,400 feet or upwards of a mile in circumference, these ancient geometricians must have had instruments and minute means of measuring arcs, for it seems impossible to conceive of the accurate construction of figures on such a scale, otherwise than by finding the angle by its area, from station to station, through the whole course of their delineation. It is no less obvious from the correspondence in area and relative proportions of so many of the regular enlosures, that the Mound Builders possessed a recognized standard of measurement, and that some peculiar significance, possibly of an astronomical origin, was attached to figures of certain forms and dimensions. That they possesse a crude knowledge of military engineering is evident from the remains of their fortifications, walls and ditches, How, for example, shall we account for the existence of their graded ways like unto that at Piketown, Ohio?

Here an avenue had been excavated leading up to a considerable height, terrace after terrace, and having a length of 80 feet and a width of 215. From earth taken from this approach, high embankments were constructed on each side of the ascent, which a few years ago were covered with trees of an enormous size. Further on earthworks were thrown up which, in their construction, point to a knowledge of defensive engineering.

" Clark's works" on the north fork of Point Creek, in the Scioto Valley, embraces in its main defences and uniform rectangular outworks an area of 127 acres. Here the bed of the river was changed to allow the builders freedom to carry out the original design and to admit of the completed circuit of the walls. When, in 1842, excavations were made in these works, valuable remains of ancient art were brought to light, including fragments of carved ivory, many pieces of sculpture, coiled serpents chiselled out of stone and overlaid with sheet mica and copper. Mr. Squier remarks that the amount of labor expended in the construction of this work was immense. The embankment measures three miles in length, and a careful computation shows that, including mounds, not less than three million cubic feet of earth were used in its construction.

On the Little Miami River, Ohio, is a work having a circuit of four or five miles, an embankment twenty feet high and an enclosed area that would give protec-

tion to sixty thousand men. The great mound of
Miamisburg is 68 feet high and 852 feet in circumference, while the Grave Creek Mound of Virginia is
seventy-feet high, and would require a chain one thousand feet to girdle its base.

THE GREAT MOUND, NEAR MIAMISBURG, OHIO.

"We have seen mounds," writes the American
Topographer Flint, " which would require the labor of
a thousand men employed on our canals with all their
mechanical aids and the improved implements of their
labor for months.

" We have more than once hesitated in view of one
of these prodigious mounds, whether it were not really
a natural hill. But they are uniformly so placed, in
reference to the adjacent country, and their conforma-

tion is so unique and similar that no eye hesitates long in referring them to the class of artificial erections."

To this day there are traces of military fortifications left by this ancient people through Central New York, Northern Ohio, and extending into Indiana to the banks of the Wabash. This prehistoric race made *adobe*, or sun-dried brick, mixed with rushes. They wrought in copper, silver and lead, and there are evidences that they even understood the smelting of iron. Copper axes, bosses for ornaments, spear heads, bracelets and rings, with strange characters marked upon them, have been recovered from their mounds.

At Marietta, Ohio, on the Muskingum River, a mound was opened in 1869, and, among other articles uncovered, were large circular ornaments for a sword belt, composed of copper, overlaid with a thick plating of silver. Two or three pieces of copper tubing were also found, filled with iron rust and copper rivets or nails.

Mr. Squier says: "These articles have been critically examined, and it is beyond doubt that the copper bosses were absolutely *plated*, not simply *overlaid*, with silver. Between the copper and the silver exists a connection such as, it seems to me, could only be produced by heat, and if it is admitted that these are genuine relics of the Mound Builders, it must, at the same time, be admitted that they possessed the difficult art of plating one metal upon another. There is but one alternative, viz.: That they had occasional and constant intercourse with a people advanced in the arts, from whom these articles were obtained. Again, if Dr. Hildreth is not mistaken, oxidized iron or steel was also discovered in connection with the above remains, from which also follows the extraordinary conclusion that the Mound Builders were acquainted with the use of iron, the conclusion being, of course, subject to the improbable alternative already mentioned."

From these mounds have been taken squares of matting delicately woven, pieces of double and twisted fibre cloth, mouthpieces and stops for wind instruments, and quaintly and curiously wrought lovers' flutes,* reminding one of Bryant's lines :

> " Till twilight came and lovers walked and wooed
> In a forgotten language ; and old tunes
> From instruments of unremembered forms
> Gave the soft winds a voice."

They plated stone with copper, possessed various mechanical contrivances, were acquainted with the lathe, knew the use of the mould, and excelled in carving.

There is a conflict of opinion among writers on these ancient people as to how far this forgotten race penetrated westward. Mr. Fontaine wrote that the Mound Builders never inhabited either the New England States nor the State of New York. Mr. Squier who,

---

* The " flute " is used principally by the young man whose fancy lightly turns to thoughts of love.—A. C. Fletcher, on " Omaha Indian Songs," p. 425.

for a long time held the opposite opinion, acknowledges that the force of evidence compelled him to alter his conviction that traces of the Mound Builders were evident in the lands of Western New York. Mr. Squier says: "In full view of the facts, I am driven to a conclusion little anticipated when I started upon my trip of exploration, that the earthworks of Western New York were erected by the Iroquois or other western neighbors, and do not possess an antiquity going very far back of the discovery of the country."

Sir Daniel Wilson agrees with Mr. Squier, and writes: " These large earthworks and mounds, essentially dissimilar from the slight structures of the modern Indian, appear to stretch from the upper waters of the Ohio to the westward of Lake Erie, and thence along Lake Michigan nearly to the copper regions of Lake Superior."

DeWitt Clinton, in his " Memoir on the Antiquity of the Western Part of New York," holds the opposite opinion. He writes : " Previous to the occupation of this country by the progenitors of the present race of Indians, it was inhabited by a race of men much more populous and much further advanced in civilization. I have seen several of their fortifications in the western part of this State. There is a large one in the town of Onondaga, one in Pompeii, and one in Malens ; in a word, they are scattered all over the country." From the Niagara River to the Genesee there is a line of these fortifications, and a considerable number of burial mounds, of whose history the Iroquois had no knowledge. Eleven miles east of the present village of Lewiston, on a farm formerly occupied by John Gould, was found a huge ossuary and the remains of an ancient fortification, called by the Tuscarora Indians "Kienka." Nearly in the middle of this fort was a burial mound. When the earth was removed, flags of sandstone were uncovered, and beneath them was a huge pit filled with human bones of both sexes and of all ages. In the position of the skeletons there was none of the signs of ordinary Indian burial. Remains of earthenware, pieces of copper, and instruments of rude workmanship were ploughed up within the area. The ancient works at Fonthill, in Western New York, discovered forty years ago, show a knowledge of defence upon the part of the builders, surpassing that possessed by the American Indian. The skeletons found within the fortified enclosure were those of a race of men one-third larger than the Iroquois or Huron. The giant forest trees that grew upon these works were over five hundred years old, and there were traces that another growth existed before them.

In 1856, Dr. Reynolds, of Brockville, found at the head of the Galops Rapids on the River St. Lawrence, about fifteen feet below the surface, twenty skeletons. "Some of the skeletons," he wrote, "were of gigantic proportion. The lower jaw of one is sufficiently large to surround the corresponding bone of an adult of our generation."

About one and a half miles west of Shelby, in Orleans County, N.Y., is a mound from which were taken skeletons of a giant size, pieces of pottery and earthenware, covered with patterns in relief, wrought with great skill. " This was doubtless a spot," writes the Hon. S. M. Burroughs, " where a great battle had been fought. Were not these people a branch of the Aztecs ? "*

In the year 1809, in one of these ancient fortifications, on the middle branch of Buffalo Creek, three and a half miles from the village of Aurora, was ploughed up a copper plate, twelve inches broad and sixteen inches long. Upon it were engraved characters extending its whole length, which have not yet been deciphered. That its mysterious import will ever be known is scarcely to be expected. The language of the race, like the race itself, is unknown. Like the Palenque hieroglyphics, or those on the walls of the Temple of Philo, at the first cataract of the Nile, it has defied the ingenuity of scholars, and awaits the birth of an American Champollion or a Grotesfeud to unveil its secrets.

In 1847, prospectors of the Minnesota Mining Company discovered an abandoned mine, in which were found ladders, masses of broken rock, tools and implements, proving that the mine had been opened and worked by a race of men who knew the value of copper for decorative, ornamental and other purposes.

* " North Americans of Antiquity, N.Y., 1851."

The American Indian, before the coming of the French, knew nothing of copper, iron, or any other metal than stone. These ancient copper workers had opened mines for over a hundred miles along the southern shore of Lake Superior and on Isle Royale centuries before the Algonquin was driven northward. "At a locality," writes Sir Daniel Wilson, "lying to the east of Keweena Point, in the rich iron district of Marquette, in what appears to have been the ancient bed of the River Carp, and about ten feet above the present level of the channel, various implements and weapons of copper were found. Large trees grow on this deposit also, and the evidences of antiquity seemed not less obvious than in that of Ontonagon. The relics included knives, spear or lance heads, and arrow heads, some of which were ornamented with silver. One of the knives made, with its handle, out of a single piece of copper, measured altogether about seven inches long, of which the blade was nearly two-thirds of the entire length, and of oval shape."

The great Ontonagon block of pure copper found in the Minnesota mine, near Ontonagon River, and now in the Smithsonian Institute, Washington, weighs over six tons, and showed when found numerous marks of the tools of these ancient people. The miners had sunk a trench twenty-six feet deep, detached the copper block from its matrix, and raised it on to a platform eight feet high, which was preserved by the water in which it was standing. The mining tools and implements which were found near its mouth seemed to imply that the miners left the diggings in confusion, and pointed to a sudden attack or a devastating pestilence, like that which nearly exterminated the New England Indians before the landing of the pilgrims. If these people were not of a gigantic size, endowed with a corresponding strength, how was it possible for them to lift this enormous mass of copper into its cradle without machinery? Again, what use did they make of the great quantity of copper taken from the storm-beaten and castellated shores of Lake Superior? They left behind them adzes similar in shape to our own, with bevelled edges, tempered drills, and gravures of copper, the use of which was not even known to the Algonquin.

This mysterious race has left no other records behind it than those found in their mines, fortifications and mounds, and as to what manner of people they were, or where they came from, historians are unable to agree.

> "Yet all these were, when no man did them know,
> Yet have from wisest ages hidden been;
> And later times things more unknown shall show,
> Why then should witless man so much misween
> That nothing is but that which he hath seen?"
>
> —FAERIE QUEEN.

Caleb Atiwater, in his "Archæologia Americana," is of the opinion that they were of Asiatic origin, but admits that this is only a supposition, and Morgan (Peab. Rept. XII., p. 552) holds that they cannot be classed with any known Indian stock. It would appear that this ancient people never crossed into or dwelt on the Niagara Peninsula, for no traces of them have ever been discovered in any part of the land. The Attiwandarons of the Huron-Iroquois stock, or a kindred tribe, were in all probability the first and only race of men that ever occupied the Peninsula before the advent of the European, and save a few flint arrow heads and stone axes recovered at times from their burial mounds, there remains nothing to remind us that even they ever lived. From Niagara to Detroit there is not a stream or river bearing their name, and all that is left of their language are the words preserved in Brebeuf's dictionary. Fifty years after their destruction by the Iroquois, over their corn fields and clearings, over their very graves, there sprang up a luxuriant growth of vine, wood and timber, that obliterated all traces of the slaughtered nation. The earth alone in kindness preserves their memory, and to the student of archæology occasionally delivers up the relics which, for two hundred and fifty years, it has sacredly preserved from decay. Longfellow, in his embodiment of the Algonquin legends, represents Hiawatha lamenting the decay and death of all things, and that great men and their achievements perish and are forgotten.

> "Great men die and are forgotten.
> Wise men speak ; their words of wisdom
> Perish in the ears that hear them ;
> Do not reach the generations

> That as yet unborn are waiting
> In the great mysterious darkness
> Of the speechless day that shall be."

And so the Attiwandarons, the wind-dried and sun-scorched hunters of the Peninsula, await the speechless Day of Judgment when all things shall be made known.

CHAPTER II.

A FORGOTTEN PEOPLE.

The Attiwandarons—Champlain and Sagard—Chaumonot's Map—Origin of
the Neutrals—Their Dress and Habitations—Knowledge of Surgery—
Their Sweat Bath — Their Physical Development — Sorcerers and
Witches—Hospitality of the Neutrals—Burial Customs—The War
Dance—Nation of Fire—Fasting—Harangue of a Neutral Chief—On
the War Path—Attack of the Mascoutins—Fate of Prisoners—The
Torture—War With the Iroquois—Slaughter and Ruin—Flight of the
Neutrals—Destruction of the Tribe—Savage Ferocity—Superstitions.

> " A warrior race, but they are gone,
>   With their old forests, wide and deep,
> And we have built our homes upon
>   Fields where their generations sleep.
> Their rivers slake our thirst at noon,
>   Upon their fields our harvest waves ;
> Our lovers woo beneath their moon—
>   Ah, let us spare, at least, their graves."
>
> —BRYANT.

AT the time that the Jesuit Fathers had established their missions among the Hurons, in
1626, the desolation of forest stretching from their
frontier town to the Niagara river and beyond was
occupied by one of the most powerful and ferocious
tribes of the great Canadian wilderness. To their
Indian countrymen at a distance the members of this
tribe were known as the Attiwandarons, but from the

3

fact that in the continuous wars between the Iroquois and Hurons they took no part, they were called by the French, Neutrals.

As they roamed the forests which covered the land now tilled by us, and were those with whom are associated all the Indian legends and romances woven into the history of Niagara Falls and River, they will ever have a melancholy interest for the immediate dwellers on both sides of the mighty cataract. The historians of our country and of the Indian tribes have only incidentally noticed them. Champlain and Sagard refer to them as a people in their time unvisited by any white man. Father de la Roche Daillon, in 1626, fearlessly plunged into their gloomy forests and passed a trying winter with the tribe, leaving an interesting description of their habits and morals. In 1640 Fathers Brebeuf and Chaumonot—the one to perish nine years after in the fires of the Mohawk and the other to outlive all his companions on the mission —also spent a winter among them, enduring suffering and disappointment so great as to almost stagger faith.*   Father Chaumonot, on his return to the shores of Lake Huron, wrote a graphic description of the people, including a valuable narrative of his experience among them. Brebeuf also wrote the only dictionary of the Neutral language ever compiled.

* For a more extended notice of the Neutrals and the visit of Brebeuf and Chaumonot, see the writer's "History of the Early Missions of Western Canada."

Chaumonot drew a map of the country, which seems to have been lost. This map no doubt was the model for Sanson's chart of 1656 and Ducreux's Latin map of 1660. On Sanson's map the Neutral towns are marked as St. Francis (north-east of Sarnia), St. Michael (east of Sandwich), St. Joseph (County of Kent), and Notre Dame des Anges (on west bank of Grand River, between Brantford and Whiteman's Creek*). Only Chaumonot or Brebeuf could have named and sited these towns, which proves that Sanson and Ducreux copied Chaumonot's map.

This tribe was of the parent stock of the Huron-Iroquois, speaking a Huron dialect and wedded to many of their superstitions and customs. In summer the men went naked. They tattooed their bodies with powdered charcoal and vermilion, and painted on their faces images of beasts, birds, reptiles and fishes. In winter they clothed themselves with skins of bears and other animals, wore moccasins of curried hide, often ornamented with porcupine quills wrought into various shapes and forms. The women were decently clothed, except that in summer they went with bare breasts and naked arms, wearing necklaces of wampum and bead-worked ornaments. The Neutrals lived in bark cabins, with a fire in the centre and an opening in the roof for the smoke to escape. One or two deer or bear skins sewed together served for a door. Here every night during the winter months whole families,

*Letter of General I. A. Clarke.

almost stifled with smoke, huddled together, suffering at times the pinchings of hunger and the alternations of heat and cold.

They possessed a rude knowledge of surgery, and utilized herbs, sassafras roots, and barks of certain trees for medicinal purposes. If in the depths of the forest a Neutral broke his leg or arm, splints of softest material were at once improvised. Branches of uniform length and thickness were cut, which were lined with down-like moss or soft material gathered in a neighboring marsh. If the accident occurred in winter, cedar or hemlock shavings interlaid with fine twigs were used for padding, and, if near a marsh or cedar swale, wild hay was gathered and a cushion made for the wounded limb. Withes of willow osier or young birch bound the splints to the limb. The patient was then placed upon a stretcher of four young saplings, interwoven with cordings of basswood, and carried to his lodge. Here the splints were taken off, the bone examined and reset by some member skilled in bone-setting, and the patient made as comfortable as circumstances permitted. Fractured bones soon united, for the recuperative power of the Neutrals, like that of cognate tribes, was remarkable. The reparative power of the Neutral when injured was only equalled by the stoicism with which he bore the agony of pain and the torture of their rude surgery. They amputated limbs with stone knives, checking the hemorrhages with heated stones, as was the

custom of European surgeons in the days of Ambrose
Pare. Abscesses were cut into with pointed flints.
They were also familiar with the use of warm fomen-
tations, and in every clan of the nation were some
venerable men or women who possessed a knowledge
of medicated decoctions and of the potency of the
extracts of certain herbs found in the forests. If one

A SHAMAN, OR MEDICINE MAN, EXORCISING AN OKI.
(Old Engraving.)

of the tribe suffered from fever or from the effects of
long exposure to cold, a steam bath was readily improvised. A small tent, thrown up for the purpose, was
tightly closed, the patient placed in the centre, a fire
built a short distance from him and stones heated.
On these stones water was poured, till the confined air
was saturated with vapor. Any degree of heat or

moisture was obtained, till the powerful sudatory produced copious sweatings. They were also familiar
with the use of emetics and laxatives, astringents and
emollients. The so-called medicine man, or *Shaman*,
who practised incantations, and was supposed to be in
familiar intercourse with the *okies*, was only called in
when natural remedies failed.

In times of peace the men occupied themselves
chiefly with hunting and fishing. All the menial labor
of the village, the hoeing and planting of corn, in a
word, all servile and outdoor work, was woman's
allotted portion. For a warrior to put his hand to any
kind of work was demeaning, and to assist the women
in their daily labors a degradation. The Neutrals
were physically the finest class of Indians on the
American Continent—tall, straight and well built,
remarkable for their endurance and activity, and free
from deformity. They had no knowledge of God as
we understand the Word, but recognized supernatural
beings, known as manitous or okies, to which they
offered propitiatory sacrifices. They held sorcerers
and witches in detestation, and when a sorcerer was
accused of practising his malign art any member of
the tribe was free to kill him. They put great faith in
dreams, for they believed that their tutelary manitous
took this method of giving directions and warnings
to them. As a result, they were slaves to superstition,
and given over to the grossest and most revolting form
of spiritual debasement. They were a brave and cour-

ageous people, endowed with extraordinary powers of
endurance, and gifted with a discernment of the senses
almost incredible. They held eloquence in high
repute, and frequently chose as their chief the man
who was most endowed with oratorical gifts. Nowhere
were the laws of hospitality more honored. A
stranger was always welcome, the place of honor in
the wigwam allotted him, and while he remained

A NEUTRAL GRAVEYARD.
(*Old Engraving.*)

under their roof he was regarded as one of the family.
A singular custom obtained among the Neutrals from
time immemorial, mention of which we do not find
among any of the other tribes. When one of their
number died, the corpse, if that of a man, was dressed
in his best clothes, his face painted, and the body
exposed at the door of the wigwam. Around him were
placed his weapons, his totem drawn upon his naked

breast, his medicine bag suspended from his neck, and the distinctive symbols which he bore during life attached to his jerkin.   After three days the body was brought into the wigwam and there retained for weeks or months, till the odor of putrefaction became unbearable. His wife and daughters, while the body remained in the cabin, blackened their faces and gave themselves over to grief and lamentation, uttering cries and groans and weeping incessantly. When at length compelled to dispose of the body, they bore it sorrowfully to the scaffold, placed a tobacco pipe in the mouth, and laid his war club and bow and arrows by his side. In a few months they buried the bones, then closed the grave and covered it with large stones, to protect the remains from profanation by wild beasts.

The Neutrals were inveterate gamesters. They played with a kind of dice, and so completely were they the victims of gambling, that the game frequently lasted for whole days and nights amid hideous noise and clamor, the joyful shouts of the winners, and the imprecations of the losers.

One predominant and ruling passion was common to the great Neutral Nation ; and, indeed, it might be said to all the tribes of North America. The Neutral was an inveterate gambler, shamelessly licentious, and devoted to the chase, but when he once took to the war trail all other emotions and feelings became absorbed in the devouring craving for blood. Each member, when able to bear arms, became a warrior, and was privileged to assist at the meetings of the tribe and exercise his right to vote and to be heard in debate. In 1638 the Neutrals declared war on the Mascoutins, or Nation of Fire, a numerous people of Algonquin stock, speaking the same language as the Foxes and Sacs. They dwelt on the southern shore of Lake Michigan, and fortified many of their towns with strong palisades. Before issuing declarations of war, the Neutrals assembled in Council and were harangued by their chiefs. After several had spoken, the tribal orator arose and thus addressed the braves : " The bones of our slain brethren are bleaching on the ground. They cry to us for vengeance, and the cry must be answered. Paint yourselves with the deepest colors ; take up your terror-inspiring arms ; let your war songs and our demands for vengeance gladden the shades of our departed warriors, and cause our foes to tremble. On then ! take captive our enemies, and fight as long as wood grows or water runs. Let the sun and the stars leave the firmament before we quit the field of battle until the victory be gained ! "

A chief experienced in stratagems of war and distinguished for former exploits, was then chosen to command the expedition. That night the warriors assembled in a body, entered upon the Scalp Dance, with movements and gestures suggestive of the coming battle. The neighboring woods re-echoed with their war cries. A white dog was sacrificed to propitiate the demon of slaughter, the inferior chiefs delivered vaunting discourses, dwelt upon the deeds of their ancestors, and their own past and prospective exploits. In the meantime the leader of the band retired to his wigwam, and entered upon a fast of two or three days, to propitiate the military guardian of the tribe, and invoke assistance in the campaign he was about to enter upon. It would be an interesting and perhaps an instructive study to trace the origin of fasting among the American Indians. From the mouth of the Mississippi to the coast of Labrador, fasting was regarded as a religious rite among all the tribes, and was ineradicably associated in their minds with propitiation. Among the Hurons and the Algonquins the custom of fasting twelve and fourteen days before entering upon a hazardous expedition was not rare. The American Indian regarded it as a sacred rite, and believed that the supernal powers were more pleased with this self-inflicted punishment than even with human sacrifices.

When the Neutral chief had finished his fast, he issued from his wigwam, chanted his ominous war song, gathered his braves around him, and struck the trail leading to the land of the Mascoutins. While the path lay through their own country no order was maintained, the warriors being free to scatter during the day in quest of game, returning to the appointed rendezvous as night approached. Once they crossed into the enemy's country an extraordinary change took place. They advanced with caution, spoke in bated breath, and took note of every feature of the country. They scanned the water courses, noticed the elevation of the land, marked every tree, so that in case of defeat they could turn their observation to advantage. Their sense of vision was so developed that they would note marks of a trail of man or animal which would escape the observation of the keenest trapper.* To conceal all traces of their march, the warriors, when necessary, would move in single file, so that to the ordinary observer it would appear as if only one or a few men had passed by the way. They so timed their journey as to reach the neighborhood of the enemy's camp when night had already closed in upon it. In this particular instance, however, the Mascoutins had received notice of their coming, and their fortified village was prepared for the attack. After a siege of ten days, the Neutrals captured the town, and indiscriminately slaughtered men, women and children. They took eight hundred prisoners, whom they dragged back with them to the Neutral villages to be reserved for the torture. "Last summer," writes Father Lallemant, "two thousand warriors of the Neutral Nation attacked a town of the Nation of Fire, well fortified and defended by nine hundred warriors. After a siege of ten days they stormed the palisades, killed many, and took eight hundred prisoners—men, women and children. After burning seventy of the best warriors, they put out the

* See Appendix A, "On Indian Scouts and Trailers."

eyes of the old men, cut away their lips, and then left them to drag out a miserable existence."—" Relations des Hurons," 1644.

The woful fate which awaited the Mascoutins was only too familiar to them from the treatment they themselves had measured out to their Neutral captives in other days. Runners were already sent in advance to notify the Attiwandarons of the success of the campaign, and the number of prisoners the warriors were bringing back with them. When the conquering braves reached their own villages the women, with the old men and children, rushed out to meet them with cries of welcome and rejoicing. The unfortunate prisoners were then portioned out among the Neutral cantons, and the scenes of horror, which for days and nights were witnessed, baffle description. After running the gauntlet, when the prisoners were mercilessly pounded and beaten, they were tied to posts and their torture began. Torches were applied to their quivering bodies, the flesh torn in shreds from their limbs, insulting epithets of cowardice and poltroonery the meanwhile heaped upon them. In many instances the torture was prolonged for days, until at length the unfortunate prisoners sank from sheer exhaustion, or had their heads split open with the murderous tomahawk. It seems inconceivable that men could endure such atrocious torture and continued pain without giving expression to a suffering moan or shriek of despair. Yet, we are assured that the victims, either from pride of spirit or more probably the hope of the glory that would be theirs when they met their friends in the other world, sustained their awful torture without a groan. Nay, more! from the midst of the burning brands they taunted the Neutrals with cowardice, upbraided them with their inability to inflict pain on brave men, and challenged them to multiply their tortures, and see how bravely a Mascoutin could die. Five hundred of the Mascoutins were burned alive, and the remaining two hundred adopted into the tribe to fill the places left vacant by the warriors slaughtered in the war. The Mascoutins were literally wiped out, but their death was soon to be avenged, for the Iroquois were preparing to turn the first sod of the huge grave that was soon to close in forever over the doomed Neutral Nation.

After the slaughter and dispersion of the Hurons of the Georgian Bay region by the Cayugas and Mohawks, a fugitive band of that ill-fated nation fled for shelter to the Neutrals, and received a hospitable welcome. They were allowed to take up their dwellings in the Neutral cantons, hunt in their forests, fish and trap in their streams, and invited to become one people with them.

The Iroquois, for a long time, had been waiting for a pretext to declare war upon the Neutrals, and the hospitality extended to the Hurons was regarded as a sufficient provocation to excite the anger of the Five Nations. In 1650, the Senecas and Mohawks took the war trail and entered the Neutral territory 1,200 strong. They stormed two of their frontier towns, one of which contained a population of 1,600 souls, captured a great number of prisoners, and slaughtered the old people and children. The Neutral warriors retaliated, killing two hundred of the enemy, and putting fifty captives to the torture.*

When the Iroquois learned of the death of their braves they threw 1,500 men into the Neutral country, stormed one of their fortified towns, having a population of two thousand souls, and made it a slaughter-house. In rapid succession they captured village after village, butchered the inhabitants, and recrossed the Niagara River with troops of prisoners reserved for the fire. This campaign led to the ruin of the Neutral Nation.

> " The barriers, which they builded from the soil,
>   To keep the foe at bay—till o'er the walls
>   The wild beleaguers broke, and, one by one,
>   The strongholds of the plain were forced and heaped with corpses."

The inhabitants of the other towns took fright and scattered in all directions. They fled into the woods, and thousands of them perished from starvation and exposure.

* Father Lafiteau states, on the authority of the Jesuit Garnier, that when the Iroquois had destroyed their enemies and were in danger of losing, from want of practice, their warlike dexterity and skill, Shonnonkeritoin, an Onondaga, proposed to the great Chief of the Neutrals that their young men should meet in occasional combats. The Neutral, after much hesitation, at last reluctantly consented. In a skirmish that took place soon after the agreement a nephew of the Iroquois Chief was captured and burned at the stake. The Onondagas, to avenge his death, attacked the Neutrals. The Mohawks and Senecas joined their countrymen and destroyed the Attiwandarons.—"Lafiteau," Vol. II., p. 176., Paris Edition, 1724.

Father Paul Ragueneau, the Superior of the Jesuits, wrote in 1651: "The Iroquois, contrary to our expectations, have not given us (the French) much trouble this year. They turned their arms against the Neutrals, and sent most of their fighting men to the Neutral country. They were everywhere victorious, capturing two of the enemy's frontier towns, in one of which there were 1,600 men. The first village was taken towards the end of August, and the second early in spring. The slaughter of the old people and children, who were too weak to accompany the Iroquois to their own country, was frightful. The number of prisoners, principally young women, whom they saved for their villages, was very great." The destruction was complete, and led to the ruin of the Neutral Nation. The inland and remote towns were struck with panic. People fled from their villages, and whole families left the country, preferring the horrors of retreat and exile to the rage and cruelty of their ruthless conquerors. The unfortunate fugitives were devoured with famine, and separating, wandered through the forests, through marshes, and along the banks of distant streams in search of anything that would stay the devouring pangs of hunger.

So perished the great Neutral Nation, the fierce and weather-tanned Attiwandarons, who dwelt amid forests that once covered the territory now known as the Niagara Peninsula. If they were a savage and, in war, a cruel race of men, it must not be forgotten, when judging them, that they were the creatures of circumstances and of an adverse environment. The Neutral had his affections, and the image of God was not completely destroyed in him. He could not escape the influence of customs, of prejudices founded on his own imperfect knowledge, and controlled by the imperfect knowledge of others. He had a soul, and could not help meditating. False or true, his thoughts would impress a direction on his tendencies. He was the slave of superstition. Custom ruled him remorselessly. Suffering, when it does not excite sympathy, excites the ferocity of man, and as ferocity in a nation of savage warriors is deemed a virtue, the Neutral could not be other than cruel and blood-thirsty to his enemies.

A remarkable instance of savage fierceness is given in Kohl's " Kitchi Gami ": " Once we Ojibbeways set out against the Sioux. We were one hundred. One of ours, a courageous man, a man of the right stamp, impatient for distinction, separated from the others and crept onward into the enemy's country. The man discovered a party of the foe, two men, two women and three children. He crawled round them like a wolf, he crept up to them like a snake, he fell upon them like lightning, cut down the two men and scalped them. The screaming women and children he seized by the arm, and threw them as prisoners to his friends, who had hastened up at his war yell ; and this lightning, this snake, this wolf, this man, my friends, that was—I. I have spoken ! "

Nor should we marvel that a chain of superstitious practices held them in hopeless slavery. We must remember that they were wholly unaccustomed to trace effects to causes except in the most superficial manner. Somewhere in Lafiteau's "Les Moeurs de Sauvages," it is recorded that when the Ottawas wished to bring about the death or calamity of a neighbor, they made a small image of wood representing their victim, and pierced holes with a needle in the region of the head or heart. If the victim really died, they boasted that it was their spells which killed him. A similar process was supposed to cure the sick. They made a dummy, stuffed with straw, to represent the evil spirit which tormented the sick man. They then carried the figure into the lodge of the patient, and shot.arrows into it till it was reduced to tatters. If we reflect for a moment, we will discover that even among ourselves there still lingers much of what even the American savage would regard as childish and absurd. That tying a mutton bone to the bed post, or carrying a chestnut in the pocket, or wearing an iron ring on the third finger of the left hand should cure a man of rheumatism, is a belief which displays the most lofty disregard for cause and effect. That a child's caul should save a sailor from shipwreck; that a sight of a piebald horse should influence the order of events; that setting off on a journey on Friday, spilling salt by accident, or thirteen sitting down to a table should be unlucky; that amulets, "lucky" stones

4

and horse shoes over the door should bring good fortune, and many other superstitions of a like kind which exist among us, prove that civilization and education have not entirely destroyed the childish superstitions of the past. That we live in an age of Christian civilization is a blessing which we owe to our Divine Redeemer, and if mercy, tenderness and compassion be our inheritance, we have reason to be thankful to the "Orient Sun of Justice," who, two thousand years ago, brought to man the message of peace and good-will.*

* The remnant of the Neutrals joined with the Petuns, or Tobacco Nation, the Algonquin League, in 1754 ; those who were not absorbed in the Confederacy drifted into the Hurons, and with them formed what was known as the Wyandots, or Dionondadies. They are mentioned for the last time as a separate people in " Le Journal des Jesuites," p. 183, July, 1653.

CHAPTER III.

A VALIANT PRIEST.

The Missionaries—A Daring Franciscan—The Huron Flotilla—Outward Bound—Forest Scenery—On the Ottawa—The Portage—De la Roche Daillon—Enters the Priesthood—Opposition of Friends—Leaves for New France—With the Hurons—Goes to the Neutrals—The Neutral Chief—The Council—Hospitably Entertained—Huron Liars—From Friendship to Hatred—Alarming Threats—Returns to Huronia—Description of Niagara Peninsula in 1626—Daillon Sails for France—Death of the Franciscan.

> ". . . . He went forth
> Strengthened to suffer—gifted to subdue
> The might of human passion—to pass on
> Quietly to the sacrifice of all
> The lofty hopes of manhood, and to turn
> The high ambition written on his brow
> From the first dream of power and human fame."
>
> —WHITTIER.

ON the 19th of June, 1625, Fathers Charles Lallemant, Enemond Masse, and John Brebeuf, members of the great Jesuit Order, arrived at Quebec ready to devote themselves to the conversion and elevation of the roving hordes that filled the forests of New France, now the Dominion of Canada. Just one year before, members of this extraordinary society had reached the confines of Thibet and the sources of the Ganges. The three priests were now about to establish a mission which was destined to carry the cross from the St. Lawrence to the Mississippi and the Hudson's Bay. With them came Father de la Roche Daillon, a distinguished priest, a member of the Franciscan Order, whose missionaries for ten years labored among the Hurons of the northern region, and followed the shiftless and roving Montagnais to the head waters of the Saguenay and along the northern banks of the St. Lawrence. It was a member of this venerable order who, in 1615, greeted Champlain on the shores of Lake Huron.

When the Jesuit priests arrived at Quebec they were hospitably received by the Franciscan priests, who tendered them the freedom of their monastery and sheltered them for the two years they remained at Quebec awaiting a dwelling-place of their own. "At this epoch," writes Charlevoix, "there was in all Canada but a solitary fort at Quebec, surrounded with a few wretched buildings and bark cabins, two or three huts on the Island of Montreal, a like number at Tadoussac, and a few trading posts along the Lower St. Lawrence. At Three Rivers they were beginning to form a settlement."

In the spring of 1626, Father Daillon, accompanied by the Jesuits, Brebeuf and De la Noue, left Quebec with a Huron flotilla, whose canoes were headed for the Huron hunting grounds in northern forests. The trees on either side of the St. Lawrence were budding into verdant foliage, cakes of ice were still floating on the waters, and the startled deer gazed upon the voyageurs in awe and wonderment. On the afternoon of the 14th of April they entered the dark waters of the Ottawa. The eternal silence of the wilds around them, the rank and luxuriant growth of vine and timber, the giant trees that lined the river on either side, amazed the priests, while the desolation of forests that lay in endless stretches around them excited their wonder and admiration. As the canoes moved into the upper waters of the Ottawa, the river opened at times into spacious lakes, fringed with the primeval forest, and sown with picturesque islands that floated on their placid surface. They portaged the Rideau Rapids and, reaching La Chaudiere, lingered for a time to allow their swarthy companions to offer to the tutelary Manitou of the cataract the propitiatory gifts of tobacco and tobacco smoke. The priests witnessed this idolatrous act with horror, but, powerless to intervene, they observed a discreet silence, "praying to the only and true God," as Father Brebeuf wrote, "to enlighten the minds of these poor savages."

At length they reached the waters of the Matawan, crossed the last of the thirty-five portages, and relaunched their canoes on the calm bosom of Lake Nipissing. Coasting its southern shores, they entered French River, whose pleasant current bore them to the great Lake of the Hurons, or Karegnondi, as it was called by their Indian companions. Skirting its western shore line, they sailed on, and after a weary voyage of seven hundred miles, the Huron flotilla paddled into Matchedash Bay, where, after a few hours, the canoes were beached and the journey was ended.

The priests, after a short rest, began their heroic labors. From the eighteen towns, having a population of thirty or forty thousand souls, they selected two in which to open their missions. At Ihonatiria, Fathers Brebeuf and De la Noue began the Mission of St. Joseph, while Father Daillon went to Caragowha, on the western coast of the Huron peninsula, where he opened the Mission of St. Gabriel. Here he built a bark chapel, in which every morning, clothed in simple vestments, he offered up the Holy Sacrifice on an altar decorated with vines and wild flowers.

Joseph de la Roche Daillon was a man of extraordinary force of character; "as distinguished," wrote Champlain, "for his noble birth and talents as he was remarkable for his humility and piety, who abandoned the honors and glory of the world for the humiliation and poverty of a religious life." Of the aristocratic family of the Du Ludes, society tendered him a courteous welcome, the army and the professions were open to him, wealth, with its corresponding advantages, too, were his, when he startled his friends, shocked society, and grieved his family by declaring his intention of becoming a member of the Order of St. Francis, a religious association of bare-footed beggars. The ranks of the secular clergy offered him the probabilities of a mitre, and the hope of a Cardinal's hat. His family's wealth and position in the State, his father's influence at Court, his own talents, and the prestige of an aristocratic name, all bespoke for him promotion in the Church. His friends in vain pleaded with him to associate himself with the secular priesthood, and when they learned that he was not only inflexible in his resolution to join the Franciscans, but had asked to be sent into the frozen wilds of

WIGWAM.
(Old Engraving.)

Canada, they thought him beside himself. He left France in the full flush of his ripening manhood, and, for the love of perishing souls, entered upon the thorny path that in all probability would lead him to a martyr's grave. He remained at Caragowha for some months, when he received a letter from Father Le Caron, the Superior of the Recollects at Quebec, to set out for the great Neutral tribe or Attiwandarons, whose tribal lands lay between the Hurons and the Iroquois.

In obedience to this request, he left Huronia, October the 18th, 1626, accompanied by two French traders, Grenolle and LeVallée, and struck the trail leading to the nearest village of the Tobacco Nation. Here he was fortunate enough to make a favorable impression on a Petun chief, to whom he made known his desire to visit the great Neutral Nation. The Petun volun-

DAILLON PREACHING TO THE ATTIWANDARONS.
(Old Engraving.)

teered to escort him in person, and as he noticed that he and his two companions were heavily laden, he prevailed upon some of his men to carry the packs and provisions. Towards noon of the sixth day they entered the first village of the Neutrals. After the women and children had satisfied their curiosity gazing upon them, as men fallen from the clouds, they were

invited into a large tent and hospitably entertained.
The Petun chief made known the object of the priest's
visit, and after commending him to their care and
kindly offices, he retraced his path to the Tobacco
towns. "All were astonished," writes Father Daillon,
" to see me dressed as I was, and to see that I desired
nothing of theirs, except that I invited them (by signs)
to lift their eyes to heaven, make the sign of the cross,
and receive the faith of Jesus Christ. What filled
them with wonder was to see me retire at certain hours
in the day to pray to God, and attend to my spiritual
affairs, for they had never seen *religious*, except
towards the Petuneux and Hurons, their neighbors."
Invitations now poured in upon him from the neighboring towns, for the report of his arrival with his companions, their peculiar dress, the devotional practices
of the priest, passed from town to town, and village
to village, until it reached even to the last canton, on
the banks of the Genesee. The sixth village, Ounontisaston,* was a place of considerable importance, and
as Souharissen, the most distinguished chief and
warrior of the Neutrals, dwelt here, the priest deemed
it expedient to establish his headquarters in this town.
After the customary savage civilities and formalities
were exchanged, Daillon expressed a wish to meet
some of the prominent chiefs and warriors. The

* Gilmary Shea, in an article which he wrote for the " Narrative and
Critical History of Canada," Vol. IV., is of the opinion that he took up his
residence in one of the villages on the eastern bank of the Niagara River.

Council met in a large wigwam, and after the members had seated themselves on the ground and lighted their pipes, Daillon opened the Council. He explained that he had come on the part of the French to enter into a friendly alliance with them, that the French had goods to exchange for their peltries and furs, and that it would be for the benefit of all to trade the one with the other. He then begged of them to allow him to remain in their country, that he might instruct them in the laws of the one true and only God, which are the only means of obtaining Paradise. He then advanced and placed before them the gifts and presents, offering collectively to the members of the Council as a unit a bundle of French wares, and separately to each individual a knife or some trifle that was almost worthless to a Frenchman, but esteemed by the Neutrals as of great and precious value. Souharissen, after the priest had finished his address, began his harangue. He was a man of fine personal appearance, of undoubted courage, and of unquestioned superiority over the whole Neutral nation. "This man," writes Father Daillon, " is the chief of the greatest credit and authority that has ever been in all these nations ; for he is not only chief of this village, but of all those of his nation, composed of twenty-eight towns, cities and villages, made like those in the Huron country, and also of several little hamlets of seven or eight cabins, built in various parts convenient for fishing, hunting or agriculture. It is unexampled in other nations to have so absolute a chief. He acquired this honor and power by his courage, and by having been repeatedly at war with seventeen tribes, which are their enemies, and taken heads or brought in prisoners from them all. Those who are so valiant are much esteemed among them, and although they have only the club, bow and arrow, yet they are, nevertheless, very adroit and warlike with these arms." Striding from end to end of the tent, the Neutral warrior first repeated sentence by sentence Daillon's speech, and then, on behalf of his people, expressed the pleasure it gave them to have him among them. He assured him of his protection, and declared from that day the priest should regard him as his father. He then presented the priest with a wampum belt, and dissolved the Council.

Daillon now advised Grenolle and Le Vallée to return to Huronia, and after escorting them some distance on their way, bade them an affectionate farewell, and retraced his steps to the Indian town. He now began the study of their language, endeavoring by signs and the few words he had acquired to instruct them in the truths of religion, seeking, as he says, to advance the glory of God. He acknowledges that at this time he was the happiest man in the world. He went from cabin to cabin on friendly visits, was received with warmth and cordiality, studied their customs and manners, and to the naked, unkempt and gabbling children taught the sign of the Cross. He believed that if he could succeed in establishing a treaty of commerce between the French at Quebec and the Neutrals, it would be much to the advantage of both. He was also satisfied that if he once found the mouth of the Niagara River, the great obstacle to trade would be overcome. He submitted to the chiefs a proposition embracing a voyage to Quebec, and they readily consented to allow four canoes to undertake the voyage if he would accompany them. When the Hurons learned of the priest's intentions, they began to fear that the trade would be diverted from themselves. Runners were at once despatched to the Neutral villages, informing them that Daillon was a dangerous magician, that he had poisoned the air in their country, and as a result many of their best men had died. They warned the Neutrals that he was with them for no good purpose, and if allowed to live would undoubtedly introduce a plague which would sweep away whole villages. The messengers further stated that the French were unapproachably rude, a morose and melancholy people, who devoured snakes and poison as other men eat the flesh of the deer, adding a thousand other absurdities which terrified the Neutrals. It was in vain that the priest stigmatised these calumnies as lies, invented by the Hurons to prevent the Neutrals from trading with the French. The people became paralyzed with fear, and if one of their number fell ill, the relatives threatened Daillon with death unless he cured him. They now subjected him to repeated abuse, and conceived for him a hatred that was fast developing into a murderous intent. In the meantime a rumor reached Fathers Brebeuf and De la Noue that he had been killed, and they at once despatched Grenolle to hasten with all speed and return with the priest if he found him alive. Realizing that for the present he could make no favorable impression on the Neutrals, he bade them good-bye, and returned to the Huron country. This was the first recorded visit of any white man to the Niagara Peninsula. In his letter he expressed himself charmed with the Neutral country, which he pronounced incomparably greater and more beautiful than any he had visited up to that time. He records the incredible number of deer that roamed the forests, the native manner of taking them by driving them into an enclosure, and the superstition which led them to kill every animal of the herd, lest if any should escape alive they would tell the others how they had been taken, so that afterwards the deer would be so cautious and wary that the Indians would not be able to capture them. He speaks admiringly of the large quantities of moose, beaver, wild cats, black squirrels, bustards, turkeys and cranes which he saw. The first fall of snow was on the 22nd of November; on the 26th of January it began to thaw, and on the 8th of March the snow was gone from the open places. Their streams, he tells us, were filled with good fish, and the ground produced corn, pumpkins, beans and other vegetables in abundance. He tells us of the oil he saw oozing from the ground; adverts to the laziness and immorality of the people, who, during the summer, went entirely naked, and closes an interesting letter with an expression of surprise that the Merchants' Company had not already sent some of their men to live in the country. Father Daillon* remained but a short time with the Hurons. He returned to Quebec, and on September 9th, 1629, sailed for France.

One of the Jesuit Fathers (Brebeuf), who was dwelling among the Hurons, having heard that his life was in danger, sent two Frenchmen to bring him back. In "Les Voyages de Champlain," Canadian Edition, Book 2nd, chap. 1, 1625, he is first mentioned as coming over from France in the same ship with Sieur de Caen, that he was an exemplary priest, connected with the family of the Count Du Ludes, and that he abandoned all worldly honors and temporal benefits for things spiritual. He arrived at Quebec, June 19th, 1625. He is again mentioned in " Les Voyages de Champlain " as having accompanied the Jesuit Fathers, De la Noue and Brebeuf, to the Huron country. He is referred to again, and for the last time, by Champlain, in 1629. Champlain was at Quebec, and short of provisions; in fact, the colony was threatened with famine. He says : " I called on Father Joseph

* Very little is known of Father Joseph de la Roche Daillon. He is mentioned in the " Relations of 1641," p. 74. In "Pierre Margry," Vol. I., p. 4, I find the following extract : "One of our fathers was the first to visit the Neutral Nation, a tribe occupying a large extent of country, and hitherto comparatively unknown."

de la Roche, a very good *religious*, to know if I could obtain provisions from the Fathers, if they had any to spare." He replied : " So far as he was concerned, he was ready to give every assistance, that he would at once see Father Joseph Le Caron and speak to him about it." In Noiseux's "Liste Chronologique," the date of his death is given July 16th, 1656.

PORCUPINE.

CHAPTER IV.

THE JESUITS AND THE NEUTRALS.

Chaumonot and Brebeuf—Leave Huronia—Reach the Neutrals—Chaumonot's Letter—Among the Neutrals—Population—Conditions of Neutrality—Dress and Manner of Life of the Neutrals—Hunters of Wild Cats and Bears—Tanning—Stature of the Neutrals—The Dead—Burial of the Dead—Echon—Preaching to the Tribe—Superstition—Courage of the Priests—Good-bye for Ever—A Neutral Woman—Her Affection and Kindness—Homeward-Bound.

FOURTEEN years after the visit of Father Daillon to the Attiwandarons, and his return to France, two Jesuit priests, John de Brebeuf and Joseph Marie Chaumonot, started in the fall of 1640 from the shores of Lake Huron, and after a fatiguing journey of four days reached the first village of the Neutrals. During their stay of five months they visited eighteen towns, and made heroic efforts to instruct the people. They reaped but a harvest of barren regrets, and after a season of disappointments and disheartenings they bade good-bye to the Neutrals and retraced their path to the Huron villages. It was good-bye forever, for in less than ten years the Iroquois had burned Brebeuf at the stake, driven Chaumonot with a handful of Huron converts to the ramparts of Quebec, and swept out of existence the Neutral Nation. So awful and complete was their annihilation, that a few burial mounds and the name of their great river* are all that is left of this once brave and numerous people. On the return of the priests to their headquarters, near Penetanguishene, they wrote a very interesting and graphic account of their experiences with the tribe. This remarkable letter we now publish for the first time in the English language, and as it deals with an unknown and forgotten race of savages, who once peopled the land now tilled by our farmers, and dotted with our towns and villages, it will have, especially for the people of this Peninsula and Western New York, a fascinating interest. It was probably written by Father Chaumonot and signed by Father L'Alemant, the acting Superior of the Huron Missions.

"From 'Relations des Jesuites'
(Vol. I., Year 1641).

"*An account of what happened at the Mission of the Angels among the Attiwandarons or the Neutral Nation. Addressed to the Reverend Father James Dinet, Provincial of the Society of Jesus in the Province of France.*

"My Reverend Father:

"Christ's peace be with you.

"This is the new mission that we have begun this year in one of the most numerous nations of this country. It is a long time since this land was visited,

---

*Parkman is of the opinion that the word is of Iroquois origin, but as the river flowed through the lands of the Neutrals, and their town, Onghiarra, was near its banks, it is more probably of Neutral origin.

according to the testimony of many people. But many acquainted with strange languages are not easily found, if the Holy Ghost does not give extraordinary grace, particularly when one is deprived of the assistance of masters, teachers, and interpreters to instruct them, as we are in this locality.

"Moreover, it is not customary to go to the extreme end without passing the centre, or engage in the work of civilizing the farthest nation before having attended to the nearest. This having been done, we found ourselves able at the opening of fall to devote two laborers to this mission without doing any injustice to those now in our care. The lot fell upon Father John de Brebeuf, who first introduced and established us in this country, God having endowed him with a special grace and gift for languages. It would seem that when it is a question of becoming acquainted with a strange people differing somewhat in language, he is always chosen for the work. It is our intention, if it be pleasing to God, to build in this new country a permanent residence, such as we have here, which will also serve as a house of retreat for missionaries.

"His companion was Father Joseph Marie Chaumonot, who came from France last year, and who has a natural gift for languages.

"This nation is very populous, settled in about forty towns. The first and nearest town to the Hurons is about four or five days' journey; that is to say, about one hundred and twenty miles, keeping straight south. According to the last and most accurate observation that we could make, if our new house of St. Mary's, which is in the centre of the Huron country, is in north latitude 44 degrees and 25 minutes, then the beginning of the Neutral territory from the dividing line of the Hurons would have an elevation of $42\frac{1}{2}$ degrees. It is impossible for us to think of making a more exact survey or observation in the country for the present, as the sight of an instrument is all that would be necessary to carry to extremes those who

A NEUTRAL CAMP.

cannot look upon an ink bottle without emotions of awe and fear.

" The first town of the Neutral Nation at which we arrived, following the road south or south-east, is about four days' journey from the mouth of the celebrated river of this nation which empties into Ontario or Lake St. Louis. On the west side of the river, and not on the east, as marked on some charts, are most of the towns of the Neutral Nation. There are three or four villages on the other side running from east to west towards the Raccoon Nation, or Eries.

" Into their river the great lake of the Hurons discharges itself, flowing first into Lake Erie, or Lake of the Raccoon Nation, and then through the Neutral country, taking the name of Onguiaahra ; thence it flows into Ontario or Lake St. Louis, and finally into the river which passes Quebec, known as the St. Lawrence. If our people (the French) were masters of the shores of the lake nearest the Iroquois country, we could ascend the St. Lawrence without danger, reach the Neutral Nation, and go even farther.

" It is the opinion of the Fathers who have been there, that there are at least twelve thousand souls in this country. They can call out four thousand warriors, notwithstanding the wars, famine and pestilence which for the past three years have desolated them.

" But I am of the opinion that those who claimed for this nation an incredible number of souls and an importance out of all proportion to their merits, included with the Neutrals all the other nations which are south and south-west of our Hurons, but who in the beginning were scarcely known, and thus became associated with their name. The knowledge which we have obtained, since those early days, both of the language and the country, has furnished us more accurate information. Moreover, of the different nations with which we are now acquainted, there is not one among them that does not trade with others at a distance. This convinces us that there is yet a great multitude of people to be visited, and before we can reap an abundant harvest, there are yet mighty fields to sow and till.

"Our French, who were the first to visit the country, called this people the Neutral Nation, and for a good reason; for through their forests overland is the ordinary route by which the Iroquois and Hurons, sworn enemies, pass and repass, and with whom the Neutrals are at peace. Sometimes the Hurons and Iroquois met each other in the same town, and even in the same cabin, but they gave pledges that they would not violate the peace; but, of late, the hatred of one against the other is so great, that no matter where they meet there is no security for the weaker party, particularly if he be a Huron, for whose people the Neutrals seem at present to have little love.

"Our Hurons call the Neutral Nation Attiwandarons, meaning people with a slightly different language. They call the people who speak a tongue which they do not understand Akona Ake, meaning a strange nation. Those of the Neutral Nation also call the Hurons Attiwandarons.

"We have every reason to believe that it is not long since they all—Hurons, Iroquois and Neutrals—were one people; that they descended from the same family or from some primitive stock dwelling in these lands; but that in the course of time they became separated from each other, influenced more or less by localities, self-interest and choice; so that some have become enemies, others Neutrals, and some brought into relations of friendship.

"This nation, which remains neutral in the wars between the Hurons and Iroquois, enters upon cruel campaigns with some western tribes, and particularly with the Atsistaehronons, or Nation of Fire, of whom last year they took one hundred prisoners, and having this year renewed the war, they have captured already more than seventy, whom they treated with the same cruelty as the Hurons do their enemies. At times, when the number of prisoners is very great, they burn the captive women as well as the warriors, which the Hurons do not; for, instead of putting the women to the torture, they are satisfied with slightly mutilating them.

" The clothing and manner of life of this people seem little different from the Hurons. They possess Indian corn, beans and citrons in equal abundance. The fishing here is as good as with us, certain kinds being found in one place that are not found in another.

" These people are very expert in hunting deer, moose, wild cats, wolves, bears and other animals, the hide and fur of which are very valuable. Flesh meat is plentiful this year, for the great quantity of snow which has fallen helped the hunters in the chase. Rarely does snow fall in this country deeper than one foot and a half, but this year there has been three feet. In the fields and woods are to be found many flocks of wild turkeys.

" The crab apples are larger and chestnuts more plentiful than among the Hurons; other fruit is about the same in quantity and quality.

" They go about in winter covered with skins, like all savages, but with less regard for decency than the Hurons. Many of them, indeed, observe very little modesty in their apparel; however, the women are always covered at least from the waist to the knees. They seem to be more shameless in their lasciviousness than the Hurons.

" They tan skins with much care and labor, and study to adorn them in different ways, but still more so their own bodies, on which from head to foot they make all sorts of figures with burnt charcoal picked into the flesh. Formerly they traced their descent on their bodies, so that sometimes from the face to the abdomen they were completely tattooed.

" In their customs and manners they are very much like all other savages of this land, particularly in their superstitions and forms of government, whether political or economical.

"But they differ in some other respects from our Hurons. They appear larger, stronger, and better formed than our people. Again, their affection for the dead seems to be greater. The Hurons, immediately after death, carry the body to the cemetery, and do not return again except for the Feast of the Dead. The Neutrals do not take their dead bodies to the cemetery until putrefaction renders them insupportable ; hence it happens that the bodies remain sometimes the whole winter in the cabin ; and having been put outside on a scaffold, they then collect the bones, after the flesh has rotted away, and expose them, arranged side by side in their cabins, until the Feast of the Dead. Their reason for preserving the bones in their cabins is to continually remind them of their dead. At least they so state. At intervals during the day the women in a plaintive chant utter doleful lamentations, and give expression to their grief in sorrowful accents. Unlike the Hurons, they tolerate a great number of pretended fools or maniacs, whose antics are grotesque. Everywhere are to be met with these impostors, who are permitted every license, lest their protecting okies should take offence. They throw and scatter the coals of the hearths, tear and break whatever they meet as if they were mad, when, in fact, most of them are as much masters of themselves as people in their proper senses They act in this manner to please their okies, who, they claim, exact these performances from them, speaking to them in dreams, promising them success in the hunt and the fulfilment of their desires.

"The Fathers learned that the Senecas, one of the Five Nations of the Iroquois, have a different mode of government. Men and women conduct affairs alternately, so that it is now a man who governs them, but after his death it will be a woman, who, during her life, will rule in all things excepting what relates to

A SCENE IN A NEUTRAL FOREST.

war; and after the death of the woman a man will again assume the direction of affairs.

" Some old people told our Fathers that they knew of a certain western nation with whom the Neutrals were often at war, who lived not far from the sea; that the inhabitants of the place fished for large shell-fish—a species of oyster, from the shell of which are manufactured the pearls of this country. Here is how they describe their mode of fishing:

" When the sea rises they wait near the places where these shell-fish abound, and when the violence of the waves throws them towards land, they jump into the water and seize all they can carry. They sometimes find them so large that it is all they can do to hold one. Many assert that only the young men who are virgins can capture this fish, and if they be not so the fish disappear. I vouch not for the truth of this. They state that these same people hunt certain aquatic animals, larger and quicker than the deer. The young braves enter the water to tempt this animal to follow them on to dry land, and when the pursuit becomes dangerous, the young men turn and throw down pieces of leather, old moccasins and the like, which, exciting the curiosity of the beast, detain and amuse it till the hunter gains time. This device is repeated every time the monster gains on them, till they arrive at a place where a number of hunters are in hiding, who rush out and finally destroy it. We have been told these stories of this strange land.*

" French traders have before now visited the country of the Neutrals, but we have not heard of any other priest than Rev. Father de la Roche Daillon, Recollect, who preached the Gospel and passed the winter of 1626 among them. The French who were in the Neutral land at the time of his visit returned, having heard that some of their companions in the remote places were roughly handled.

---

* Evidently this alludes to the alligators of the Mississippi.

" The above mentioned Father, who undertook this great journey, soon after his arrival among the Hurons, was not acquainted with their language, and, being without an interpreter, he endeavored to instruct those around him more by signs than by voice, as he himself related in one of his own printed letters. This ignorance of their language, joined to the lies which the Hurons, who feared to lose the profits of the trade they carried on with this people, circulated about him, prevented the Father from doing as much for the service of God as he desired.

" Fourteen years after his return, two Fathers of our society, who had charge of a Huron Mission, left St. Mary's November 2nd, 1640. When they arrived at St. Joseph's, or Tean Austajae, the last town of the Hurons, where they were to obtain provision for the journey and meet the guines, they learned that those who had promised to accompany them failed to keep their word, so they had no other alternative than to address themselves to heaven. After praying, Father Brebeuf met a young man, who had no intention of making this journey. I do not know why the Father addressed himself to him, but he simply said : ' Come with us and be our companion.' This young man, without hesitating, followed them, and remained their faithful companion. Two of our Frenchmen went with them on their journey to assist them, and trade as merchants in the country, for, without this excuse, the doors of the cabins would have been closed against them, as, in fact, they afterwards were. They slept four nights in the woods, and on the fifth day arrived at the first town of the Neutral Nation, called Kandoucho, which they christened ' All Saints.'

" As they knew something of the ill-will of these people, whose minds were poisoned with the lies and calumnies circulated among them in other days, they deemed it prudent to wait upon the chiefs and elders of the tribe, present their offerings, and make known their intentions. For this reason, it was necessary to wait upon the chief who conducted public affairs, and who was called Tsohahissen. His town was in the middle of the country. To arrive there it was necessary to pass through other towns and villages, the doors of whose cabins were closed against the Fathers by reason of the fear which filled the people.

GRAND COUNCIL OF NEUTRALS.
(Old Engraving.)

"The name Echon, which is the Indian name of Father Brebeuf, was known everywhere as that of one of the most famous sorcerers or demons of whom they had ever heard. The hope of a prosperous trade, however, at times pacified them, and it was owing to this expectation that the Fathers were hospitably entertained at the village of the principal chief, where they were compelled to wait until spring for the return of the warrior who was on the war-path.

"Our Fathers spoke to those who conducted affairs

during his absence; made known to them their desire to preach the Gospel in the country, and for this purpose wished to contract an alliance with them. In proof of the sincerity of their statement, they offered a wampum belt of 2,000 grains. The principal men, after consulting together, replied that they could not accept the gift before the return of their chief, for, according to their custom, they would be compelled to offer gifts in return; but, if we wished to wait until then, we were at liberty to do so, and give such instructions as we wished. Nothing, it would appear, could happen more opportunely, for it gave the missionaries time to converse with the older heads, and to soften the more angry spirits. But, before they began to preach, the Fathers deemed it prudent to retrace their path and escort their attendants out of the country, then return and begin their duties, which they did. But now that there was no longer a hope of barter, the Fathers were subjected to a renewal of the calumnies which had confronted them on their arrival.

"The Hurons had already told these people that before Echon entered their country he publicly thus expressed himself: 'I will remain so many years, during which time I will cause the death of many, and then I will go elsewhere until I have brought about the destruction of the whole nation.' Others again said that after Echon had communicated a mortal disease to some of the Hurons, he left to make an alliance with the Senecas, one of the Iroquois tribes, sworn enemies of the Hurons, who dwelt but a day's march eastward from the Neutral town, Onguiaahra, which is also the name of the river. He said that when he met them he would make them presents of wampum belts and arrows, and induce them to come and effect the ruin of this country.

"Others were continually dinging into our ears that we should be on our guard, lest we be massacred, as was one of our Frenchmen who had undertaken a similar voyage, excited their jealousy and aroused a fear of losing trade. Others, again, said that when they had buried an excellent Christian named Joseph Chivuatenhua, Echon turned towards the country of the Senecas, who had killed him, and exclaimed aloud: ' Senecas, it is all over with ye, ye are dead men,' and soon after the Fathers faced towards their country and introduced disease which, in effect, was raging among them (the Senecas) during the stay of the missionaries in the Neutral Nation.

" I am sure that from the day of the departure of the Fathers for the Neutral country until their return, not a week passed that the Neutrals did not report their death. Yet I am of the opinion that, very often, these rumors were circulated by our own pagan Hurons, who, suspecting that some of their own friends might have killed the Fathers, wished to make strangers responsible for the deed.

" Be that as it may, it is certain that a Huron named Aouenhokoui, nephew of one of our principal chiefs, went in company with another through several towns of the Neutral Nation when our Fathers were there, saying they were sent by their chiefs and elders with presents of axes, to warn the warriors to be on their guard and watch the French if they did not wish the ruin of their country; and, above all, to have nothing to do with our gifts. And these messengers of evil suggested that, in case the Neutrals refused to strike the blow, the Hurons had resolved to destroy the two upon their return; adding, that the design would already have been executed, only that all the Fathers were living together in the same house.

" This man, Aouenhokoui, having arrived on the same day with the missionaries at one of the villages, bestowed a thousand endearing caresses on them, inviting them at the same time to accompany him still further into the country; but they, having other matters to attend to, left him to proceed alone. Afterwards, having heard of certain of his speeches and propositions, they took counsel with some of the members of the tribe, and asked what could have been the motive of Aouenhokoui in so strongly urging them to accompany him. The answer portended no good. This man, although the most dangerous, was by no means the boldest, for another, named Oentara, filled the ears of the people with lies and calumnies. He said that we harbored disease at our house, that our writings were symbols of sorcery, that we brought death to almost everyone in the Huron country, and that we had resolved to destroy all that still remained. He advised them, furthermore, to close the doors of their lodges against us, if they would prevent desolation coming upon the nation. He was even bold enough to make his charges against the Fathers in their very presence, and in the hearing of the elders of the country. However, though Father Brebeuf effectually refuted all his lies, the poison which was injected into the hearts of these poor savages was not easily neutralized, and they still held in mortal dread one whose name was so ominous of evil. Other Hurons, who arrived about this time, confirmed what had been said against us, and awakened much suspicion in the minds of the chiefs and leading men of the tribe.

"Now, although those very men refused to hold a consultation with us in the beginning, stating that they had no authority to act till Tsohahissen, their head chief, returned, they now, after two months and a half, declared that they had the authority to act and to decide pressing affairs in the absence of Tsohahissen; adding that they considered our business of such an important nature as to call for immediate action.

"Having come to this conclusion, one of them waited on the Fathers to communicate the result of their deliberations, which was that they refused to exchange presents. The Fathers replied that the exchange of gifts was not the only motive which induced them to visit the country; that their principal object was to bear to them a knowledge of God and

His Son, Jesus Christ our Saviour, and they now
wished to know if the people refused to hear their
instructions since the chiefs refused to receive their
gifts. The Chief replied that they had nothing to say
against the faith which was preached, having found in
it nothing but what was good; nevertheless, they could
not accept any gift from them. Though the Fathers
were pleased with this reply, as it conceded the principle for which they were contending—that is, liberty
to preach and proclaim the Gospel throughout the
land—they deemed it wise, however, to enquire the
reasons for refusing the gifts, saying that they had a
duty to discharge and an account to render to those
who sent them. At first, the Chief replied that the
people were poor, and were not able to make suitable
returns for our gifts. The Fathers made answer that
if that was their only difficulty, they need not refuse
the presents, for they would not expect or ask for any
return of the same nature, and that, if they accepted
them as brothers, it would be sufficient. He persisted
in his refusal, however, adding trivial excuses; till, at
length, the Sachem of the Council appeared and exclaimed : ' Hear me, ye black robes. Are your ears
deaf to what Aouenhakoui stated when he came here
to warn us, or are you blind to your own danger and
the consequences of your stay in our country ? '

" Father Brebeuf attempted to reply, but he turned
a deaf ear to him, and the Fathers were compelled to
retire. The result of the meeting, however, did not
induce the Fathers to leave the country. They decided to remain, satisfied that if in the past they had
to endure insults and sufferings, they would now have
to suffer more in the future. In fact, in more than
one town which they visited, they were met on every
side with contumely. ' Look ! ' they shouted out, .
' the Agona (this was the name they applied to their
most hated enemies) are coming ; fasten your doors.'
So that when the Fathers stood before the doors of
the wigwams they were confronted with determined

opposition by those who looked upon them as sorcerers, scattering death and disease around. If sometimes there was found one who received them, he was moved to act more through fear of refusal than by reasons of hospitality.

"It is hard to credit the tremendous effect produced upon these poor savages by the stories of the Hurons. The report circulated among them of our great power for evil wrought upon their naturally defiant and courageous spirits a fearful and withering effect. The very appearance of the Fathers, their movements and dress—so different from their own—their manner of walking, their gestures, and, in fact, their every action, seemed to be a confirmation of the ominous tidings borne to their ears. The breviaries, ink-horns and materials for writing were regarded as instruments of magic, and their very posture, when on their knees praying to God, was associated with the practice of sorcery. When they went to the stream to wash their plates, they were said to be poisoning the waters. It was reported of them that whenever they visited a lodge, the children began to bleed and were seized with a fit of coughing, and the women struck with barrenness. In fact, there was no misfortune so great for the present and the future of which they were not considered to be the cause. At some of the cabins where the Fathers lodged the inmates slept neither night nor day, refused their presents as things malign, and skulked in the farthest ends of the tents. The good wives already looked upon themselves as lost, and mourned for their little ones, who would not live to people the earth.

"The chiefs hinted to the Fathers that the Senecas were coming, and would soon arrive in their country; others stated the reason for which they refused to accept our presents was that they could not give us any assurance of safety while we remained in the country.

"The insolence and tyranny of some of those who

received us were almost unbearable. They ordered us around as slaves, insisting on immediate obedience. Sometimes we had nothing to eat, and at other times they forced us to visit their relatives, eat what was put before us, and pay whatever they demanded. In short, they began to speak of killing and eating us.

"The pretended maniacs ran wildly from cabin to cabin. On one occasion three of them, as naked as one's hand, entered the lodge where we were, and after performing a series of foolish antics, disappeared. On another occasion some of them rushed in, and seating themselves beside us, began to examine our bags, and after having taken away some of our property they retired, still conducting themselves as fools. In short, we could only compare ourselves to a football, with which the demons enjoyed themselves in this barbarous country; still, Divine Providence watched over us so that we needed nothing for our support, and aided us to bear affronts and injuries more easily imagined than described.

"The Fathers, during their stay in the country, visited eighteen towns, to each of which they gave a Christian name, by which they could, in the future, if the occasion arose, recognize them. They stayed for a considerable time at ten of the villages, where they gave instruction to as many as would listen to them. They counted in these ten villages five hundred fires and three thousand souls, and it will be strange if the sound of the Gospel which they preached there be not heard throughout the whole land. In our calculations we have only taken into account these three thousand souls. At last the Fathers, seeing that the people were not disposed to receive their teachings, and finding that the terror and confusion of the people increased with time, deemed it wise to retrace their path and return to the village of Kandoucha, or that of All Saints, where they were in the beginning more graciously received, and there, awaiting the opening of spring, instruct its inhabitants. God, however, disposed otherwise ; for, having arrived at Teotongniaton, or St. Williams, midway on their route, a great quantity of snow fell, preventing them from continuing their journey. This misfortune, if it may be so called, was for them the greatest blessing and consolation they had experienced since they left home, for, being unable to remain anywhere in peace and quietness, even for the purpose of studying the language of the country, they now found themselves lodged with a hostess who made it a special object to make their stay here as pleasant as others made it unhappy. She welcomed them to her lodge, and, seeing they did not eat. meat, it being the season of Lent, she took particular care to make a special dish for them, seasoned with fish, and much better than that which she served to her own family.

" It was for her a special delight to instruct them in the language, dictating the words, syllable by syllable, as a teacher would to a scholar, and relating to them narratives and stories touching her people. Moved by her example, her little children, who at first were seized with terror and fled away, now rendered them a thousand friendly attentions, and vied with each other in showing kindness to them. Nay! more. While all the other people of the town implored her to send away the Fathers, reminding her of all the misfortunes and dangers associated with them, she laughed at their fears, and persistently refuted their calumnies, saying, that they themselves were imposed upon by the lies told them by others.

" When some of them warned her of the destruction and death that would surely overtake her upon the departure of the Fathers, she replied that it was a common thing for people to die, and that she awaited the consequences with indifference ; saying, at the same time, that they themselves were sorcerers who wished her death and that of her children ; adding, moreover, that she would rather expose herself and her family to death than to send the Fathers away at this season, when they would surely perish from cold and exposure.

Not only had she to contend against those of the villages, but she was even annoyed with one or two in her own lodge who, among other things, said that her own father had been a sorcerer, and that consequently it was not to be wondered at that she consorted with sorcerers. This charge, however, had no more effect on her than the others. Even her little children quarrelled with their playmates, going to the extent of fighting in defence of the Fathers.

"It is, indeed, surprising that this good woman remained indifferent to her persecutors, and continued her care for and her hospitality towards the Fathers, even to the day of their departure. Their only regret in leaving was that her disposition towards the Faith was not sufficient to warrant them in baptizing her. They, however, hope that the prayers of those who now hear of her hospitality will obtain for her the blessing of conversion.

"The greatest cause of sorrow to this poor woman was that she could not always prevent the insults which were offered to them. A pretended maniac threw himself on Father Chaumonot, tore his cassock and shouted out that the priest ought to be burned, and, night after night, he kept up such a continuous noise, that the Fathers could not sleep. Others entered the cabin, and in her presence took from the Fathers their articles of devotion, and even threatened to burn the missionaries, which threat, perhaps, if their good angel had not intervened, would have been carried out. At length, the father of this good woman interfered, approving of all things she had done for them, testifying a particular affection, and promising to visit them at their own house in the Huron country. May our Divine Lord guide his footsteps.

"It was, without doubt, a special providence of God which protected them in this village ; for, during the twenty-five days which they remained there, they

6

added to their Huron dictionary the idioms of this people, a work which well repaid them for their long voyage.* The savages receive with more kindness those who speak their own language, and regard those who do not as aliens and foreigners. Amid all the vicissitudes and misfortunes which the Fathers experienced during their stay in the country, they did not neglect the infants, the old people nor the sick, to whom they gave the consolations of religion.

"Among all the villages which they visited, there was only one, Khioetoa, named by them St. Michaels, where they were received with any show of courtesy becoming their mission. In this town there dwelt a number of refugees belonging to a strange nation, named Auenrehronon, that lived on the shores of Lake Erie, near the Raccoon Nation, who fled here from their enemies, and were directed, as if by Providence, to this town to listen to the teachings of the Fathers. They were fairly well instructed by the missionaries, who, however, did not deem it opportune to baptize them. The Holy Ghost will fructify the seed which has been sown in their hearts.

"I remain, your very humble and obedient servant in our Saviour,

"H. L'ALEMANT.

"From our residence at St. Mary's of the Hurons, May 19th, 1641.

---

* See Appendix B. on "The Jesuit Stone," found here in 1869.

CHAPTER V.

THE FLINT WORKERS.

Neutral Remains—The Beothics—The Andastes—The Tobacco Nation—
The Five Nations—Wars of the Neutrals—Population—Hunters of
the Moose—Flint Workers—Wood and Bone Carvers—Neutral Wigwams—Building of the " Long House "—Mechanical Skill—Weaving
and Mat-making—Tanning—Tally Bones—Beginnings of Literature—
Wampum Belts—Clay Pipes—The Shamans.

> " Ye say their cone-like cabins,
>   That clustered o'er the vale,
> Have fled away like withered leaves
>   Before the autumn gale ;
> But their memory liveth on your hills,
>   Their baptism on your shore ;
> Your everlasting rivers speak
>   Their dialect of yore."
>   —MRS. SIGOURNEY.

IN contemplating the history of our race, there is
no sadder, no more pathetic thought than that
so many nations and peoples have been " improved
off the face of the earth," if one may use an expressive
though utterly feelingless modern phrase. On this
continent alone there have been numerous examples
of tribal extermination during its brief historic period:
The Beothics, of Newfoundland ; the Andastes, of the
Susquehanna ; the Hurons, of the Georgian Bay ; the

Mascoutins, of Michigan; the Attiwandarons, of Southern Ontario; and the Eries, of Northern Ohio, have all disappeared. For this state of things European influence is scarcely at all responsible, unless in the case of the Beothics—those abnormally guileless savages who, as common game, were ruthlessly hunted down by the British and French settlers and the Micmac Indians. The Newfoundland Indian never knew the white man but as a murderer, and when he could he retaliated.

ATTIWANDARON CARVED STONE HEAD.
Probably worn as a Neck Pendant.

Internecine war was wholly accountable for the extirpation of all the other tribes, except in so far as disease may have had a share in carrying off the unfortunate Andastes.

It is not at all improbable that the presence of the white man, by attracting no small proportion of attention, actually tended to retard the mutually vengeful and destructive tendencies of the natives. Until very recently the Five Nations have been regarded as the parent stock from which the Hurons, Neutrals, Eries, Andastes, Tuscaroras, and some smaller tribes or clans,

were offshoots.   Linguistic study, coming to the aid
of tradition, now makes it abundantly evident that
the Huron Nation was the oldest member of the stock
which is now known ethnologically as the Huron-
Iroquoian; and that, of the clans forming the Huron
confederacy, the Tionnontates, or Tobaccos, claimed
seniority.   Dr. Horatio Hale, in a recent paper,
refers to the traditional ancestral abode of these
people on the shore of the Gulf of St. Lawrence,
previous to the misunderstanding and consequent
bloodshed that led to separation and eternal hate.
Following the south shore of Lake Ontario, after
ascending the St. Lawrence or River of the Iroquois,
the main body of the migrants, afterwards known as
the Hurons, or Wyandots, reached the Niagara peninsula.   Having remained here for a period, they
eventually rounded the western end of the lake, and
in course of time took permanent possession of all the
country lying south of the Georgian Bay; there, after
a while, they were joined by the Tionnontates, who
had pursued their journey up the Ottawa.   In this
tradition there is nothing to account for the presence
of the Attiwandarons on the north shore, or of
the Cats* on the south shore, of Lake Erie.   And

* General John S. Clark, of Auburn, N.Y., than whom perhaps there is no
better authority on Iroquois ethnology, in answer to a letter of the author,
writes as follows: "The scholars of the country have for two hundred years
persisted in calling the Eries, ' Wild Cats.'   The *chat sauvage* of Canada is the
well-known raccoon, called by the Onondagas *tchou-e-a-gak*, hence the name
Era or Erie.   The real wild cat was, and is, called, '*jego-sasa*.'   The raccoon
was abundant in the country of the Eries, and they used the skins for clothing."
Sagard gives the name of "*chat sauvage* as ' *Tiron* ' (Raccoon), which in Mohawk
s called at the present day, *A-tiron*."

yet it appears certain that they, too, came from the old home below Quebec. We are left to conjecture, therefore, as to whether the Attiwandarons reached the country chosen as their own before or after the great Huron migration. What seems to favor the former supposition is that, during the chronic condition of war that subsequently existed between the Five Nations and the Hurons, they stood aloof. As confirmatory of the belief that they were of a more recent removal from the east, it may be urged that some of their practices corresponded more closely to those of the Five Nations than to those of the Hurons, and that their neutrality was chiefly the result of the peculiarly advantageous position they held between the contending parties. It is not, however, impossible that they actually formed a part of the great secession, and chose to remain in the south country, while their kindred moved farther north. In point of numbers they may have felt themselves able to cope with the Five Nations if followed by them, and in after years, when the latter were on their way westward, it may have been thought expedient to come to some arrangement with the Attiwandarons which would leave the Iroquois free to carry on their feud with the offending Hurons; or the Attiwandarons themselves may have been sufficiently powerful to defy the Iroquois, who henceforth proceeded to wreak their vengeance on the weaker people.

However this may have been, we are warranted in

accepting: first, that the Attiwandarons were of Huron-Iroquois blood, corresponding more or less closely in language, manners and mode of life to the Hurons on the one hand, and the Five Nations on the other; second, that their presence on so extensive a vantage ground had long been a source of jealousy on the part of the Five Nations; and third, that when all fear of an alliance, offensive and defensive, between the Hurons and the Neutrals had been rendered impossible by the

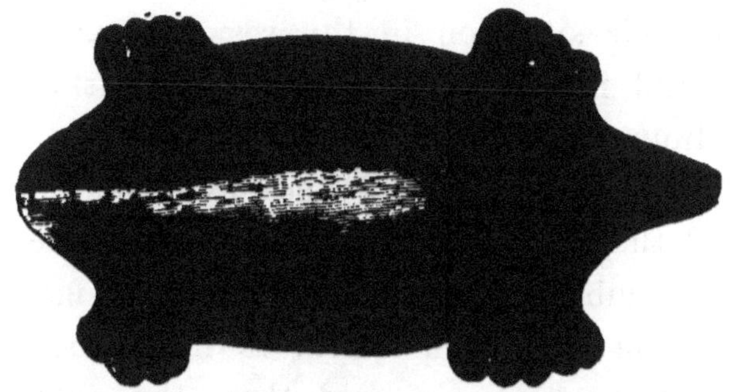

ATTIWANDARON TURTLE TOTEM OF STONE.

destruction of the former, the Neutrals were also exterminated by the relentless American Goths, the "Indian of Indians." Geographical position, non-combatant relationship to the Huron and Iroquois, fertility of soil, abundance of game, and command of a "flint" supply, all tended to the rapid increase of the Attiwandarons in wealth and population. Otherwise than to gratify their own bloodthirstiness, war was unnecessary, but, like their congeners—their ultimate vanquishers—they fought for the love of fighting, for scalps and for pillage ; and those who suffered most at their hands were the Mascoutins, one of several Algonquin tribes, all of which were liable to invasion by them at any moment. Had it been in the nature of the Attiwandarons to live a reasonably peaceful life, they might have become the most powerful branch of the great Huron-Iroquois family. Long immunity from attacks from without induced them to devote their leisure to the enjoyment of every animal luxury their savage nature could appreciate. Among northern peoples their situation in this respect was probably unique, and its effect corresponded with the results arising from " riotous living " everywhere else.

Freedom from national and domestic cares had rendered them " women " to all but their inferiors in point of number. They quailed before the face of the Five Nations, and even appear to have stood in awe of the Hurons, who refused them the right-of-way through their country to the Ottawa ; but, as a bloody pastime, they carried on cowardly, ferocious wars against weak, western Algonquin tribes.*

* Lallemant stated the population of the Mascoutins (Nation of Fire, or preferably, as Parkman says, Nation of the Prairie) to outnumber that of the Neutrals, Hurons and Five Nations combined, but this is plainly an Attiwandaron estimate for the purpose of glorifying their own prowess. Again, according to Daillon, they had also been carrying on war with seventeen other Algonquin tribes—this, too, was probably gasconade. In 1635, Brebeuf reckoned the Hurons at 30,000, and it would appear undoubted that the Five Nations were quite as numerous : but making due allowance for any unintentional over-estimate, it is safe to compute both populations at the number given for one. Parkman asserts that at any time the population of the Neutrals exceeded that of the Hurons and Iroquois united, which would give the Neutrals at least 35,000. Then we have the above statement that the Mascoutins exceeded all

In point of cruelty, licentiousness and superstition they were not surpassed by any native American people of whom we have any record. "Compared with the Hurons," says Parkman, "their licentiousness was even more open and shameless; and they stood alone in the extravagance of some of their usages." Leading a life of comparative ease and comfort between their western forays, they had ample time to cultivate savage art, to repeat old myths and invent new ones, to tattoo, paint and otherwise adorn their bodies, to engage in dances and ceremonies of various kinds, to practice juggleries, to gamble, to indulge every low appetite, and, in a word, to act the part of aboriginal sybarites. Although they are credited with good faith as treaty-makers, their reputation as liars was equalled only by their susceptibility to deceit. That they were expert in the chase we may readily believe, for few people had better hunting opportunities, whether we consider the abundance of game or the nature of the country. As a beaver-breeding ground Attiwandaronia was all that could be desired, and herds of moose and deer stalked through their woods. Wild turkeys were numerous, and predatory animals of various kinds were not scarce. Their simple agricultural operations were performed

the rest together, thus assigning them a population of at least 70,000. Add to this the seventeen other tribes with which the Neutrals were said to have been at war, and allow for each tribe a population of only 2,000, or 34,000 in all, and we have an aggregate of more than 100,000! No doubt most of the information relative to such estimates was supplied by the natives themselves.

by the women, who cultivated sun flowers (for oil, probably), pumpkins, tobacco, coarse hemp and maize. The ground planted was not in our sense a field. No clearing was done by way of cutting down trees. These were simply deadened by "girdling" the bark, which process consisted in pounding it with stone axes until it separated from the stem. Light and heat then reached the ground through the leafless branches. That his clothing was made from prepared skins, that both sexes dressed much alike, and that the *brave* was as fond of bedecking himself with gew-gaws as was the woman, it may be unnecessary to say; more to the purpose is it that the preparation of the raw material was an art requiring great skill and patience, and one in which the Attiwandaron had attained, we may believe, perfection. House cleaning was not an institution among them, and year after year filth accumulated on the floors of their dwellings. Hard substances, like broken bones, horn and shell, were consigned to a "dump" or midden close by, and sometimes articles now valuable to the student of archæology found their way there also, as a close examination of one of these heaps seldom fails to yield a profitable return. It was only when the accumulation of *debris* and offal, either on the floor or outside, became inconvenient that the residents of the long-house erected a new structure and removed to it.

Their mortuary customs corresponded more closely

to those of the Five Nations than to those of the
Hurons, but partook to some extent of the practice in
vogue among both these peoples. In Beverly township, for example, we find the veritable Huron ossuary,
while farther south the graves appear to have been
single. Several of the latter have been found near
Point Abino, and elsewhere in Bertie township, as well
as at intervals near the Erie coast to the western
limits of the Nation, and in numerous places, in
what are now the counties of Brant and Middlesex.

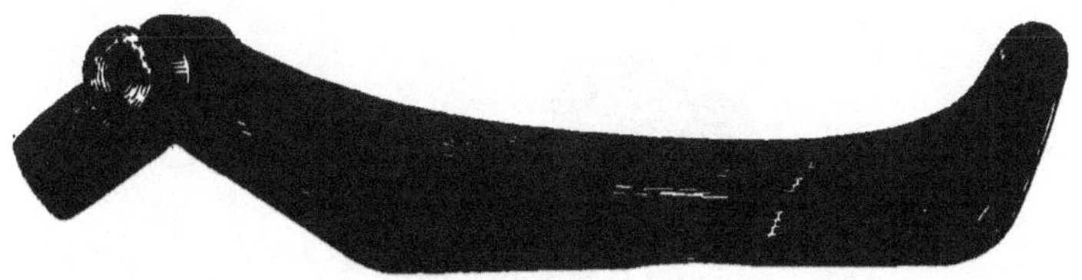

BIRD-LIKE OBJECT, PROBABLY A TALISMAN CHARM OR AMULET,

For success in the chase, or for ceremonial use.

At Port Colborne a low mound was found to contain
several bodies, with which were associated many valuable offerings in the shape of wampum and pottery.
This very exceptional burial place is within a few hundred yards of the shore, and on low ground, although
high enough to be beyond the effect of even the most
violent wave-action from the lake. It is not to be
wondered at that among people scattered over so large
an extent of country, and affected at various points
widely separated by diverse influences, there should
have been less uniformity in burial customs than we

find among those who occupy a more circumscribed area, and who are on this very account more likely to conform to what may be called some national usage. Still, the custom of placing offerings in the grave maintained its hold, on account, no doubt, of the pan-spiritism that formed so large a factor in the Indian's belief. Thoroughly convinced that the spirit-world implied not alone the ghosts of the deceased braves, but of everything material, the graves were furnished with clay pots, arrow-heads, wampum, bone needles and numerous other articles, including

BIRD AMULET OR TALISMAN.

probably bows and various objects of wood, all traces of which have now disappeared.

Primitive methods of manipulating raw material and of handling tools must ever prove attractive to the student of ethnology. In these we observe the dawn of ideas which, after the lapse of many centuries, have, by degrees almost imperceptible, developed through the minds of superior families of the human race, into those almost miraculously automatic devices that are the crowning mechanical glory of the nineteenth century. The distance is great from the pebble in the hands of a savage, whether used to crack a bone or bring down a bird, to the steam-engine of fifty thousand horse-power, and the gun that can propel hundreds of pounds of metal eight or ten miles, but all the steps may be traced between the simple and the highly complex forms. There is little similarity between the satisfied grunt of an uncivilized man and the soul-inspiring strains of an oratorio, but the one is respectively the origin of the other.

When the Romans landed in Britain they found our ancestors in a condition not much, if at all, superior to that of the aborigines of this continent four hundred years ago, and as, indeed, many of them are still. It is, therefore, to be noted that in the study of aboriginal life, among no matter what people, possessing the capacity for advancement, we are simply holding the mirror up to nature. We are, in effect, doing in a very universal sense something akin to the desire expressed by Burns, for if not seeing ourselves "as others see us," we are at all events trying to see ourselves *through* others.

The Attiwandarons, when discovered by Father Daillon in 1626, were like the Britons when first seen by Cæsar, many degrees advanced beyond the lowest condition of savagery. In this respect they resembled neighboring peoples, and a few lines may here be devoted relative to their methods of working.

Knives, arrow-heads and spear-heads were made by flaking flint (chert), of which a large supply existed in

Attiwandaronia. The process is a difficult one to describe, but is said to have been effected (after the articles were roughly blocked out with stone hammers) by means of a piece of notched bone or horn, held in the right hand and pressed with a dexterous twist against the edge of the flint held on a pad in the left hand. Specialized forms, having more or less regularly serrated edges, were probably intended for sawing the bones of birds crosswise to form beads, for separating heavy and solid bones lengthwise to make awls, and for cutting small pieces of wood like arrow-shafts. The serrations may have been made by means of slight blows with a sharp stone tool, or they may have been pinched off with a bone flaker.

When tools like axes, adzes and gouges were required, the material was procured from some surface boulder of primary rock, which was broken up into fragments by being first heated, and then suddenly cooled by the application of water; or, perhaps, much work like this was performed during cold days in winter, when the stone, after being heated, was simply left exposed to the atmosphere. At any rate, it is easy to understand that if separation failed to take place during the heating process, it would be almost certain to occur when, after having been thoroughly heated, the surface was quickly contracted by cooling, however effected. Suitable fragments and splinters were next shaped by means of persistent pecking with other hard stones, perhaps large flint flakes; and when something approaching to symmetry was obtained in this way, the tool was finished by being rubbed either on, or with, gritty stones, like sandstone.   Many specimens have so high a polish that limestone or other fine-grained material must have been employed for the final operation.

The methods of pecking and rubbing apply to every class of stone object during the last steps in their production.   When imported material, like the beautiful but comparatively fragile striped (Huronian) slate, was employed, the method resorted to for the purpose

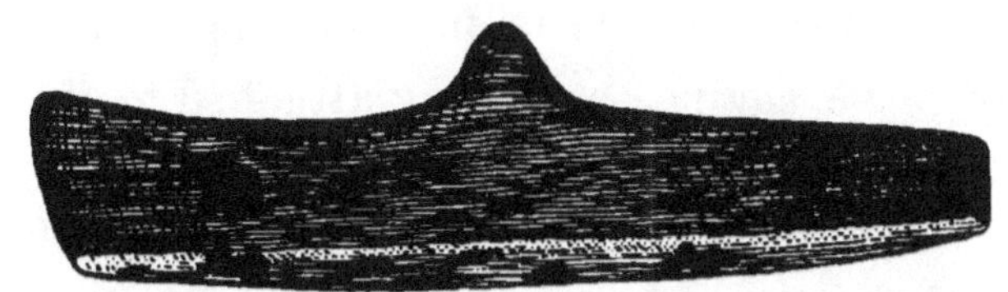

VERY UNUSUAL FORM OF AMULET OR CHARM STONE,

Or may have been employed by the shaman or sorcerer in his juggleries and incantations.

of reducing the size of the stone, or of bringing it into shape, illustrated some advancement in mechanical ideas.   Deep notches were sawn with flint flakes so closely together that the intervening portions of stone were easily broken off; another method was to bore a series of holes along the line of desired severance, when with little difficulty the piece was detached either by a blow or by carefully sawing through the connecting portions.

Incidental reference has been made to the boring of holes. Of course the boring tool must have been of flint, and specimens of drills are not uncommon ; but we are not certain as to how these drills were put in motion. Various ingenious devices for this purpose have been observed among savages in different parts of the world, but perhaps the simplest, apart from actual hand pressure, is that known as the fiddle-bow, or simply the " bow," on account of its form. The cutting portion, or drill proper, being fastened to a shaft, not more than eighteen inches in length, the string of the bow is given a twist around the shaft, which now becomes a spindle, the upper end being held in place against a bearing attached to the forehead, the breast, or sometimes even the teeth, and while the stone to be operated on is held by the left hand, motion is communicated to the drill by moving the bow backwards and forwards with the right, the necessary amount of pressure being afforded by the action of the head or body Among some savages this plan is used to produce fire.

Regarding the woodcraft of the Attiwandarons but little can be said, any more than in the case of other departed tribes. That they did employ various articles of wood we know, but these were no doubt of an exceedingly simple kind as to form. The paddle of a canoe, the ever-necessary bow with its accompanying arrow-shafts, war-clubs, and stakes for various purposes were all made by splitting and scraping. If

these people ever did anything worthy of being regarded as wood-carving, no evidence of such remains
to-day. Judging by aboriginal performance generally,
we have good reason to believe that at least rude
attempts at ornamentation in this way were indulged
in by the Attiwandarons, but these no doubt consisted chiefly in sawing lines and notches by means
of flint flakes. Patterns thus formed on the bow or
on the handle of the paddle would then be stained
with some bright-colored juice extracted from root,
bark, leaf, flower or berry. Spoons (or rather dippers
of wood) were no doubt used by them, as it is certain they were by other tribes; but the production of
these necessitated little aptitude, as the hollowed
portion could be made by a repetition of charring and
scraping.

As makers of snow-shoes and toboggans they must
have possessed some skill, although articles of this
kind were of less extensive use with them than
among tribes living farther to the north and in areas
of more rugged configuration.

Even among people in the lowest degree of savagery
much ingenuity is often exemplified in producing
water vessels and cooking utensils from materials that
to us appear most unlikely for such purposes. Our
Indian selected bark no doubt because the natural
shape of it suggested a vessel, and partly, perhaps, on
account of its abundant and great variety. Birch
affords the best material for making vessels; but this

7

tree was not a common one in southern Ontario, and the Attiwandaron had to do the best he could with the covering of the elm, ironwood, basswood, and some other trees. From this material he made vessels for carrying water and even for cooking, the latter operation being performed by dropping hot stones among the contents of his rudely-formed pot. Of bark, too, were formed receptacles of various kinds in the shape of boxes or baskets for the collection and preservation of seeds, fruits and roots. Articles of this kind were the equivalent of our chest, pail and pantry. From a shallow cup of bark he could drink ; a piece of bark he might use as a plate, should he care to indulge in such a luxury ; with a strip of bark passing round his brow and attached to a sheet of the same material, on the ice he could convey for a long distance the victim of his bow or spear ; a piece of perforated bark shielded his eyes from the glare of the sun on the snow ; thus in numerous ways bark ministered to his necessities ever since he had been bound to the back of his mother in a swaddling of bark and leather bands.

In another part of this chapter reference will be made to the Attiwandarons' lack of skill as boatmen ; still, they must have found canoes of great use in some parts of their territory, and certainly employed them crossing the Niagara on visits of kinship, as well as when on their Algonquin raids they found it necessary to reach the western banks of the St. Clair and Detroit. The want of birch-bark necessitated

the employment of elm for this purpose, as with
the Five Nations; but vessels of this material were
indeed of poor quality, and it is probable that their
best canoes were "dug-outs," the making of one of
which required a prodigious amount of time and
toil, from the felling of the tree by means of stone
axes and the use of fire until the completion of the
work involved in shaping and hollowing by similar
tedious methods. But the Indian was a patient
workman; time was of little value to him so long as
present needs were supplied, and he was no doubt
quite well satisfied if he could complete his tiny ship
during the course of a whole season or, mayhap, of
two. It is most likely that when the making of such
a canoe was undertaken it was rather the work of the
village or community, than of individual achievement.

Of more importance, although of less difficulty, was
the erection of his "long-house," so-called because,
being intended for the dwelling of from five to fifty
families, it extended sometimes to the length of four
hundred or even five hundred feet, its width seldom
exceeding fourteen or fifteen feet. A house of this
kind was made by placing saplings in the ground at
regular distances, bending and fastening the tops
together to support the roof, and covering the whole
of this rude framework with sheets of bark. Cross
bars between the sapling-poles gave strength to the
structure, and at intervals of ten or twelve feet parti-
tions of bark separated the apartments of the various

families. A hole in the roof over the middle of each space served as a chimney, through which the smoke from the fire on the ground sometimes found its way, but, as a rule, so permeated the whole house as to produce infinite discomfort and not unfrequently diseases of the eye, resulting in total blindness, especially among the women, who, from the nature of their occupations, were compelled to remain much of their time within.

The mechanical skill requisite to construct a house of this kind was not high. Of what we call carpentry there was none. Joints of all kinds were made simply by lashing one piece to another with strips of rawhide or ropes, made of some fibre like basswood bark, or the roots of certain trees—in more northernly latitudes those of the spruce were chosen. The bark covering was pinned and laced in sheets overlapping each other, the interstices being filled in with grass, moss and leaves. In winter a similar arrangement formed a lining within, while in warm weather most of both coverings would be conspicuous by its absence.

It should be observed, in connection with these peculiar dwellings, that no pretension was made to construct them regularly or in straight lines. From two well-marked fire-rows, respectively 130 and 360 feet long, marking the sites of long-houses on Point Abino, it would appear, in one case, that the ground-plan was made to correspond with the configuration of the neighboring bank; and in the other, that the irregularity was merely the result of carelessness or want of mechanical ability. However this may be, both form obtuse angles about midway in their length. We learn incidentally that single dwellings were also in use among the Attiwandarons. Chaumonot and Brebeuf frequently mention having entered places of this kind, and it was in one such, in all probability, that these missionaries received shelter on their memorable return to Ste. Marie in the spring of 1641.

But the operations of the Indian mechanic were not confined to wood and stone. In some respects bone occupied an equally important place, although in working both bone and horn he had to follow exactly the same methods as with stone, cutting it and boring it with flints and rubbing it down or sharpening it with sandstone.

It was, perhaps, as a potter that he (or rather she in this case) showed to best advantage. When suitable clay was found for making vessels it was not only kneaded but tempered. One cannot even surmise how the art of tempering was discovered by our Indians, perhaps it was a common heritage from the parent stock, whether that stock came from Asia or Polynesia on the one side, as many think, or Europe on the other, as is contended by Dr. Brinton.

Attiwandaron pottery was fashioned wholly by hand, and without the assistance of a wheel or any substitute for one, and the work is creditable to the women who were engaged in it. Pipes were formed by the men, but nothing beyond this can be said about them, except that no two pipes are exactly alike, for the reason that no mould was used, and every man 'made pipes according to his own caprice.

Weaving, as a matter of course, was woman's work, and a slow operation it must have been.   Strong,

RUDE ATTIWANDARON CLAY BOWL.
(About five inches in depth.)

coarse threads or strings were twisted from bark and root fibres, and from the stalks of wild hemp. These threads were fastened at each end to a bar, the distance between the bars corresponding to the length of the mat or " blanket " to be woven. The woof threads were then passed in various ways through

and among the others according to the fancy of the
weaver, or the kind of fabric to be produced. No
implement corresponding to a shuttle was employed,
for the operation of interstacing threads was rather
what we now call darning.

Grass mats were made in the same way, and
patterns showing considerable taste in design and
skill in execution were, presumably, fashioned by the
women of Attiwandaronia, just as we may suppose
they excelled in quill work. Flowers, fruits, leaves,
roots and some kinds of earth yielded the expert
woman a variety of brilliant dyes, with which she not
only stained her grasses and porcupine quills, but was
able to supply material for colored borders and devices
of various kinds, on the light yellow, soft leather
garments necessary for winter use; for it must be
observed that in their modes of preparing the skins of
deer, bears, wolves and other beasts, our Indians could
not be excelled. Their methods of skin-preparation
could not properly be called tanning, it was rather a
prolonged system of *massage*, part of which consisted
in the women sitting down deliberately to chew the
raw hides hour after hour. The brains of the slain
animal were usually employed to smear the inner side
of the skin after it had been freed from flesh, and
been effectively chewed. Other operations consisted
in stretching, rolling up for a time, again opening out,
kneading, pulling, rubbing, smearing, drying and again
rubbing and kneading until the desired quality of

softness and pliability was secured. Many Indians
yet possess and practise this art, the product of which
is superior in many respects to the results of chemical
processes as employed by ourselves.

Doggedly and superstitiously conservative as are all
low grade communities, even to minutiæ of unim-
portance in time-honored customs and observances,
circumstances connected with a change of habitat,
arising either from voluntary or enforced migrations,
suggest, if they do not compel, modifications in the
manner of life. The Huron-Iroquois do not appear at
any time to have been skilful canoeists. They were,
at any rate, not to be compared in this respect with
many Algonquin tribes, and we have, therefore, no
cause for wonder when we learn that the Attiwandarons appear to have become comparatively helpless
in moving on or over large bodies of water. They
feared, even during later years, to coast the shore of
Lake Ontario or to glide down the rapids of the St.
Lawrence for the purpose of trading directly with
the French at Montreal, preferring to effect their
barter through the Hurons. Dr. Parkman attributes
this to a want of " sense or reflection enough to take
the easy and direct route of Lake Ontario, which was
probably open to them though closed against the
Hurons by Iroquois enmity." But surely this is an
imputation that cannot be accepted regarding a people
who had " sense and reflection enough " to profit by
dissensions among their kinsmen in every other way,

to say nothing of the long and tedious marches they must frequently have undertaken to attack their enemies—perhaps to pursue them beyond the spot on Lake Michigan where Chicago stands to-day. Mr. J. H. Coyne,* with more reason, says this was because they "did not understand the management of canoes, especially in the rapids." Their only knowledge of rapids on a large scale must have been derived from the awe-inspiring examples of these on the Niagara, and if we bear in mind the extraordinary credulity and superstition of the Attiwandarons, which would in no small degree tend to magnify the dangers and terrors of the voyage on the St. Lawrence, we may have an additional reason why timid or inexpert canoemen should hesitate about venturing on a voyage of nearly four hundred miles by lake and river. War parties may have used the stream we now so stupidly call the Thames, but considering the almost uniform level of Attiwandaronia, its consequent freedom from natural obstacles beyond an occasional swamp or shallow ravine, and the fact that most of its water-courses lie across the great routes of travel, it is quite as likely that expeditions for hostile and other purposes were chiefly confined to well-beaten trails through the magnificent forests.

Not many of our northern tribes appear to have had either taste or leisure to produce fanciful or unusual

* "The Country of the Neutrals," by Jas. H. Coyne, B.A., in Canadian Institute Archæological Report for 1893.

forms of arrows or other flaked objects from flinty
stones, but within Attiwandaron limits more specimens of this kind have been found than in all the
rest of Ontario, and we are warranted in believing
that the articles so shaped were not intended for use
with the bow or even as spears. At least in some
instances, the purpose was probably a decorative one;
nor need this seem at all surprising when it is noted
that even among ourselves swords, daggers, arrows,
hammers, horse-shoes and many other every-day
objects serve as models for jewelry. Perhaps even
the most degraded savage has within him somewhat
of the æsthetic beyond the instinct that dictates the
picking up of glittering substances; but at all events
nothing in the history of the American Indian is better
attested or more widely known than his love of finery,
and there is little doubt that the voluptuous Attiwandarons excelled surrounding nations in this respect.
In proof of this we find throughout his country a
larger number of well-formed, highly-finished objects
than in any other portion of the Province, and our
inability to assign uses to many or most of them with
any degree of certainty is probably owing to their
having originated in connection with the numerous and extravagantly superstitious practices of this
people.

No doubt other reasons may be adduced for the
comparative profusion of these objects, as, for example,
the plundering raids of the Attiwandarons, in which

they would aim to appropriate the best of everything belonging to their enemies, their commercial relations with the Hurons and the Iroquois, and their ability to procure by exchange the choicest specimens of veined or striped slate and other foreign stone; the security of their position; the fixed nature of their towns or villages and the corresponding comfort of their dwellings; their excessive desire for show in connection with the frequency of their warlike excursions and ceremonial parades; their large supply of chert for tool-making, and the occurrence of various kinds of drift-boulders on the surface of the ground in many parts of their territory. However much or little these reasons may be worth, it is a fact that the Attiwandaron was particularly well skilled in the manipulation of such material as he employed in fashioning his tools, weapons and ornaments, although, except in respect of what we call ceremonial objects, it cannot be said that he made any advance on traditional forms. The tomahawk, the drill and the arrow, generally speaking, are like those of neighboring peoples, but individual specimens show attempts at improvement.

On the accompanying figure of a tomahawk or stone celt it will be observed that the workman, by the laborious process of pecking, has left in low relief a not ungraceful design, and this, so far as known, is the only one of its kind in Canada, perhaps in America —at any rate such specimens are exceedingly rare. Another unusual type of axe is here shown (see opp. page), also having a rude carving, probably to represent a man.

Attiwandaron pottery was in no respect superior to that of the Hurons and Iroquois, or to specimens found that are probably the work of Algonquins; indeed, at least one clay vessel from the shore of Lake Erie is of an extremely low type both as to form and decoration (see cut on page 94), but it may have been the work of previous occupants of the soil, for evidences are not wanting that a people preceded those

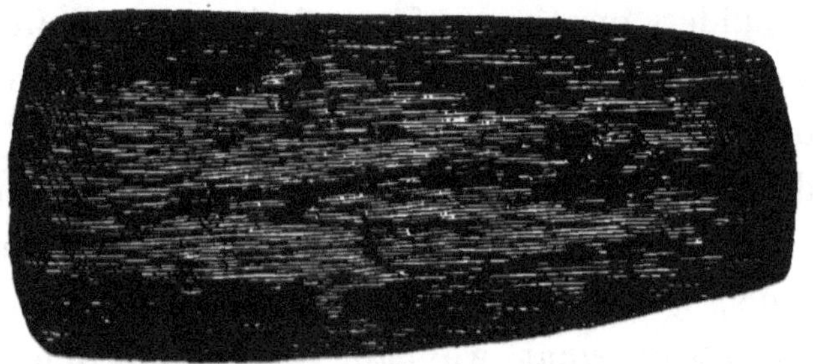

ATTIWANDARON STONE AXE,
With elaborately formed pattern left in low relief, on one side.

who were found in the country when it became known to Europeans.

Workmanship in bone is of a better quality than we usually meet with in Huronia or farther east, where the only efforts made were to produce awls or, as they are often called, needles. Now and then carving in bone was attempted. Small bones, seldom exceeding three-fourths of an inch in diameter, and from three to four inches in length, were used as records or tallies.

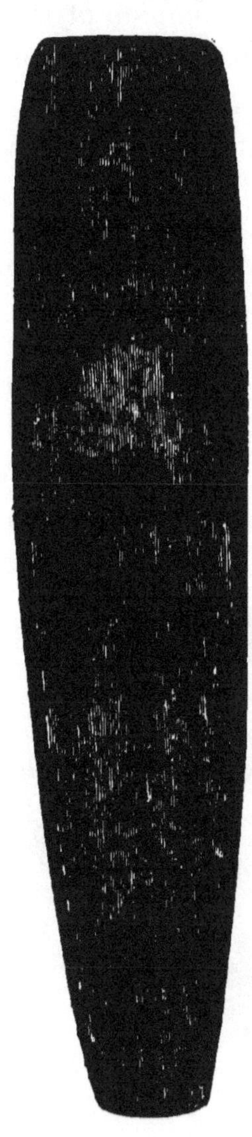

ATTIWANDARON STONE
AXE OR CHISEL,

Bearing conventional human
figure in the T-like form.

On these were cut, with a flint edge, slight notches in one or more rows, by means of which count was kept, it may have been of scalps taken, prisoners captured, numbers of men in a war-party, or days travelled. As most of the tally-bones are thin, smooth and well squared at both ends, they may have been worn about the neck either singly or as part of a necklace.

Here, it will be admitted, we have the beginnings of literature ; but, given sufficient time, were the Attiwandarons or other Indians who employed this simple mnemonic system likely to make any advance on what had no doubt been a widely-spread practice for, who knows, how many centuries? Besides such numeration marks, they pictured rude forms of human beings and of the lower animals, and by highly conventionalizing some of these (see figured axe or chisel), at least one step was taken beyond pure pictography and towards an alphabetic form. Notwithstanding this, it is the opinion of the best American ethnologists living that the Indians of this part of the continent possessed not the capability of extraneously unaided advancement in this

ATTIWANDARON BONE AWL OR NEEDLE.

direction. In view, however, of what has been accomplished by the natives of Mexico and Central America, such a conclusion, arrived at by no matter how high an authority, need not be accepted without demur or doubt.

ATTIWANDARON ORNAMENTAL BONE PIN.

Dire fate, at any rate, has forbidden our aborigines the opportunity to work out a destiny that would either prove or disprove their capacity to develop a

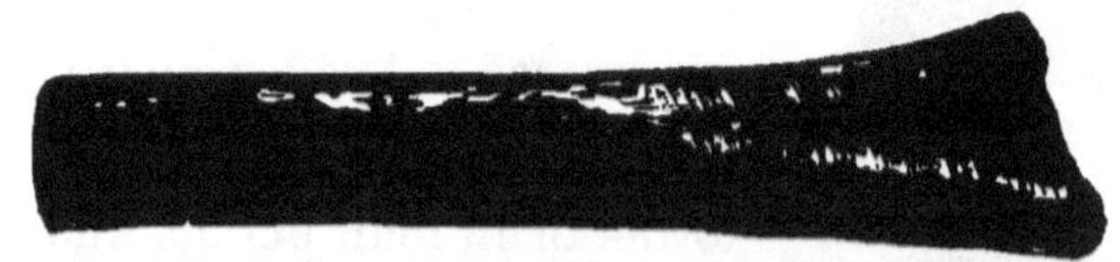

ATTIWANDARON RECORD OR TALLY-BONE.
Notched to keep count of numbers.

literature, in other words, to attain an autochthonous civilization, and all we can now do is to amuse ourselves with theorizing as to possibilities. In any case, the process of development must have been, as always, exceedingly slow, and our knowledge of the Attiwandarons does not warrant a shadow of belief that they were other than magnificent savages ; in a few unimportant respects superior to the Hurons and Iroquois, while from many points of view they were quite the opposite, despite the advantageous nature of their position, topographically and politically.

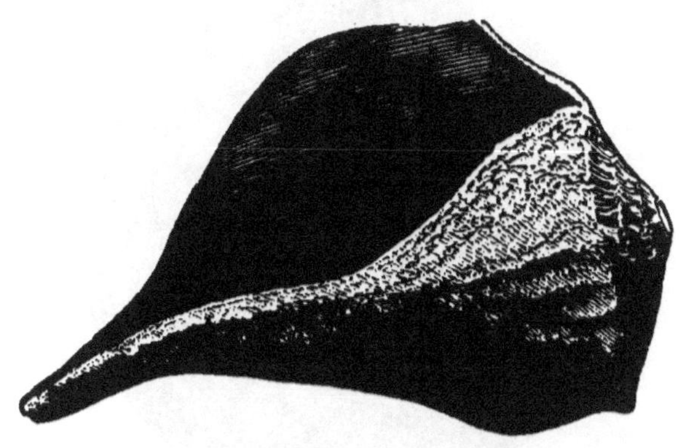

SHELL FROM COAST OF FLORIDA.

Busycon Perversum, material used in making Gorgets and Wampum or Beads.
(About one-fifth full diameter.)

Objects made from a large shell, and sometimes the shells themselves, are found in graves, but copper articles are scarcer. As the shell came from the coast of Florida and the copper from the south shore of Lake Superior, it would seem that communication was more easily maintained through the country of the Iroquois than through that of the Algonquins. This, we may suppose, from what we know of the relationship that existed among the peoples concerned, or we may conclude that, in any event, shell was more highly prized than copper—an opinion not without some weight, in view of the scarcity that characterizes finds of the latter, even where the natives of other tribes had more easy access to the copper-bearing localities. Without the knowledge of smelting, and the still higher knowledge of amalgamating, copper

ATTIWANDARON GORGET OR BREAST ORNAMENT.
Made from *Busycon Perversum.*

tools must have been of but little practical value to an Indian, otherwise than as objects of display. At any rate the native metal, whether in the shape of tools or ornaments, is not of common occurrence in Attiwandaronia.

The large conchs or shells referred to were mainly utilized for making gorgets and wampum or beads. The latter were formed both as discs and as cylinders,

and had a high place in the Indian estimation. Not
only were they worn in strings as personal adornments,
but they seem to have answered the purpose of money,
and belts composed of them were exchanged as pledges

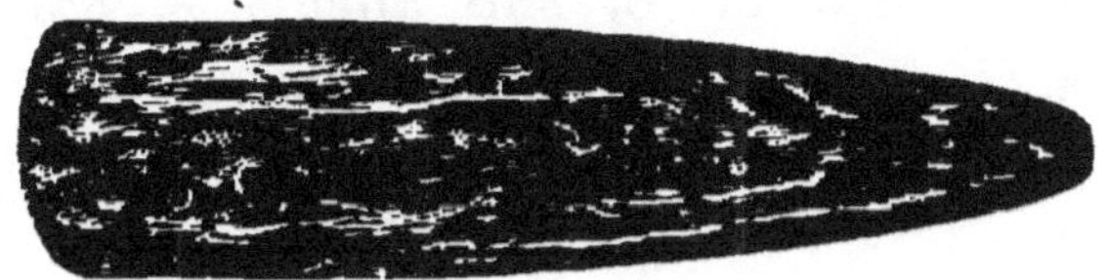

COPPER CHISEL.

of good faith at the ratification of treaties. High as
its value must have been, considering the distance
the heavy shells were carried and the amount of work
required to form each bead, wampum* has been found
deposited, sometimes in quantities amounting to

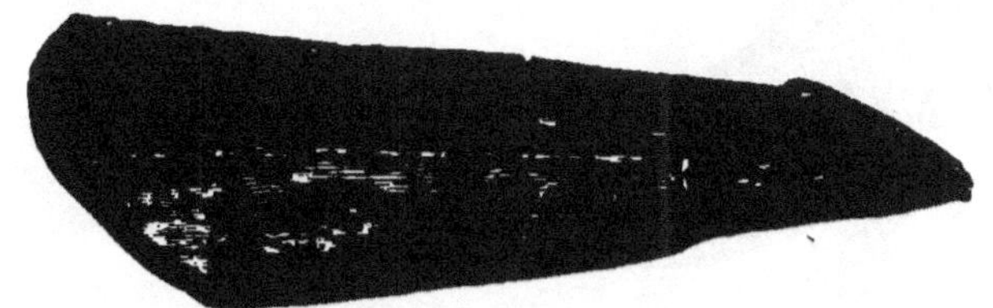

COPPER AXE, WITH SOCKET.

thousands of specimens, along with human remains.
Pins and pendants were also made of this material,
but next to wampum, most interest attaches to the

* Wampum was a sort of beads of several colors, perforated and formed into
belts, collars, and strings for records   It served for many purposes : for money,
for ornamentation and as historical records of the tribe.   Wrought into belts
of various devices, each having its particular meaning and significance, wampum
preserved the substance of treaties, and a belt was delivered to ratify every
specific article of negotiation.

8

breast-plates or gorgets. These varied somewhat in form, but most of them are circular and perfectly plain, except for the presence of two or more holes, the largest of which is in the middle. So far as we know, only one object of this kind has been found bearing such an engraved scroll as is not uncommon on shell gorgets farther to the south.

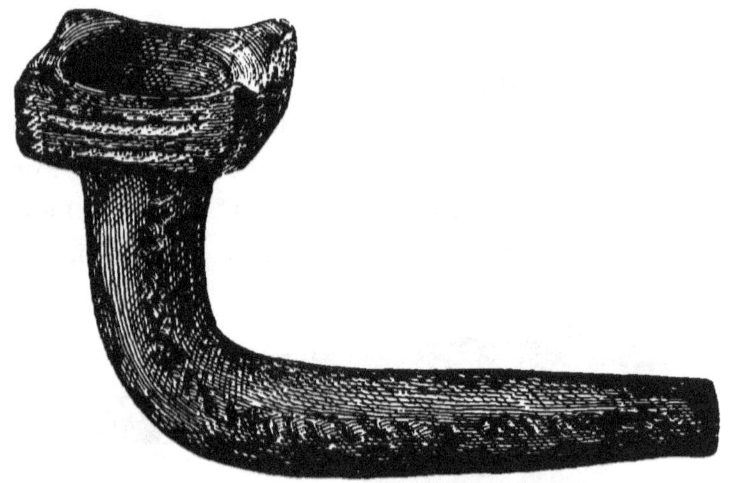

ATTIWANDARON SQUARE-HEADED CLAY PIPE.
(Full size.)

Smoking, an almost universal aboriginal American habit, was held in especially high favor among the Huron-Iroquois, and although it was rather a matter of ritual than of personal gratification, still it may readily be conceived how prevalent the use of tobacco was among the Neutrals. At council meetings of all kinds the pipe was an important object—no man spoke

until everyone present had taken a draw or two from
the ceremonial pipe. To smoke one with another on
any occasion was to make a solemn pledge of friendship, as to refuse was a declaration of enmity. All

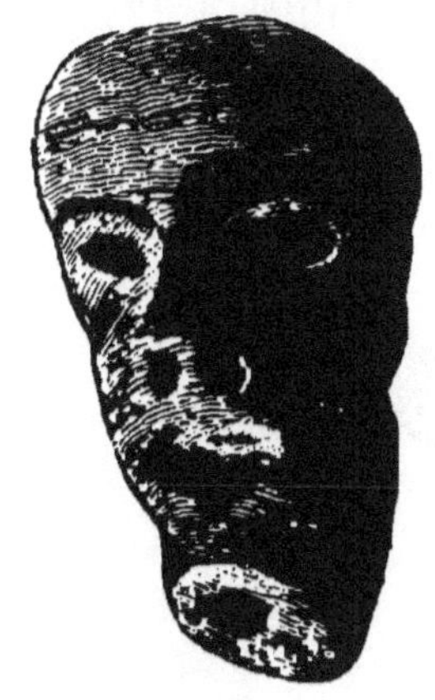

ATTIWANDARON CLAY PIPE
HEAD (full size).

ATTIWANDARON STONE PIPE
HEAD (full size).

ATTIWANDARON "WHITE STONE" PIPE (six inches long).

this we know, and yet we are at a loss regarding the
fundamental *why*, as it appeared to the Indian mind.

Pipe-making, whether in stone or clay, was a favorite occupation among the men, and many specimens of

their work show considerable taste in design as well as
skill in execution. In the production of clay pipes
they were perhaps inferior to the Hurons, especially
the Tionnontates, but they surpassed these people in
the art of making stone pipes. The illustrations show
a few types of the latter.

But it was in talismans, amulets, luck-stones or

ATTIWANDARON PIPE HEAD OF LIME-
STONE (nearly full size).

fetiches that the Attiwandaron took his highest rank
as an artist-mechanic. In all ages and everywhere,
religion, even in its grossest forms, has been favorable
to the development of the art instinct. The best
efforts of the most skilful and ingenious have aimed
at the production of something elaborate and unique
in honor of their deities, whether true or false —
hence painting, statuary, architecture. In obedience

to this inclination (little as the crude imaginings of
the Indian deserved the name of religion) he selected

HIGHLY-FINISHED OBJECTS OF VARIEGATED SLATE.
Probably used by the shamans or medicine men in their ceremonies.

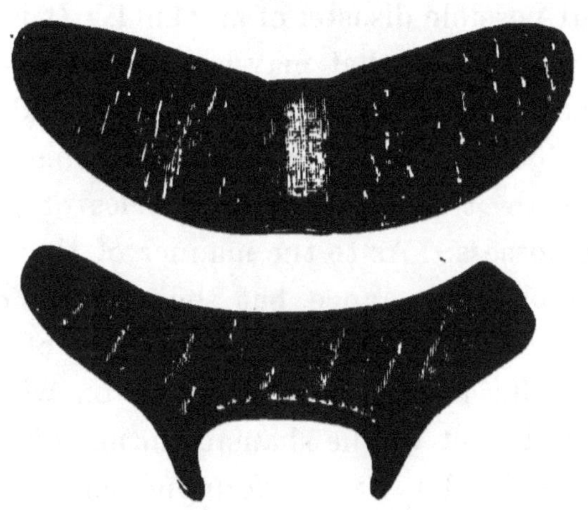

FINELY-MADE SLATE OBJECTS.
Probably for shaman or ceremonial use.

what appeared to him the most beautiful stones,
and these he fashioned in such a manner as most
likely, according to his ideas, to please one or more.

of his innumerable okis or spirits, and thus lead to success in his enterprises, for this was the sum of Indian worship, if worship it could be called. The accompanying illustrations show a few of the forms found in Attiwandaronia, to which are attributed some such fetichtic value as is here referred to. But it is not to be supposed that objects like these were at all common, or even in common use. What is more likely is that they were the property of the shamans —the medicine men—and were employed by them only on important occasions, as when performing jug-gleries for victory in war, for abundance of food, for dry weather, for rain or snow, to drive away disease, or to avert possible disaster of any kind. It is difficult for us to appreciate what may be called the commer-cial value of such laboriously-wrought and highly-finished objects, but we may compare them, in this respect, with the best prized articles of gold and silver we possess. As to the manner of their use, we are in complete ignorance, but the presence of a hole through the middle of each is suggestive of wands or slender shafts having been inserted, on which they were carried aloft by the shaman during his incanta-tions, or while he was performing some grotesque dance accompanied with discordant noises. It is also allowable to suppose that if so mounted they were decorated with a profusion of dyed feathers, porcupine quills and grasses, perhaps also with stone or bone beads, and even with the scalps of a few Algonquins.

To gorgets of shell, already mentioned as having
been worn suspended from the neck, and to stone
tablets like those shown in the illustrations, are usually

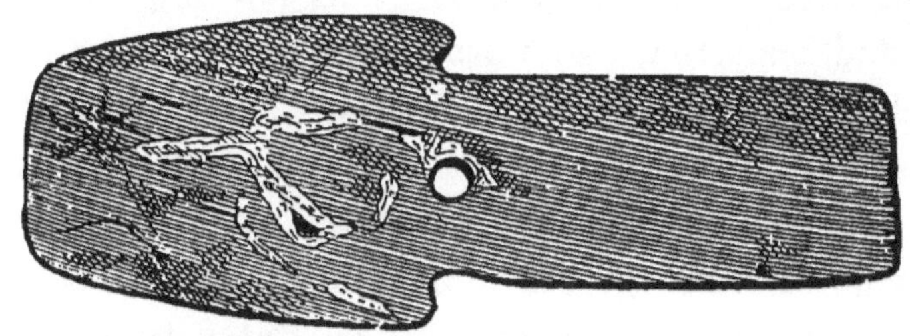

ATTIWANDARON SLATE TABLET OR GORGET,
Or object employed in ceremonies, perhaps simply a Charm or Luck-stone.

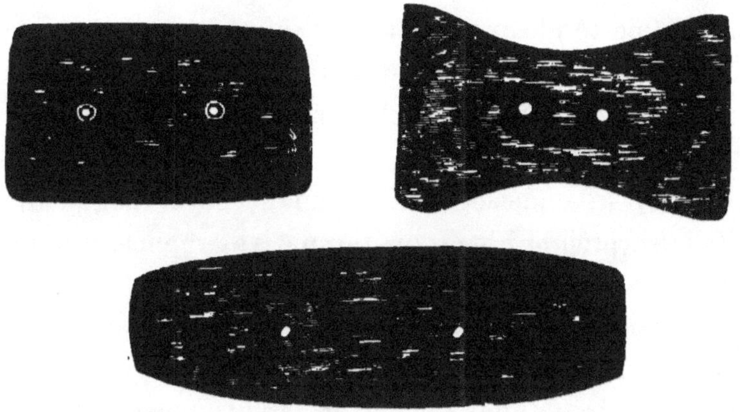

ATTIWANDARON SLATE TABLETS OR GORGETS.
(From four to six inches long).

ascribed a similar use. In every case they are perforated with one, two, or more holes, and it is, of
course, chiefly on this account that they are spoken of
as gorgets; but most of them we have seen do not
lend any favor to this opinion, because not only are

the holes frequently bored without any apparent reference to convenience for suspension, but they seldom
show marks of wear.   Besides this, the faces are generally free from such abrasions as one might expect
to find on articles so worn.   The condition of these
tablets rather suggests that they have been kept by
the owners carefully wrapped in some soft leather or
fur as talismans, for some other and unknown purpose
in connection with the multiplicity of Attiwandaron
superstitions, although it must be stated that similar
objects are found in Huronia and farther east.

From living representatives of the Red Man, it is
impossible to glean a particle of information regarding
the uses or purposes served by such relics as have been
but briefly adverted to in this chapter.   In " Notes on
Primitive Man in Ontario," Mr. David Boyle puts this
difficulty in concise form, when he says (page 93):
" It is surprising how soon the natives themselves not
only lose all knowledge of former practices, but even
adopt the absurd theories or beliefs of white men.
Confusion of ideas begins in the second generation
following desuetude, and utter forgetfulness speedily
succeeds.   Nor is this to be wondered at among a
people devoid of power to record their thoughts otherwise than by means of rude pictographs."

Louis Hennepin

(Portrait, from Frontice in Edition of 1703.)

CHAPTER VI.

FATHER HENNEPIN.

A Wilderness of Wood and Marsh Land—The Coming of Father Hennepin—
Sketch of His Life—His Birth—Enters the Franciscan Order—Ordina-
tion to the Priesthood—Adventurous Longings—His Love for Travel
—Sails with La Salle—Arrives at Fort Frontenac—Visits the Iroquois
—Enters the Niagara River—View from Queenston Heights—Leaves
for the Falls—His Journey Described—The Imperial Cataract—Hen-
nepin's Description of the Falls—At the Mouth of the Chippewa River
—Return to Queenston—The First Mass—The Beautiful River.

> " No wigwam smoke is curling there,
>   The very earth is scorched and bare ;
>   And they pause and listen to catch a sound
>   Of breathing life, but there comes not one,
>   Save the fox's bark and the rabbit's bound."
>
> —WHITTIER.

THE dispersion of the Neutrals left the Niagara
Peninsula a solitude. The clearings gradually
disappeared, the abandoned lodges rotted and fell to
pieces, and where acres of pumpkins, tobacco and
Indian corn once grew in abundance, the maple, birch
and hemlock again began to cover the ground. A
wilderness of wood and marsh land, whose silence was
unbroken save by the bark of the wolf or the dismal
cry of the screech-owl, stretched from the Niagara

River to the Detroit Narrows. Now and then a Seneca hunting party crossed at Fort Erie or Lewiston, and the startled moose gazed upon them unconscious of danger. The land was fast returning to its primal state ; the streams began again to teem with fish, wild animals to increase and multiply, while over all— over forest, river and marsh, over the graves of the slaughtered—there brooded the silence of a starless night.

> " This is the forest primeval ; but where are the hearts that beneath it
> Leaped like the roe, when he hears in the woodland the voice of the
> huntsman ?
>
> .   .   .   .
>
> Scattered like dust and leaves, when the mighty blasts of October
> Seize them, and whirl them aloft, and sprinkle them far o'er the ocean."

Such was the state of the country when, almost forty years after the ruin of the Neutrals, the Franciscan Friar Hennepin, in company with the Sieur de le Motte, La Salle's lieutenant, entered the mouth of the Niagara River. It was on the 6th of December, 1678, when they anchored on the Canadian side opposite the now historic fort of Niagara. They chanted a *Te Deum* in gratitude to God for their safe arrival, the members of a Seneca fishing party looking on in mute surprise.

This romantic and adventurous priest left France with La Salle, the explorer, and Bishop Laval. He went with La Salle to Fort Frontenac (now Kingston) as a missionary, and when that daring and adventurous Frenchman was preparing to leave on his second expedition to the Mississippi, the distinguished priest, accompanied by La Motte, sailed in advance, and after a stormy passage of eighteen days, safely reached the entrance to the Niagara River, where they awaited the coming of their leader.

As Father Hennepin will ever be intimately identified with the history of our country, it becomes us to dwell at some length on his extraordinary career. Of his early life we know comparatively little. He was born at Ath, in Hainaut, France; though Margry, on the faith of documents, says that he was born at Roy, adding that his family originally came from Ath. In his "Nouvelle Decouverte," he writes that while pursuing his studies he felt a strong inclination to leave the world and lead in retirement a life of strict purity and virtue.

"With this view," says he, "I entered the Order of St. Francis, in order to spend my days there in a life of austerity. I accordingly took the habit with several of my fellow students, whom I inspired with the same design."

He made his novitiate in the Recollect Convent at Bethune, in the Province of Artois, where his master of Novices was Father Gabriel de la Ribourde, a man eminent alike for his high social position and for a most exemplary life, and who was destined at a later day to die for the faith, while laboring as a missionary in America. "As I advanced in age," he continues,.

" an inclination for travelling in foreign parts strengthened in my heart. One of my sisters, who was married in Ghent, and for whom I entertained a very strong affection, used every argument, indeed, to divert me from this project, while I was in that great city, to which I had gone in order to learn Flemish. But I was urged by several of my Amsterdam friends to go to the East Indies, and my natural inclination to travel, supporting their entreaties, shook my resolution greatly, and I almost resolved to embark in order to gratify this desire.

" All my sister's remonstrances could not divert me from my first design. I accordingly set out to see Italy, and by order of the General of our Order, I visited the finest churches and the most important convents in that country and Germany, in which I began to satisfy my natural curiosity. At last, returning to our Netherlands, the Rev. Father William Hernix, a Recollect, who died not long since Bishop of Ipres, opposed my project of continuing my travels. He placed me in the Convent of Halles, in Hainaut, where I discharged the duty of a preacher for a year. After that, with my Superior's leave, I went to Artois, and was thence sent to Calais, during the season for salting herrings. In this place my strongest passion was to listen to the stories which sea captains told of their long voyages. I then returned to our Convent of Biez, by Dunkirk ; but I often hid behind the tavern doors, while the sailors were talking over their cruises.

Whilst thus endeavoring to hear them, the tobacco smoke sickened me terribly ; yet I listened eagerly to all that these men told of their adventures at sea, of the dangers they had encountered, and the various incidents of their voyages in foreign parts. I would have passed whole days and nights without eating in this occupation, which was so agreeable to me, because I always learned something new about the manners and mode of life of foreign nations, and touching the beauty, fertility and riches of the countries where these men had been.

"I accordingly was more confirmed in my old inclination. With the view of gratifying it the more, I went as a missionary to most of the cities of Holland, and at last halted at Maestricht, where I remained eight months. There I administered the sacraments to more than three thousand wounded. While there, engaged in this occupation, I was several times in great danger among these sick people. I was even myself taken down with purples and dysentery, and was within an inch of the grave. But God at last restored me my former health by the care and aid of a very able Dutch physician.

"The following year, by an impulse of my zeal, I again devoted myself to labor for the salvation of souls. I was then at the bloody battle of Seneff (August 11th, 1664), where so many men perished by fire and steel. There I had abundant occupation in relieving and comforting the poor wounded men. At last, after enduring great hardships and encountering extreme dangers in sieges of cities, in trenches, and on the field of battle, where I exposed myself greatly for the salvation of my neighbor, while the soldiers breathed only blood and carnage, I beheld myself in a condition to satisfy my first inclinations."

Canada had become for a second time a field of labor for the Recollect missionaries. The Count de Frontenac, Governor-General, was especially anxious to have them in the colony, having quarrelled with the Jesuits and the Bishop, who, with his secular clergy, held very strict rules of morality, especially on the point of selling liquor to the Indians.

The King of France, Louis XIV., yielding to the appeal of the Count de Frontenac, wrote to him on the 22nd of April, 1675: "I have sent five Recollect religious to Canada to reinforce the community of these religious already established there."* Father Hennepin was one of those selected. "I then received orders," he proceeds, "from my superiors to proceed to Rochelle in order to embark as a missionary for Canada. For two months I discharged the duties of parish priest two leagues from that city, because I had been requested to do so by the pastor of the place, who was absent. At last I abandoned myself entirely to Providence, and undertook this great sea voyage of twelve or thirteen hundred leagues, the greatest and perhaps the longest that is made on the ocean."

---

* Gilmary Shea, Preface to "Nouvelle Decouverte."

On reaching Canada he assures us that Bishop Laval entertained him hospitably. "Considering that during the voyage I had displayed great zeal in my sermons and in my assiduity in performing the divine office, and had moreover prevented several women and girls, who were sent over with us, from taking too much liberty with the young men of our crew, to whose hostility I thus frequently exposed myself— these reasons and several others obtained for me the encomiums and good-will of this illustrious bishop. He accordingly obliged me to preach the Advent and Lent sermons in the cloister of the Hospital Nuns of St. Augustine in Quebec.

" However, my natural inclination was not satisfied with all this. I often went twenty or thirty leagues from our residence to visit the country. I carried on my back a little chapel service, and walked with large snowshoes, but for which I should have fallen into fearful precipices, where I should have been lost. Sometimes, in order to relieve myself, I had my little equipage drawn by a large dog that I took along, and this I did the sooner to reach Three Rivers, Saint Anne, Cap Tourmente, Isle Royal, Pointe de Levi and the Isle of St. Laurent. There I gathered in one of the largest cabins of these places as many people as I could ; then I admitted them to confession and holy communion. At night I had usually only a cloak to cover me. The frost then penetrated to my very bones. I was obliged to light my fire five or six times

during the night for fear of being frozen to death, and
I had only in very moderate quantities the food I
needed to live and to prevent my perishing with hunger
on the way. During the summer I was forced to
travel in a canoe to my mission, because there are no
practicable roads in that country. I was sent, as it
were to try me, to a mission more than 120 leagues
from Quebec.

"I made several different voyages, sometimes with
Canadian settlers, whom we had drawn to our Fort
Catarokouy (Kingston) to live, sometimes with Indians
whom I had become acquainted with. As I foresaw
that they would excite the suspicion of the Iroquois
in regard to our discoveries, I wished to see the
Indians of their Five Cantons. I accordingly went
among them with one of our soldiers from said fort,
making a journey of about seventy leagues, and both
having large snowshoes on our feet on account of the
snow, which is abundant in that country during winter.
I had some little knowledge of the Iroquois language.
We thus passed to the Honnchiouts (Oneidas) Iroquois
and to the Honnontagez (Onondagas), who received us
very well. This nation is the most warlike of all the
Iroquois. At last we arrived at the Gannickez Agniez
(Mohawks). This is one of the Five Iroquois Nations,
situated a good day's journey from the neighborhood
of New Netherland (New York). We remained some-
time among this last nation, and we lodged with a

Jesuit Father (Bruyas), born in Lyons, in order to transcribe a little Iroquois dictionary."*

After this brief autobiography we take up the strand of our story and continue the narrative.

On the morning of December 7th, Father Hennepin, with five or six companions, ascended to Queenston. They climbed the steep ascent, and from that lofty elevation looked over the intervening forest, and saw the waters of Lake Ontario stretching northwards in chaste and peaceful slumber. On their left extended the limitless forest, whose desolation of unbroken solitude shrouded in eternal silence the bones of the slaughtered Neutrals. Below them poured with accumulated grandeur the waters of four inland seas. Above the moaning and swaying of the pines rose the thunder of the distant cataract, breaking the mystic stillness. Far away, high above the tree tops, the spray of the Falls, suspended in mid-heaven, floated like a bridal veil o'er its virgin beauty.

The hardy adventurers strapped their snow-shoes to their moccasined feet and began their journey in quest of an acceptable site to build a vessel that would bear

* His subsequent voyages and journeyings he recounts in his "Descriptions of Louisiana" and in his "New Discovery," the former of which he dedicated to William Prince of Orange, King of England, who afterwards gave him valuable aid and support. In these works he relates the History of La Salle's Expedition to Niagara, Michilimakinac, Green Bay, the Forts of the Miamis and Crevecœur. He also tells us of his own expedition down the Illinois to the Mississippi and up to the Falls of St. Anthony. Descending then to the Wisconsin by way of Green Bay, back to the St. Lawrence and Quebec. He sailed for France in 1682, but history does not record the date of his death. I found his signature in the Baptismal Register at Quebec for the month of May, 1676.

La Salle and his party on their voyage to the Mississippi. The Franciscan, clothed in the coarse grey habit of his order, the peaked hood drawn over his head, the cord of St. Francis girdling his waist, and the familiar rosary and crucifix hanging by his side, at the head of his companions pushed his way through the primeval solitudes. The river narrowed as they advanced along its lonely and savage banks till, like a watery monster writhing in torture, it hurried on impatient to die on the bosom of welcoming Ontario.

They emerged from the gloomy forest, ploughed into an oak opening sheeted in snow, passed the whirlpool rapids, rounded the great bend, and again entered the darkling woods. At length, lost in speechless admiration, Hennepin, first of white men, looked upon the imperial cataract. Before his wondrous vision the great Falls,

"Charming the eye with dread—a matchless cataract,"

glorified by the dying sun, poured its majestic wealth of waters. Long after he had recovered from his awe and wonderment, he wrote for his friends in Europe a graphic description of the cataract. He thus describes the Falls:

"Between the Lakes Ontario and Erie there is a vast and prodigious fall of water, which rushes down after a surprising and astonishing manner, insomuch that the universe does not hold its parallel. 'Tis true, Italy and Switzerland boast of some such things, but

NIAGARA FALLS FROM THE FERRY.

we may well say that they are sorry patterns when compared with this of which we now speak. At the foot of this horrible precipice we meet with the river Niagara, which is not above a quarter of a league broad, but is wonderfully deep in some places. It is so rapid above the descent that it violently carries down the wild beasts while endeavoring to cross it to feed on the other side, and not being able to withstand the force of its current, which inevitably casts them headlong above six hundred feet high. This wonderful downfall consists of two great cross-streams of water, and two falls into an isle sloping along the middle of it. The waters which fall from this horrible precipice foam and boil after the most hideous manner imaginable, making an outrageous noise, more terrible than that of thunder; for, when the wind blows out of the south, their dismal roaring may be heard more than fifteen miles off. The river Niagara, having thrown itself down this incredible precipice, continues its impetuous course for two leagues together, to the great rock above-mentioned, with an inexpressible rapidity; but having passed that, its impetuosity relents, gliding along more gently for two other leagues, till it arrives at Lake Ontario, or Frontenac. From the great fall into this rock, which is to the west of the river, the two banks of it are so prodigiously high that it would make one tremble to look steadily over the water, rolling along with a rapidity not to be imagined. Were it not for this vast cataract, which interrupts navigation, they might sail with barques or greater vessels more than 450 leagues, crossing the Lake of Hurons, and reaching even to the further end of Lake Illinois, which two lakes, we may easily say, are little seas of fresh water.

"After these waters have thus discharged themselves into this gulf, they continue their course as far as the Three Mountains, which are on the east of the river, and the Great Rock, which is on the west, and lifts itself three fathoms above the waters, or thereabouts."

Pushing on they reached Chippewa Creek, constructed a temporary cabin, lighted a fire, and throwing themselves upon a bed of spruce boughs, slept the sleep of travel-worn and wearied men. The place was not suitable for the building of a vessel, and the following morning Hennepin and his companions began their return journey. Herds of startled deer and flocks of wild turkeys gladdened their hearts, giving promise of abundant game for their subsistence during their stay in the country. The following morning, December 11th, 1678, Father Hennepin, in the presence of La Motte and his men, nailed a crucifix to a tree, improvised an altar, placed the sacrificial stone thereon, and robed in chasuble, stole and alb, offered to the adorable God the clean oblation, realizing the vision of the poet:

> "A crucifix fastened
> High on the trunk of a tree, ...
> Looked with its agonized face on the multitude kneeling beneath it,
> This was their rural chapel."

This was the first mass ever said on the banks of the Niagara River.* La Motte served the mass, his companions knelt in adoration, while the openings of the temporary chapel were darkened with the faces of the swarthy Senecas, who, confused and astonished, watched with wonderment the white-robed priest. Daillon, the first of consecrated men to raise the emblem of man's redemption among the Neutrals, was dead and mouldering in his grave; Brebeuf perished as became a hero of the cross; and now, from the land sanctified by their labors, the consecrated Host is elevated in benediction, and the angelic hymn, " Glory to God in the highest," breaks the eternal silence of the primeval forest, and dies away in its infinitude of desolation.

THE FIRST MASS.

I.

Deep, and silent, and heavy, and tall,
   The forest swept to the water's edge ;
The wild deer fled at the eagle's call,
   The wild fox crept through the laurel hedge,
And the blue sky bent o'er the river's flow,
The " Beautiful River "†—long ago !

* The first mass ever said on the Niagara Peninsula was offered up at or near the mouth of the Grand River, where the Sulpician Priests, Galineé and De Casson, wintered in the year 1669, and, according to the "Journal" of Father Galineé, said mass every morning.

† The beautiful river Niagara, into which no barque similar to ours had ever sailed.—" Hennepin, N. A.," p. 74.

II.

And then, in the light of the winter sun,
  In the glorious flush of the morning sky,
A wonderful scene on the shore is begun—
  A scene half earth, half heaven brought nigh ;
While the musical waves of the river flow
Past the wonderful vision—long ago !

III.

Red men stood there on the snow-clad sod,
  With the dark-eyed soldiers of sunny France,
And the vested priest of the living God
  Lifts the sacred Host to their rev'rent glance ;
And nought broke the hush but the river's flow,
That wintry morning—long ago !

CHAPTER VII.

THE PRIEST AND THE EXPLORER.

Hennepin Leaves for the Seneca Towns—Journey Through the Forest—
Father Garnier—Mass with the Senecas—The Iroquois Council—
La Motte Speaks—Torture of a Prisoner—Frightful Cruelty—Galineé
and the Andaste—Return of the Embassy—René La Salle—His
Journey to the Senecas—Building of the "Griffon"—History of La Salle
—The Spanish Explorers—La Salle's Dream of Conquest—Journey to
the Grand River—Meets Joliet—On his Second Expedition—The
Recollects—Outward Bound.

LA MOTTE, acting probably on instructions from
La Salle, now prepared to visit the Seneca
chiefs. His object was to obtain permission to build a
fort near the mouth of Niagara River, enter into a
friendly alliance with the tribe, and secure their good
will and approval while building the *Griffon*. Father
Hennepin, with four men and one or two of the Seneca
fishing party, accompanied him. The priest, as we
have seen from his own account, was in a measure
familiar with the language of the tribe; and as he was
something of a diplomat, and a man of indomitable
courage and endurance, he was an invaluable companion of La Salle's lieutenant. Leaving a guard at
the foot of the mountain ridge (now Lewiston) they

set out on snow-shoes, well-armed and equipped, and plunged into the depths of the cheerless forest. It was the Christmas morning of 1678, after the sacrifice of the mass had been offered up, when they began their journey, bearing on their backs five hundred pounds of gifts of considerable value, and some sacks of dried corn. For five days they held the Indian trail, and on towards noon of the 30th entered the Seneca town of Taegarondies, near the present city of Rochester. The Iroquois received them with distinguished consideration, and conducted them to the lodge of the head chief, where their travel-worn feet were bathed and rubbed with bear's oil, while a gaping crowd of women and children stared at them with awe and curiosity. Here, to Father Hennepin's intense delight, he met Fathers Julien Garnier* and Peter Raffeix, the Jesuit missionaries. In 1654, Fathers Chaumonot and Le Moyne opened the missions to the Five Iroquois Cantons, and from that year, with hardly an intermission, the heroic members of the great Jesuit Order labored among these savages with an

---

* Father Julien Garnier was the first Jesuit ordained in Canada, and the last missionary of that Order among the Senecas. At the early age of 25 he began (in 1668) his labors among the Oneidas, and during the same year preached to the Cayugas and Onondagas. The following year we find him with the Senecas, having charge of the mission of St. Michael and also that of St. James. In 1671, according to the "Relations," he had charge of the three missions of the Senecas. After sixty years of a missionary life, filled with examples of heroism surpassing belief, he calmly died at Quebec in the month of February, 1730. He was well versed in the Algonquin, Huron and Iroquois tongues, and was said to be familiar with their various dialects. It was from him that Lafitean gathered his knowledge of Indian manners and customs.

intensity of zeal and heroism of self-denial that to-day excites the wonder and admiration of the historian.

The following morning Father Hennepin celebrated mass in the bark chapel of the Jesuits, and after he had finished his thanksgiving and breakfasted, he was told that the Seneca chiefs, to the number of forty-two, met in Grand Council and awaited himself and La Motte. When the priest and his companion entered the Council-house they were received with courteous silence. The tall and lithe forms of the Iroquois, enveloped in ceremonial robes of beaver, wolf and black squirrel, were as motionless as statues. When Hennepin and La Motte advanced to pay their respects to the assemblage, the chiefs squatted on bear skins, lighted their calumets, and, with a dignity and stateliness becoming the importance of the occasion, invited the strangers to speak. La Motte made known the object of their embassy, accompanying each request with valuable gifts, for, adds Hennepin, " the best arguments in the world are not listened to by these Indians unless accompanied by presents." They accepted the gifts with apparent satisfaction, gave wampum belts in return, but answered La Motte's demands so evasively that the Council ended without any satisfaction. Their gravity and diplomacy excited the surprise of the priest, and their bearing during the whole interview he compared to that of the Senators of Venice. Before the discomfited embassy returned, two prisoners of war, captured near the borders of

Virginia, were brought to the village, one of whom, out of compliment to the French, was put to death with unspeakable torture. The priest and his companion, to show their abhorrence and condemnation of the scene about to be enacted, refused to witness the awful spectacle, and withdrew to a neighboring lodge.

Ten years before, in this very town, when the Sulpician priest Father Galinee visited these people, the same awful tragedy took place, and the graphic description given by the illustrious priest in his journal still exists to record the ferocious thirst for blood and the delight in human agony that devoured the North American savage.

"During this interval," he writes, " I saw the saddest spectacle I had ever witnessed. I was informed one evening that some warriors had arrived with a prisoner and had placed him in a cabin near our own. I went to see him and found him seated with three women, who vied with each other in bewailing the death of a relative who had been killed in a skirmish in which the prisoner had been captured. He was a young man 18 or 20 years old, very well formed, whom they had clothed from head to foot since his arrival. They had inflicted no injury upon him since his capture. They had not even saluted him with blows, as is their custom with prisoners on entering a village. I thought, therefore, that I would have an opportunity to demand him for our guide, as

they said he was one of the Tongenhas.* I then
went to find M. de La Salle for that purpose, who told
me that the Senecas were men of their word, that
since they had promised us a captive they would give
us one, that it mattered little whether it was this one
or another, and it was useless to press them. I therefore gave myself no further trouble about it. Night
came on and we retired. The next day had no sooner
dawned than a large company entered our cabin to
tell us that the captive was about to be burned, and
that he had asked to see the " Mistigouch."† I ran
to the public place to see him, and found he was
already on the scaffold, where they had bound him
hand and foot to a stake. I was surprised to hear
him utter some Algonquin words which I knew,
although, from the manner in which he pronounced
them, they were hardly recognizable. He made us
comprehend at last that he desired his execution
should be postponed until the next day. If he had
spoken good Algonquin I would have understood him,
but his language differed from the Algonquin still
more than that of the Ottawas, so I understood but
very little. I conversed with the Iroquois, through
our Dutch interpreter, who told me that the captive
had been given to an old woman, in place of her son
who had been killed; that she could not bear to see
him live; that all the family took such a deep interest
in his suffering that they would not postpone his

* The Andastes.   † The priest.

torture. The irons were already in the fire to torment the poor wretch. On my part, I told our interpreter to demand him in place of the captive they had promised, and I would make a present to the old woman to whom he belonged; but he was not at any time willing to make the proposition, alleging that such was not their custom and the affair was of too serious a nature. I even used threats to induce him to say what I desired, but in vain, for he was obstinate as a Dutchman and ran away to avoid me. I then remained alone near the poor sufferer, who saw before him the instruments of his torture. I endeavored to make him understand that he could have no recourse but to God, and that he would pray to Him thus: 'Thou who hast made all things, have pity on me; I am sorry not to have obeyed Thee, but if I should live I will obey thee in all things.'

" He understood me better than I expected, because all the people who are neighbors to the Ontonacs understand Algonquin. I did not consider that I ought to baptize him, not only because I could not understand him well enough to know his state of mind, but for the reason that the Iroquois urged me to leave him, that they might begin their tragedy, because I believed that the act of contrition which I had caused him to make would save him. Had I foreseen this event on the preceding evening I would certainly have baptized him, for I would have had during the night time to instruct him. So I could do nothing but exhort him to endure patiently and to offer up his sufferings to God, in saying to him often, " Thou who hast made all things, have pity on me." This he repeated with his eyes raised towards heaven. In the meantime I saw the principal relative of the deceased approach him with a gun-barrel, half of which was heated red hot. This obliged me to withdraw. Some began to disapprove of my encouraging, inasmuch as it is a bad sign among them for a prisoner to endure the torture patiently. I retired therefore with sorrow, and had scarcely turned away when the barbarous Iroquois applied the red hot gun-barrel to the top of his feet, which caused the poor wretch to utter a loud cry. This turned me about, and I saw the Iroquois, with a grave and sober countenance, apply the iron slowly along his feet and legs, and some old men who were smoking around the scaffold and all the young people leaped with joy to witness the contortions which the severity of the heat caused in the poor sufferer."

The discomfited embassy began their return journey, and exhausted, half-frozen and nearly famished, reached on January 14th, 1679, the banks of the Niagara. Meanwhile La Salle, with Tonty, an Italian companion, had left Fort Frontenac, entered the Genesee River, and arrived at the Seneca village a few days after the departure of Hennepin and La Motte. Ten years before, this hardy adventurer, accompanied by the Sulpician priests, Dollier de Casson and Galineé, had, when starting on his first voyage to the Mississippi, passed some days with these people. He succeeded by his personal influence and commanding address in conciliating the Senecas, and after receiving their permission to build a blacksmith shop and storehouse, he returned to the mouth of the Genesee and sailed for Niagara. On the 26th of January he laid the keel of the *Griffon* at the mouth of Cayuga Creek, and after encouraging his workmen with promises of reward, he returned to Fort Frontenac to obtain an outfit and supplies for the new vessel. Father Hennepin accompanied him as far as the mouth of the Niagara, where La Salle traced a stockaded block-house, which he called Fort Conty, in honor of his friend the Prince of that name.

René Robert Cavelier, better known as La Salle, was born at Rouen in 1643, and was of an old and distinguished family. At an early age he was sent by his father to be educated by the Jesuits, and though never admitted as a member of the Order, it is probable he was a novice of that Society for a short time. He distinguished himself in mathematics, and being of an ambitious and self-willed nature, he turned aside from the priesthood and entered upon a career of exploration and discovery that has won for him an enviable place among the early explorers of this continent. The intense longing for adventure which was woven into his nature induced him to visit his brother, who was a Sulpician priest in Montreal. So favorable was the impression which he made upon the Sulpicians,

PORTRAIT OF RENÉ ROBERT CAVELIER, SIEUR DE LA SALLE.

(From an Edition of 1688.)

that they sold him, for a nominal sum, a large tract of land at Lachine, near Montreal. Soon afterwards he disposed of his possessions and organized an expedition for the discovery of the Mississippi.

Like all the early explorers, his ambition was to open a passage to the South Sea, to bring Cathay, Japan, and the neighboring islands into commercial union with the West, and win for his country a new field of trade and prosperity. His imagination was fired and his ambition stimulated in reading the lives of the Spanish and Portuguese navigators, those restless and daring adventurers that through the two Americas fearlessly and bravely bore the triumphant banners of Castile and Braganza. He had heard from his father the marvellous accounts of the heroic deeds of that galaxy of heroes who, at the dawn of the sixteenth century, sailed away from the Spanish peninsula. He was familiar with the history of the Pinzons, the companions of Columbus; of Balboa, the discoverer of the Pacific and the projector of the conquest of Peru, who dragged his ships in sections across the isthmus of Darien, to meet in the end with discouragement and an ignominious death; of Magellan, the stormy petrel and intrepid hero, before whose achievements even the daring of Columbus paled. His ambition was stimulated and his energies aroused to activity in perusing the official report of the Pizarros, who swept like a whirlwind to the conquest of Peru, and subdued an empire; of De Soto,

their companion in their exploits, who afterwards
traversed the States of Alabama and Georgia, and
reached the banks of the Mississippi, 128 years before
La Salle himself was visited by his dream of conquest. He was an earnest Catholic, and prevailed
upon the Sulpician Order to permit two of its priests
to accompany him to evangelize the nomad tribes that
ranged the valleys of the Ohio, the Mississippi, and
the great lakes. On the 6th day of July, 1669, La
Salle, Fathers De Casson and Galineé, with twenty-
two men in seven canoes, escorted by a party of
Senecas, began the ascent of the St. Lawrence. After
twenty-seven days of incessant toil, in which they
suffered severely from disease and exposure, they
entered Lake Ontario, and, coasting its southern
shore, landed about four miles east of the Genesee
River, on the 10th of August. He now proceeded
overland to the Seneca villages to obtain a guide to
conduct the party through the unknown wilderness
that stretched in unbroken slumber between their
villages and the sources of the Ohio. Failing in his
quest he returned to his canoes, and paddled westward till he reached Burlington Bay. He then
proceeded to the village of Otinaowataoua, where he
met the explorer Joliet, returning from a fruitless
expedition in search of the copper mines of Lake
Superior. Here La Salle was taken ill, and leaving
the two priests to proceed on their journey, he
returned to Montreal. At the period of which we

write, 1678, he was entering upon his second voyage to the Mississippi, and the indomitable courage, perseverance and endurance which he displayed on this expedition mark him as one of the grandest men that ever trod the American continent. The explorer was detained at Frontenac much longer than he expected, and during his absence the *Griffon* was completed and safely moored two and a half miles up the river, where she could ride securely at anchor. Father Hennepin now returned to meet La Salle and invite some Franciscan priests to accompany him on his mission to the great West.

On arriving at Fort Frontenac he received a generous welcome from his Franciscan brethren. La Salle greeted him warmly, and, as a mark of his friendship for the Franciscan Order and a recognition of Hennepin's services, conveyed to the Order eighteen acres of land, bordering on the lake near the fort, and about one hundred acres of the adjacent forest. He also decreed—by virtue of his authority as Governor and proprietor of the fort—that no other religious society should be established in its vicinity.* On the return of La Salle and Hennepin they were accompanied by three Recollect priests, Gabriel de la Ribourde, Zenobe Membré, and Melithon Wattaux. These priests were natives of Flanders, affiliated to the Spanish Recollects

*Hennepin's "New Discovery," Ed. 1698, p. 71. Gilmary Shea, in his "History of the Catholic Church in the United States," Vol. I., p. 322, is clearly wrong when he states that La Salle deeded a grant of land to the Recollects at Fort Niagara. There is no record showing that La Salle ever owned a foot of land in the State of New York.

THE BUILDING OF THE "GRIFFON," 1679.

Fac-simile reproduction of the original copper-plate engraving first published in Hennepin's "Nouvelle Decouverte," Amsterdam, 1704.

until Louis XIV. conquered Andalusia, and made it a French province, when the Recollects came under French jurisdiction. Wattaux and Membré were in the prime of their manhood, animated with a devouring zeal for the salvation of souls, and all aglow with a generous enthusiasm for missionary work.

Father Gabriel de la Ribourde, the Superior of the Order in Canada, and the last scion of an old Burgundy house, was a cheerful and vigorous old man of 64, whose martial bearing was equally adapted to the struggles of the camp or the hardships of the missionary field, and who, if he had been a Crusader, would have swung the sword with the same courage and loyalty with which he now bore the Cross through the wilderness three thousand miles from home. The ship which bore La Salle and the priests carried also the anchors, sails and rigging for the *Griffon*, which were with considerable trouble dragged from Lewiston to Cayuga Creek. At last the *Griffon* was finished, a party of men, with Father Melithon as chaplain, were left to guard the fort, and La Salle, with Hennepin, Tonty and their companions entered the vessel, which sailed away with swelling canvas into the virgin waters of Lake Erie. As they glided into deeper water Father Hennepin intoned the "*Vexilla Regis*," his companions took it up, and to the strains of this historic hymn the *Griffon*, outward-bound, headed for Lake Michigan.

CHAPTER VIII.

LAMBERVILLE AND THE IROQUOIS MISSIONS.

Seneca Discontent—The Fort Abandoned—Father Melithon—Governor
Dongan—The Iroquois Allies—Treachery of Denonville—Father
Lamberville—French Stratagem—Capture of an Iroquois Party—The
Onondaga Council—Address of the Tribal Orator—Escort to Lamber-
ville—Jesuit Missions—The Seneca Epidemic—Heroism of the Priests
—Fort Niagara—The Miamis' Rescue Party—Father Peter Milet—
Captured by the Onondagas—The Rescue—Fort Niagara Taken.

A FTER the departure of Hennepin and La Salle,
Father Melithon and his men abandoned the
bark chapel and the two houses thrown up for the
accommodation of the builders of the *Griffon*, and
retired to Lewiston, where La Motte had built his
stockaded warehouse. Hardly were they comfortably
settled in their new quarters when the Senecas began
to show signs of uneasiness and discontent. They
learned, to their chagrin, that the building which
La Motte constructed was something more than the
blacksmith shop and warehouse which they were given
to understand was all that La Salle asked for. The
strong palisades which protected the building, and the
armed soldiers, implied a determination on the part of
La Salle to hold possession of the adjoining country.
They at once assumed an aggressive attitude, insulted

those of the men that appeared outside the gates,
and, with scowling brows, gave them to understand
that they were no longer welcome. Father Melithon,
who knew enough of the Iroquois language to make
himself understood, in vain reasoned with them.
They insisted that he and the Frenchmen should
leave, and the priest, after consultation with the lieutenant in command, prudently decided to do so. The
detachment retired to Fort Frontenac, and La Salle's
stockade was burned to the ground.* Father Wat-
teaux, after the abandonment of the fort, spent some
time doing missionary work among a party of Cayugas,
who had temporarily settled at the Bay of Quinte.
The restless and nomadic nature of these people was
a bar to any hope of their permanent conversion, and
the zealous priest returned to France, where he died
at an advanced age. He was a man of strong religious
convictions and of an ardent piety which often carried
him into the realms of asceticism. So far as history
records, he was the last of the noble band of Flem-
mings who did duty in Canada.

Seven years after the burning of La Salle's fort, a
combination of circumstances led to an attack on the
Iroquois of the Five Cantons by the French. The
Dutch colony of the New Netherlands had, in the
meanwhile, become the property of the English, and
was now known as the colony of New York. The
Duke of York, after whom it was named, appointed

* See Appendix C, " Letters of Messrs. Bain and Severance."

Colonel Thomas Dongan its Governor. Dongan was a nominal Catholic, and nephew of the great Earl of Tyrconnel, presumptive heir to the Earldom of Limerick, and as he was a man of liberal education and had passed some years in the French army, he spoke the language of France with the ease and fluency of a courtly Parisian. The English laid claim to the territory now known as the State of New York, and as the Five Nations could, on short notice, call four or five thousand warriors into the field, Dongan saw the wisdom of attaching them to his service, foreseeing that a conflict between the French and English for control of the fur trade was inevitable. The Iroquois were inclined to side with the English, and as their own forests were almost denuded of game, their hunters pushed into the territory of tribes in friendly alliance with the French. Duchesnau had some time before written to Count Frontenac, "That it is quite evident that the Iroquois, inflated by victories they have obtained over the Illinois, propose to destroy the Nations which are in alliance with us and those from whom we obtain a great many peltries."* Towards the end of his letter the Intendant added the portentous sentence, "The Iroquois, stimulated by the success they will probably obtain over those tribes, who are but imperfectly disciplined, will almost inevitably turn on us when they will have no other enemy." The time had now come for the French to act, but

* " Paris Documents," Vol. II., p. 171.

Denonville, their Governor, wishing to conceal his intention of a sudden attack on the Five Nations, had recourse to a stratagem which will ever be a stain upon his memory. The English Governor, Dongan, had, by bribes and promises, prevailed upon four of the Iroquois Nations to send out of their country the French missionaries. The Onondagas, however, remained firm in their attachment to their priests, the Lamberville brothers, who were now the only Jesuits left in the whole Iroquois territory. Denonville wrote to Father John Lamberville to prevail upon the Onondagas to send a deputation of fifty of their chief men to meet him in council at Fort Frontenac; his intention being to make them prisoners, though conscious that in all probability, in retaliation for his perfidy, Father Lamberville would be burned at the stake.

Father Lamberville, entirely unsuspicious, endeavored to prevail with the Onondagas to comply with the Governor's request, but the chiefs, with characteristic caution, pleaded for delay. In the meantime Denonville, at the head of a large detachment of troops and a body of Christian Indians, left Montreal for Fort Frontenac. His Indian allies surprised and took captive a number of Cayugas, who belonged to the Neutral villages of Kente and Ganneious. Denonville held them prisoners and instructed his lieutenant, Champigny, to proceed by forced marches with a body of men to Fort Frontenac, and invite the neighboring

Iroquois to a feast. About thirty men and ninety women and children accepted the invitation, and to their unutterable surprise found themselves prisoners. The following day a party of Iroquois, who were peaceably fishing on an island in the St. Lawrence, were invited to the fort, and were likewise made captive. That night one of their number escaped, and striking into the forest, reached the nearest Onondaga town, and reported what had taken place. The Iroquois could hardly credit their senses, as no declaration of war had been proclaimed. The Onondagas now understood Denonville's object in inviting their deputies to meet him in council, and sending for Father Lamberville, they asked him if he was a party to the treachery. When the Jesuit heard the news he was astounded, and after proclaiming his innocence, candidly acknowledged that appearances were against him.

Beyond question, a man's honest dealing with his fellow-man will stand by him in every emergency. John Lamberville came to Canada in 1668, and three years after left for the Onondaga mission, where he founded the mission of St. John the Baptist. For fifteen years this heroic man devoted himself to the Christianizing and uplifting of this nation. By his consuming zeal, his continual life of self-denial on their behalf, his straightforward and manly bearing, he had won not only their good opinion but their friendship, and that friendship stood him now in good stead.

The scene that ensued was dramatic. The Onondaga chiefs rose as one man from the bear robes upon which they had been sitting, and forming a circle around the priest, their tribal orator thus addressed him : "We know you too well, Teiorhensere,* to believe that you meant to betray us. We think that you have been deceived as well as we, and we are not unjust enough to punish you for the crimes of others. We believe you to be innocent. Yet it will not do for you to remain here, and all will not do you, perhaps, the same justice as ourselves. When our young braves have once chanted their war-song, they will listen to nothing but their fury, from which we shall not be able to save you. Fly, then, Teiorhensere! Fly!"† Bidding him an affectionate farewell, they placed him under the care of two of their best warriors, who, by secret paths, conducted him to the walls of Fort Frontenac.

With him ended the last of the missions opened by the Catholic priests of France to the great Iroquois Nation. Thirty-four years before, taking their lives in their hands, the intrepid and heroic Jesuits plunged into the gloomy forests of New York Territory, and to souls seated in darkness and in the shadow of death,

* "*Dawning of the Day.*"   Colden's "Five Nations," p. 57.

† "Charlevoix," Vol. II., p. 346.

Dr. Canniff, in his "Settlement of Upper Canada," p. 15, and Dr. Withrow, in his "History of Upper Canada," p. 151, no doubt unwittingly, accuse the Jesuit priest of being a party to Denonville's treachery. Denonville, in his official journal, acquits Father Lamberville of any part in the business. "Col. Doc., N.Y.T.," Vol. III., p. 80.

brought the gift of hope and the message of the Gospel. Many of those whom they had won from heathenism were numbered with the consecrated dead ; others were gathered into villages along the banks of the lower St. Lawrence, where, protected by the French, they lived a life of Christian peace and quietness.

As the subject will ever have an absorbing interest for the Catholic reader, let us rapidly review the list of the priests and their work. Beginning with 1654, when Fathers Chaumonot and Le Moyne entered the Iroquois country, the Gospel was preached intermittingly until 1667, when the Catholic Church made permanent arrangements for the cultivation and care of this distant field. In July of that year, Fathers Bruyas, Pierron and Fremin left Quebec for the Iroquois country. In August of the same year they entered the Mohawk village, where a few years before the illustrious martyr, Jogues, offered to God his life for the salvation of these people. Leaving his brother priests in this village, Father Bruyas left for the Oneidas, to whom also came after a few months the illustrious priest, Garnier. Resting here for a short time, he passed on to the central Canton of the Onondagas, where he remained at their request, and writing to Quebec for more laborers, the Superior of the Order sent to his assistance Fathers Milet and Carheil. Father Carheil, bidding good-bye to his brother priests, westward held his way till he reached the

Cayugas, with whom he remained several years. This great priest died in Quebec in 1726, having lived for sixty years with different tribes of Indians.

The Senecas, jealous of the advantages and benefits reaped by their neighbors from the presence of the priests among them, sent in November, 1668, a deputation of their most influential chiefs, begging the Jesuits to send Black Robes to their villages. The Superior gave them a letter to Father Fremin, who with Father Pierron was with the Mohawks, requesting him to go to the Senecas. To him a request coming from such a source was a command, and though at this time the small-pox was ravaging the Seneca villages, Fremin, with the courage and magnanimity that became a soldier of the Cross, plunged into the intervening forest and arrived at Tsonnontonan. The epidemic increasing, Fremin summoned to his assistance, from the Onondagas, the heroic Father Garnier. For months these priests labored with untiring energy. Their self-denial and courage excited the wonder and admiration of the Senecas. Here were men alien in language and birth, seeking no earthly reward, despising the profits of the fur trade, and influenced only by a love for perishing souls, surpassing the understanding of their savage companions, exposing themselves to the horrors of a disease from which the Seneca shrank with fear and loathing ; their flinty hearts were softened, and when the small-pox had spent itself, the Jesuits rose from beside the last of the graves of its victims heroes and saints.

Their influence over the tribe was complete, and when, through the machinations of Orconahe—called by the French "Le Grande Guele"—Father Milet was driven from Onondaga, the Senecas· welcomed him to their villages as a conquering brave returning from the battle. Father Fremin now chose for his residence the village of Gannagaro, where he founded the mission of St. Michael, which he served until 1671. Father Garnier settled at the village of Gaosaegaah, where he remained for a number of years.

In 1669 Father Fremin, the Local Superior, summoned a Council at Onondaga of all the priests laboring among the Iroquois cantons. The object was to discuss the best means of promoting their missionary work, or, as Father Bruyas said, "to advance the salvation of souls, the glory of God, and do the best they could for the Iroquois mission." This was on the 29th of August, 1669. It was to attend this Council that Father Fremin left the Seneca mission of St. Michael on the morning of the very day that La Salle and his two Sulpician companions arrived at the Seneca town of Gannagaro. With this brief but useful review we finish with the Iroquois missions, and return to our subject.

After destroying the Seneca towns, Denonville, leaving his army at Arondequoit Bay, proceeded with a hundred men to Niagara and began the building of

Fort Denonville, on the present site of Niagara fort. He built eight cabins, erected a house for the chaplain, constructed a church, and invited Father Lamberville to take spiritual charge of his men. The fort was abundantly supplied with provisions, which, however, turned out to be atrociously bad. Scurvy and other malignant diseases began to play havoc with the men; and to add to their wretchedness, the ever-watchful Senecas prowled in the neighboring woods and tomahawked or shot down any man who ventured outside the palisades. In a few months the enclosure became a charnel-house, and when spring opened there were only twelve men left. To all appearances the priest and his handful of men were doomed. when, providentially, a war party of friendly Miamis arrived, and offered to escort what remained of the garrison to Fort Frontenac. When they entered, Father Lamberville was apparently dying. He was eaten up with scurvy and pitiable to look upon. Under the kindly treatment of the Miamis he recovered sufficiently to be dragged on a sleigh to the French settlement, where in a few months he regained his accustomed strength. After his recovery he proceeded, in 1691, to Sault St. Louis, and returned to France in the fall of 1698. The Onondagas were so devotedly attached to him that in the course of the following year they requested the French Governor to recall him from France, that he might live and die among them. The saintly priest, however, never returned, but remained in his native

land, where he died in 1703.* Denonville regarrisoned
the fort in the following year, and appointed Father
Peter Milet chaplain. This distinguished priest came
to Canada in 1667, and left the following year for the
Onondaga mission, where he joined Father Garnier,
whose apostolic labors began to bear an abundant
harvest. Here his wondrous piety excited the astonish-
ment of his Indian converts, and they gave him the
name of Teahronhiagannra (" He that looks up to
heaven"). He was elected a Sachem of the Oneidas,
and was the only European that was privileged to vote
in the Council of the Five Nations.† In fulfilment of
a promise which Denonville made to Dongan, the
Governor of New York, the fort was after a few months
demolished. Shortly before taking their departure,
Father Milet, on Good Friday, erected and blessed a
large cross in the centre of the square, having carved
upon it the following inscription :

REGN. VINC. IMP. CHRS.‡

(Christ reigneth, conquereth, ruleth)

On his return to Fort Frontenac he was made a
prisoner by strategy. In June, 1689, some pagan

---

* " La Potherie Histoire de l' Amerique," Vol. III., p. 131.

† " Paris Documents," p. 415.

‡ Mr. William Kirby makes allusion in his poem, " Spina Christi," to this
inscription in the following lines :

> " In old Niagara fort, a cross stood loftily in view,
> And ' Regnat, Vincit, Imperat, Christus' the words did show
> Carved on it, when the Ronsillon came up in early spring
> To close the port, and guard the fort,
> And keep it for the King."

11

Onondagas approached the fort, and shouting out that peace had been proclaimed at Montreal, asked for a priest and doctor to attend a dying woman. Father Milet and Saint Amand, a physician, immediately complied with their request, and to their surprise found themselves prisoners. The missionary was stripped and pinioned, but while being conducted through the forest, Manchot, an Oneida chief, joined the party, and whispered that he and his Oneida converts would save him. At one of the Onondaga villages he was subjected to considerable abuse and ill-treatment, but Manchot claimed him as an Oneida prisoner. He was handed over to the chief on condition that he should be put to death. To save appearances he was led bound to the Oneida Canton. He was then stripped for the torture, when a converted squaw advanced and demanded to adopt him in place of a son whom she had lost in a skirmish with the French. He was, however, detained as a prisoner, but kindly treated. From Oneida he wrote to the Fathers at Quebec an account of his captivity and treatment, heading his letter thus: "*A. Onneiout, jour de l' octave de St. Pierre et St. Paul, 1691*," and concludes as follows: "*Mes rds peres, tres humble et tres obeissant serviteur in N. S. Pierre Milet, de la compagnie de Jesus.*"*

On his release Father Milet returned to Quebec, where he died, after passing fifty-four years on the Indian missions.

* A copy of Shea's "Translation of Father Milet's History of his Captivity" is in the Toronto Public Library.

In 1721 the French again took possession of Niagara, which they held until 1759, when the gallant Aubrey was defeated in his attempt to relieve it when the fort was invested by Sir William Johnston. During these thirty-eight years there was always a chaplain at Niagara, for to every post having forty men it was a rule of the French military authorities that services should be regularly held ; and the garrison at Fort Niagara had always that number or more. The only name, however, to be found is that of the Recollect, Emmanuel Grespel, as the register was probably taken away or destroyed by Sir William Johnston. Father Grespel came to Canada in 1723, and was appointed chaplain at Crown Point, from which place he came in 1733 to Niagara. He was shipwrecked off the Island of Anticosti on his way to Europe, when most of his companions perished by drowning or from exposure on the desolate island. He was, however, providentially saved, and on his return to France published an account of his missionary career.. In 1721 the great Jesuit historian, Charlevoix, said mass at the fort when on his way to the Mississippi, and in the month of July, 1751, the Sulpician priest, Father Picquet, according to his own account, said mass in the chapel of the fort, and gave instructions to a band of Senecas.

CHAPTER IX.

FROM THE OLD REGIME TO THE NEW.

Capture of Fort Niagara   Good-bye to the French—The Boundary Line—
U. E. Loyalists—First Settlement of Catholics—The French Counts —
Letter of Mr. Windham—Provision for the Settlement—Failure of the
Same—Jurisdiction of Quebec—Religious Liberty—Statutory Division
—Niagara in 1792   First Parliament—Catholic Members—The Mac-
donells of Glengarry—Flight of the Scotch Catholics   Letter of Lord
Sydney—Arrival of Catholic Soldiers—First Catholic Chaplain—Letter
of E. B. Littlehales—Lord Wharncliffe's Apprehensions.

THE capture of Fort Niagara by Sir William
Johnston carried with it the destruction of the
last altar raised by the French on the east bank of
the Niagara river.   It is possible that with the forces
commanded by Johnston there were some Catholic
Hessians, but history makes no mention of them.
The Penal Code had not yet been repealed, and as one
clause of that code prohibited Irish Catholics from
serving in the British army, none would be found
with his troops.   Some years after the Declaration of
Independence on the part of the United States, Great
Britain, in 1783, acknowledged by the Peace of Paris
the sovereignty of the United States of America.
Although by this treaty the English Government
recognized the great lakes as the boundary between

their possessions on this continent and those of the American people, yet, under various pretexts, Fort Niagara and the other military posts along the northern American frontier were not surrendered until 1796 —thirteen years after the signing of Jay's treaty. The United Empire Loyalists, who stood by the King of Great Britain during the Revolutionary war, fled to Canada after the Peace of Paris, and many of them settled in the Niagara peninsula; but among these settlers, to whom large tracts of land were given, there were no Catholics. The earliest mention to be found of any Catholics settling in this section of the country is that which appears in the " Dominion Archives " for 1888. During the French Revolution, which immediately preceded the Napoleonic era, large numbers of refugees fled from France to England, where they were hospitably and kindly treated. The Duke of Portland recommended some of these French immigrants to settle in Upper Canada, and wrote to Mr. Russell, July 5th, 1798, on their behalf as follows: " The King, having taken into consideration the forlorn situation of the French noblemen and officers who have borne arms in his Majesty's service, or distinguished themselves by their attachment to his late most Christian Majesty's person and family, and by their exertions in the Royalist armies and in endeavoring to deliver their country from a cruel and oppressive tyranny, has been graciously pleased to direct that a corps of French gentlemen should be raised, under the command of Comte de Puisaye, for the purpose of forming an establishment in Upper Canada, on lands assigned by the King's commands to such French gentlemen and their families as have claims arising from the above-mentioned services, according to the following regulations."* Lands were accordingly allotted to them in the County of York and in the present township of Niagara.

Lieutenant-General the Comte de Puisaye, who was the leader of the handful of immigrants that settled at Niagara, came well recommended. "The Comte de Puisaye," writes the Right Hon. W. Windham to President Russell, "has been by far more known to me than to any other of His Majesty's ministers, the whole of his transactions with the Government having, in fact, been carried on through me. The suspicions attempted to be fixed upon him by his countrymen, and by which they seem to have succeeded best in poisoning against him the mind of his Sovereign, have been that he was sold to the British Government, and in favor of English interests betrayed those of his own country. On the whole of his conduct, in these respects, I can speak with a degree of knowledge that does not admit of the possibility of my being mistaken; and, with this responsibility for the truth of my report, I venture not only to vindicate him from every shadow of imputation of the sort attempted to be fixed upon him, but in the strongest manner to assert

* "Dominion Archives," Vol. VIII., p. 80.

his merits, and request accordingly to recommend him to your good offices, not only as a man whom I am persuaded will not fail to prove deserving of them, but as one whom we are bound in an especial manner to support, knowing, as we do, both that the calumnies circulated against him are unfounded and incurred by conduct which we must feel to be highly meritorious."

In the political and financial sketch prepared for the settlement and government of the French colonists, provision was made even for the priests who were to accompany them. "As to the priests under 40 years of age, those who on their arrival are not to be settled in parishes or convents, and for whom no ecclesiastical employment should appear to be then vacant, would be collected in seminaries of twenty or thirty in number, on the very spot of the settlement, and aided in all the hard work by the workmen who should be assigned to them, they might themselves assist in the construction of buildings and in the labor least fatiguing of the husbandry."*

The effort to establish a large French settlement never passed beyond the experimental stage. The severity of the winter, the exertion required for clearing the land, and their total ignorance of pioneer life, barred all hopes of success. De Puisaye and the Count de Chalus, his companion, abandoned their lands and returned to France. They dissuaded their countrymen in England from immigrating, stating that nothing but starvation awaited them.

* "Dominion Archives," 1888, p. 77.

The Constitutional Act, which was passed by the British Parliament in 1791, divided Quebec into Upper and Lower Canada. This political division, however, in no way interfered with the ecclesiastical limits of the diocese of Quebec, which extended from Anticosti in the east to Hudson's Bay in the North-West. Indeed, until the Declaration of Independence, the jurisdiction of Quebec's bishop extended over the States of Maine, Vermont and New York, and in the west and south over all the vast Valley of the Mississippi, Texas and the Rio Grande. A chain of French posts stretched along the Mississippi, and bound together Louisiana, Georgia, Florida, and the limitless territory that extended even to the confines of California. Three years after the fall of Quebec, Great Britain, by the Treaty of Paris, 1673, extended to her subjects in Canada the freedom, rights, privileges and immunities which they had enjoyed under the French Crown, adding, however, the dangerous-looking restriction, "so far as the laws of Great Britain permit."

As the penal laws yet disgraced the statute books of England, this last part in the clause of the treaty gave it an elasticity which might at any time be converted to the benefit of the Government. Twelve years after the Declaration of Independence, when the American people had succeeded in establishing a satisfactory and stable form of Government, Congress, by an ordinance dated July 13th, 1787, declared it to be a fundamental principle of American law, never to be changed: "That no person demeaning himself in a peaceable and orderly manner should ever be molested on account of his mode of worship or religious sentiment." This proclamation settled forever the fate of the penal laws; and whatever might be the interpretation put upon the doubtful clause of the Paris Treaty, in the face of the American deliverance, it would scarcely be prejudicial to the interests of the Catholics.*

From Jay's treaty, in 1783, to 1790, the population of the western part of the Province of Quebec increased rapidly, and the time had now come for Upper Canada to establish her own parliament. The bill of Separation was introduced on the 7th of April, 1791, by Mr. Pitt, and after debate, in which Mr. Fox, the leader of the Opposition, distinguished himself, it finally passed its third reading on the 16th of May, and Colonel John Graves Simcoe, who was in England on parole, was appointed the first Governor of Western

* The relaxation of the Penal Code dates practically from the Battle of Fontenoy, in 1745, when the Irish Brigade, led by O'Brien, almost annihilated the Duke of Cumberland's regiments. George II., on hearing the result of the battle, uttered that memorable imprecation on the Penal Code : " Cursed be the laws that deprived me of such soldiers." Davis, in his magnificent poem on " Fontenoy," records the effect of that famous charge :

" Like lions leaping at a fold, when mad with hunger's pang,
Right up against the English line the Irish exiles sprang ;
Bright was their steel, 'tis bloody now, their guns are filled with gore ;
Through shattered ranks, and severed files, and trampled flags they tore ;
The English strove with desperate strength, paused, rallied, staggered, fled—
The green hill-side is matted close with dying and with dead ;
Across the plain, and far away passed on that hideous wrack,
While cavalier and fantassin dash in upon their track.
On Fontenoy ! on Fontenoy ! like eagles in the sun,
With bloody plumes the Irish stand—the field is fought and won !"

Canada. He arrived at Montreal on January 17th, 1792, and after a short stay at Kingston, proceeded to Niagara, where he established his seat of government.

As early as 1780 the village was known as Butlersbury or Butlersburg; it was also called Lennox. In a table of distances which was made by D. W. Smith, the acting Surveyor-General,* we find the following statement : " Newark, formerly called Lennox, is situated on the west side of the entrance of·Niagara River, opposite to the fortress at Niagara on Lake Ontario.

" This town was laid out in the year 1791, and the buildings were commenced upon the arrival of his Excellency Lieutenant-Governor Major-General Simcoe, in 1792. It contains about one hundred and fifty houses. The jail and Court-house for the Home District were erected in this place by an Act of the Provincial Legislature in its first session. The courts of the General Quarter Sessions of the Peace and the Court of King's Bench sit here. The Council-house is about half-way between the town and Navy Hall, which is the residence of the Lieutenant-Governor."

At the time of the arrival of the Governor the town was known as Newark, after a town in Nottinghamshire, England, of the same name. The people, however, insisted upon calling it Niagara, and in a few

* This is the D. W. Smith whose manuscripts and correspondence were purchased in England a short time ago and are now in possession of the Public Library, Toronto. I am deeply indebted to Mr. Bain, the librarian, for his courtesy in submitting these papers for my examination.

years the latter name became finally fixed in official documents.

The first Provincial Parliament opened here on the 17th September, 1792, and among the fifteen members who represented Upper Canada, we find the names of John Macdonell, Speaker of the House, Hugh Macdonell, and Francis Baby, who, in their day, were active and zealous Catholics. On the pages of modern Canadian history there is to be found no name greater or more respected than that of Macdonell. The Macdonells of Glengarry were as distinguished for their devotion to the British Crown as for their loyalty to the Catholic Church, and the sincerity of the one or the other has never been called in question. It was a favorite saying of Bishop Macdonell, of Kingston, "That every man of his name should be either a priest or a soldier;" and, indeed, the ecclesiastical and military annals of Upper Canada are accentuated with the name. In the list of Catholic priests of Canada, published a few years ago, the name of Macdonell, or Macdonald, occurs twenty times, and as the name of the Rev. Peter Macdonald, formerly Vicar-General of Kingston, is omitted, it is probable others of the same name may have escaped the critical eye of the author of " Repertoire General."

In 1773, on the invitation of Sir Wm. Johnston, a party of Highlanders emigrated from Glengarry, Scotland, and settled in the Mohawk valley. "The Macdonells of Glengarry," writes Shaw, in his history of Moray, " never reformed. The gentlemen of that name have their sons educated in the Scotch colleges abroad, especially at Douay, and they return home avowed or concealed Papists." The Macdonells who settled in New York made no concealment of their Popery, and when a storm of bigotry, stimulated by the narrow-minded fanatic, John Jay, burst upon the State of New York, the Macdonells found themselves denounced as Tories, Papists and friends of British connection. They were disarmed by General Schuyler, and early in the year of 1776 withdrew to Canada, abandoning the homes they had made for themselves in the fertile valley of the Mohawk. Their first intention would appear to have been to withdraw at once to Upper Canada, but the fortunes of war altered their plans. In the letters of Vicar-General Montgolfier, of Montreal, there occurs the following statement, written in 1776: " Father McKenna, the missionary, has been charged to accompany a new colony of Highlanders, about three hundred in number, who, they say, are going to settle in Upper Canada, where they hope to enjoy the Catholic religion without molestation. They are now at Orange (Albany), and intend to settle altogether at the same place with their missionary, who alone understands their language. I have given him the ordinary powers to administer to his flying flock."

They had previously fought in Scotland for those whom they believed to be rightful sovereigns of Great

Britain. In the new land they were called upon to stand true once more to the principle of monarchy, although the dynasty had changed. They were prepared now "to render unto Cæsar those things which were Cæsar's," and at the outbreak of the Revolutionary war they declared to a man for the Crown and British institutions, and for that cause they fought through the long war of the Revolution.

They formed in great part the 1st Battalion of the King's Royal Regiment of New York, in which the gentlemen of the clan were immediately given commissions; no less than seven officers of the name being on the establishment when the regiment was disbanded at the close of the war; in addition to those, there were several who were killed during its progress, as well as two in the 2nd Battalion of the same regiment, three officers in Butler's Rangers, three in the 84th or Royal Highland Emigrant Regiment, and others in other corps. When the United Empire Loyalists settled in this province a list of those who had served through the war was prepared by Lord Dorchester, then Governor-General of Canada, and that list bears unimpeachable testimony to the fact that the men of this name out-rank both in numbers and service all other names on the United Empire list, and numbered more than any three English names combined. Of the merit and services of the officers mention is frequently made. Writing of one of them, some years later, Captain Matthews, who was military secretary to Lord Dorchester (Sir Guy Carleton) throughout the war, stated in an official communication to the British Under Secretary for War: "When the Rebellion broke out this gentleman's (Captain Hugh Macdonell's) family were the first to fly to arms on the part of the Government, in which they and their adherents, not less than two hundred men, took a most active and decided lead, leaving their families and property at the mercy of the rebels. I was at that time quartered at Niagara, and an eye-witness of the gallant and successful exertions of the Macdouells and their dependents, by which in a great measure the Upper Country of Canada was preserved, for on this little body a very fine battalion was soon formed, and afterwards a second. Captain Macdonell's father and uncle, at that time advanced in years, had companies in that corps, and in which his elder brother, afterwards an active and distinguished partisan, carried arms. The sons of both families, five or six in number, the moment they could bear arms, followed the bright example of their fathers, and soon became active and useful officers in that and another corps of Rangers, whose strength and services greatly contributed to unite the Indians of the Five Nations in the interest of the Government, and thereby decided to save the Upper Country of Canada and our Indian trade."

These hardy pioneers, on the restoration of peace, settled in the County of Glengarry, which they thus named after the district in Scotland which had been their home, and when British connection was attacked from either without or within the Province, the men of Glengarry were the first to take up arms and the last to lay them down.

Of these were the Macdonells who sat in the first Legislature of Upper Canada, John Macdonell, the Speaker of the House,* and Hugh Macdonell,† his brother. Of these also was Alexander Macdonell, who, at the age of 16, fought with Simcoe as a cadet in the Revolutionary war, and who, in recognition of his loyalty to the British cause, was appointed by the Governor Sheriff of the Home District, which included Niagara. In 1792 he, with his mother and the rest of the family, came from Kingston to Niagara. Mrs. Alexander Macdonell was a convert to the Catholic Church, and ever remained an active and zealous member.

On the death of Father McKenna, some few years after their settlement, letters were sent to their friends in Scotland requesting that they would use their influence with the Home Government to have a priest sent to take charge of the Glengarry mission. Rev. Roderick Macdonell placed before the Home Secretary, Lord Sydney, a petition to this effect, and the noble Lord wrote the subjoined courteous letter to Lieutenant-Governor Hamilton :

---

* See Appendix D.   † See Appendix E.

" Lord Sydney to Lieutenant-Governor Hamilton :

" WHITEHALL, 24*th* *June*, 1785.

" SIR,—Having laid before the King a memorial of
Mr. Roderick Macdonell, stating that at the solicitation of a considerable number of Scots, Highlanders
and other British subjects of the Roman Catholic
persuasion, who prior to the last war were inhabitants
of the back settlements of the Province of New York,
and to whom, in consideration of their loyalty and
services, lands have been lately assigned in the higher
parts of Canada, he is desirous of joining them in order
to serve them in the capacity of a clergyman, in the
humble hope that on his arrival at their settlement
he shall be allowed by Government an annual subsistence for the discharge of that duty. I enclose to you
the said memorial, and am to signify to you the King's
commands that you do permit Mr. Macdonell to join
the above-mentioned settlers and officiate as their
clergyman ; and with respect to the allowance to be
made to him, I shall take an early opportunity of
communicating to you His Majesty's pleasure.*

" I am, etc.,

" SYDNEY."

Francis Baby, member for the Sandwich Division,
was of an ancient French family that settled in the
St. Clair District, and contributed liberally towards
the advancement of religion in Western Canada.

Although Fort George and Fort Erie were built and
garrisoned during the Revolutionary war, we have
seen that, for reasons already mentioned, no Irish
Catholics were to be found in the ranks of the English

---

* " Dominion Archives," Series Q, 22-4, p. 279.

regiments. On the 14th of February, 1793, Mr. Hobart, Chief Secretary, brought into the Irish House of Commons "An Act for the relief of his Majesty's Popish or Roman Catholic subjects of Ireland," which was warmly supported by Grattan and Curran. The seventh clause of the Act read as follows: "And be it enacted, that it shall and may be lawful for Papists or persons professing the Popish or Roman Catholic religion to hold, exercise and enjoy all civil and military offices," and on the 9th day of April it became the law of Ireland. "Thus," says Wolf Tone, "by one comprehensive clause all penalties, forfeitures, disabilities and incapacities are removed; the army, navy, and all other offices and places of trust are open to Catholics, subject to exceptions hereinafter mentioned." When the rails which barred the entrance of Irish Catholics to the British service were taken down, large numbers of the young men of Ireland entered the army. Many of them joined the 5th Regiment, which, with the 41st and 8th Kings, was despatched to Canada and assigned to Fort George, on the banks of the Niagara River. At the solicitation of Bishop Troy, of Dublin, the Home Government requested the Bishop of Quebec to send a priest to Niagara to act as chaplain to the Catholic troops, and, in compliance with his wishes, the Rev. Mr. Le Dru, a member of the Dominican Order and a French refugee, who spoke and understood English, was appointed. The Rev. Mr. Addison was the Anglican clergyman at

12

this post.*   In the Council Chamber, a building near Butler's Barracks, the English Church service was held, one Sunday for the Protestant soldiers, and mass offered up the following Sunday for the Catholics, and thus it went on alternately while the seat of Government remained at Niagara.   Father Le Dru remained but a short time at this post, when he was practically dismissed the service by order of Lord Dorchester.

Among the Smith manuscripts I find the following letter :

"NAVY HALL, *Oct. 23rd*, 1794.

"SIR,—The ration issued to Mr. Le Dru, the French missionary, is to be discontinued on the 31st inst., of which you will be pleased to acquaint the Commissary under your command, as his Excellency Colonel Simcoe has ordered this priest to leave this province (agreeably to Lord Dorchester's directions), by the route of Oswego, by the first boat that is going there. I have the honor to be, sir,

"Your most obedient and very humble servant,

"E. B. LITTLEHALES,
Military Secretary.

"Major Smith, 5th Regiment, commanding
at Niagara."

It is possible that this priest was of strong Bourbon proclivities. Lord North was particular in the selection of priests for Canada, and, from the Haldimand letters, we learn that it was a standing order that no

---

* The Rev. Salter Mountain is also mentioned as the English Church chaplain in 1794.

priest in sympathy with the Bourbons should be encouraged to remain in Canada. Yet it is more likely that an indiscreet expression of sympathy with the Americans may have led to his dismissal, for in tracing his history we learn that he took up his residence in the States, and became a warm supporter of the government and institutions of that country. If this be so, he was not without plenty of company in Western Canada, for, on the second reading of the Canada bill in Parliament, Lord Wharncliffe thus expressed himself : " I confess that, whatever apprehensions I have had with regard to Lower Canada, I fear much more disastrous consequences from what has occurred in the Upper Province. There are a great number of discontented spirits there ; first, the settlers from the United States, who keep up a connection with it and whose views are always directed to a connexion with it ; and next, there are men who have gone from this country with little character and no means, and who have transferred to Canada the dangerous doctrines they had imbibed at home."

After the departure of the Rev. Mr. Le Dru there is no mention of any Catholic priest visiting Niagara until the early part of 1796, when Father Burke, afterwards Bishop of Halifax, remained here for a time on his way to Detroit.

CHAPTER X.

PIONEER PRIESTS.

Father Burke- Trials of a Missionary Priest—At Fort Miami—With the Chippewas—Leaves Detroit—Letter to Quebec—Plaint of a Military Commander—Meets the Chief of the Mohawks—Departure for Halifax —Col. John Macdonell—His Death—Bishop Macdonell—Sketch of His Life—Father Campion—Arrival at Niagara—Patrick McArdle and John Harris—Extent of Niagara Parish—Hardships of the Early Priest—In the Stage at Queenston—An Extraordinary Charge— Early Records.

"The life of a missionary priest is never written, nor can it be. He has no Boswell. His biographer may record the priest's public and official acts; he may recount the churches he erected, the schools he founded, the works of religion and charity he inaugurated and fostered, the sermons he preached, the children he catechized, the converts he received into the fold ; and this is already a great deal, but it only touches upon the surface of that devoted life. There is no memoir of his private daily life of usefulness and of his sacred and confidential relations with his flock —all this is hidden with Christ in God, and is registered only by His recording Angel."—Cardinal Gibbons.

THERE is no name in the glorious army of noble missionary priests who did duty on the Niagara frontier more brilliant and admirable than that of Edmund Burke. "The splendid self-devotion of the early Jesuit missions," writes Parkman, in his "Old Régime," "has its record, but the patient toils of the missionary priest rest in the obscurity where the best of human virtues are buried from age to age."

Indeed, the missionary priest is a man forsaken, as it were, by his brother men, and soon forgotten when laid to rest in the grave. Missionaries of a religious order embark for foreign fields, and prosecute their apostolic work as did the disciples of our Lord, two by two; but the secular priest went forth alone, and alone bore the burdens and responsibilities of an arduous and trying life. The shadow of a friendly tree or the rude log-cabin of the hospitable settler was his home; his labors, his sacrifices and his sufferings were known to God alone, and the end of all was frequently a solitary grave in the wilderness. But if the record of his life be unwritten for the eyes of men, the recording angel has not forgotten in the "Book of Life" his sufferings and his sorrows.

The Right Rev. Edmund Burke—who, at the advanced age of 78, died in 1820 at Halifax—believing that God summoned him to bear a message of salvation to the tribes of the West, abandoned the emoluments and ease of a professor's life, sought the companionship of wandering hordes, and labored with a zeal that has won for him an honored place among the early missionaries of this country. In the autumn of 1794 he left Quebec, and passed some time at Niagara. Thence he pushed on to Detroit, and, continuing his journey, reached Fort Miami, known to-day as Maumee City, Ohio. Writing from here to Dr. Troy, of Dublin, he says: "I am here in the midst of Indians, all heathens. This day a Grand Council was held in my house by the Ottawas, Chippewas and Pontowatomis. These people receive a certain quantity of Indian corn from the Government, and I have been appointed to distribute it; that gives me a consequence amongst them, which I hope will be useful as soon as I can speak their language, which is not very difficult." Further on he adds: "At night the howling of wolves in pursuit of deer, the growling of the bear, the hissing of the rattlesnake, the war-whoop of the Indian and the sound of his rifle are rather disagreeable sounds, but not at all uncommon." To one who had been a professor in the University of Paris, a distinguished mathematical and classical scholar, the beginning of his missionary life must have been fraught with almost insuperable difficulties, and nothing but a dominating will and the conviction that he was doing the work of God could have reconciled him to his savage surroundings. Fascinating as was for him the study of ancient, classical and Church literature, he called off his mind from their attractions and applied himself entirely to mastering the Ottawa and Huron tongues. He found the task to which he had devoted himself no child's play, and after weeks of continuous study he was almost disheartened. About this time he wrote to Father Plessis, of Quebec, and in the course of his letter incidentally remarked: "It was the devil himself, I think, who invented the Huron language, in order to exasperate men." He soon became familiar with the croaking gutturals of the Huron tongue, and to the children of the Wyandots, who, sixty years before, were driven by the Iroquois from the shores of Georgian bay, preached the same redeeming truths that Brebeuf and Lallemant preached to the dark-haired Hurons in the forests of Ihontaria.

When the limitless territory along the northern shores of the great lakes passed, in 1796, under the dominion of the United States, Father Burke, who was loyal to the English Government, crossed over into Canada, and on July 22nd we find him again at Niagara. Here he obtained from Governor Simcoe, who retained him in high repute, a grant of land, on which he intended to build, in co-operation with the Sulpicians of Montreal, a seminary for the education of priests for the Western missions. Writing to the Bishop of Quebec, he says : "If your Lordship will send me two Sulpician Fathers I shall open at once a school. There is need of a house for two missionaries at Niagara, it is the most suitable place, and I have given orders to buy an additional plot of ground for £150 or £200. I know not where I shall find the money, but God's providence will provide. If this place will afford me a maintenance I shall apply all my salary from Government towards the purchase." From Niagara he went to Quebec to plead in person his cause. From here he wrote to the Cardinal Prefect of the Propaganda, giving an account of the Western missions, and suggesting the appointment of a Vicar-Apostolic for Upper Canada. He was detained here for some time, but in the summer of 1798 we find him again on the banks of the Niagara River. On the 13th of September he wrote as follows to Bishop Plessis: " Here I am at Niagara, instead of having carried out my original design of going on to Detroit, thence returning to Kingston to pass the winter. The commander of the garrison, annoyed by the continual complaints of the civic officials against the Catholic soldiers, who used to frequent the taverns during the hours of service on Sundays, gave orders that officers and men should attend the Protestant service. They had attended for three consecutive Sundays, when I represented to the commander the iniquity of this order. He replied that he would send them to mass if the chaplain was there, and he thought it very extraordinary that, whilst a chaplain was paid by the King for the battalion, instead of attending to his duty he should be in charge of a mission, while his men were without religious services, and his sick were dying without the sacrament. You see, therefore, I have reason for stopping short at Niagara; for we must not permit four companies, of whom three-fourths, both of officers and men, are Catholics, to frequent the Protestant Church."

At York, now Toronto, he met the celebrated Indian Chief, Joseph Brant, who, for nearly fifty years, had fought the battles of England in the Western States and Canada, and whose son afterwards distinguished himself at Queenston Heights. He says: "The famous Brant, Chief of the Mohawks, declares he is a Catholic, and has told the Governor, who has spoken of it to me. The Governor looks upon this as a species of threat on the part of Brant; nevertheless, he has promised him a missionary in case the village should wish it. They were formerly Protestants; for some years they have not had a minister. Brant himself has spoken to me two or three times, and has requested me to recommend his son to the seminary, and to ask the professors to instruct him in the Catholic religion, so that he might be able to rule his village and bring them all to the faith in time. I strongly recommend him to you. The young Indian can read and write in English; he is desirous of learning a little Latin and French."

In September, 1800, he left Niagara, suffering from ague, and after passing some time at Quebec, he went to Rome, where he wrote his " Mémoire on the Canadian Missions." Shortly after his return to this country he was appointed Vicar-Apostolic of Nova Scotia, and on the 5th of July, 1818, he was consecrated Bishop of Halifax. He enjoyed the sincere and cordial friendship of the Duke of Kent, and of every military and naval officer who commanded in British America in his time. He was a tall, handsome man, of a cheerful and urbane disposition, and Great Britain had no more warm or loyal supporter of her institutions and authority than the Right Rev. Edmund Burke. Father Burke was succeeded at Niagara as military chaplain by the Rev. F. Desjardines, who remained but a short time, when the military post was intermittingly attended by priests from other places.

At the breaking out of the War of 1812, Niagara, being a frontier town and immediately opposite the American fort, was the rendezvous for many of the noble sons of Canada who took up arms in defence of their country. Among the first to respond to the call was Lieut.-Colonel John Macdonell, who, at the early age of 24 years, was appointed Attorney-General of Upper Canada. General Brock, in compliment to him and in recognition of the hereditary courage of his race, appointed him his Provincial Aide-de-Camp. At the now historic Battle of Queenston Heights he bravely bore the honor of his Scotch escutcheon untarnished, and when the chivalric Brock fell, Colonel Macdonell assumed command, and while gallantly charging up the hill at the head of the York Volunteers and 49th Regulars, fell, wounded in four places, one bullet passing through his body. He was borne off the field, but, owing to his superb constitution, survived for twenty-four hours. He was interred in the same resting-place as General Brock, and over their grave the Canadian people have erected one of the finest monuments in America. A member of the York Militia, who took part in the battle, referring to him

BISHOP MACDONELL.

in a letter written October 14th, 1812, says : "This heroic young man, the constant attendant of the General, strove to support to the last a cause never to be despaired of, because it involved the salvation of the country."* Lieut.-Colonel Macdonell was a practical Catholic, and before leaving for the frontier approached the sacrament, as if he had a presentiment of his tragic end.

On the 27th January, 1826, Pope Leo XII. formulated a bull, cleaving Upper Canada from Quebec, and canonically raised it to a separate diocese, with Kingston for its See, and by a brief of the same date created Right Reverend and Honorable A. Macdonell, first Bishop of Kingston. For many years he was the acting Vicar-General of the Bishop of Quebec, and in order to increase the powers and privileges of that office, he was consecrated bishop on the 31st of December, 1820. Bishop Macdonell was born 17th July, 1762, in Inverness-shire, Scotland, and educated in the Scotch colleges of Paris and Valledolid, in Spain. He was ordained 16th February, 1787, and was five years a missionary in Scotland. When the Highland Regiment of Glengarry Fencibles, all of whom were Catholics, went to Ireland in 1798, Father Macdonell accompanied them as their chaplain. In 1802 the regiment was disbanded, and the following year the chaplain, having obtained a grant of land for every officer and soldier who wished to accompany him, left

* Mrs. Edgar's "Ten Years of Upper Canada." p. 151.

for Canada, followed by the greater part of his men. Upon his arrival at Quebec, he presented his credentials to Lieutenant-Governor Hunter, who was Governor of the Province, and had his patents of land endorsed. They settled in the County of Glengarry, where their kinsmen of the Mohawk Valley had already pre-empted farms. On his arrival, in 1803, there were only three churches in the whole province, and only one priest who spoke English. For over thirty years the life of this admirable priest was devoted to missionary work. He may be styled the Father of the Catholic Church in Upper Canada. For ten years he was practically alone, yet in 1836, by his exertions, thirty-five churches had been built, and twenty-two priests, most of whom had been educated at his own expense, were now ministering to their scattered flocks. To record the history of this great man would require a separate volume, for his martial figure was conspicuous in the ecclesiastical, political and military life of this province for more than thirty years after its separation from Quebec. Ever vigilant and observant for the interests of religion, he noted in whatever part of his vast Diocese a handful of Catholics were gathered, and made provision for their spiritual wants.

As early as 1816 a few Catholic families settled in Niagara and along the banks of the river. They were visited from time to time by priests from Glengarry and other points, till, in 1826, they were sufficiently numerous to support a pastor of their own. Bishop

Macdonell commissioned Father Campion to take charge of the mission, and from that day until the present the town of Niagara-on-the-Lake has never been without a resident pastor.

Father Campion was met at the landing by Patrick McArdle and John Harris, and as both these gentlemen took an active interest in the success of the new mission, and largely contributed to the support of religion in Niagara, they are entitled to more than a passing notice in these pages. John Harris was of an old English family, whose ancestors had settled in Worcester a few years after the Norman Conquest. Refusing to conform after the English Reformation, they were despoiled of their property, and came under the withering blight of the penal laws. That the family retained their faith through the long night of persecution is one of those insoluble problems that baffles the Catholic historian. John Harris came to Niagara in 1818, and it is recorded of him that he conscientiously instructed his children in the truths of the Catholic religion, and before retiring at night, grouped them around him for family prayers. In 1840 he moved with his family to Guelph, where he lived until 1870, dying full of honors at the advanced age of 84 years. He was a man of fine personal appearance, ruddy complexion and robust constitution, and may be fairly classed among the early pioneers of the Catholic Church in the Niagara peninsula. His sons and grandsons are now settled in Guelph, Hamilton and Baltimore, and are respected and prominent members of these cities.

Patrick McArdle came to Niagara in 1816, and at his house Father Campion was hospitably entertained till suitable provision was made for him. When Mr. McArdle left Ireland he was well stored with the traditions which enclosed the sufferings and trials endured by the magnificent Irish people for centuries. The angel from heaven, of whom St. Paul makes mention, if he visited his house and preached any other but Catholic doctrine, would have been courteously but firmly requested to leave, for Patrick McArdle's family had the faith burned into them with the hot iron of persecution. The infant church in Niagara had no warmer friend, and from his limited means he contributed with a generosity that did him honor. He died in 1834.

"The Catholic priest," writes Archbishop Walsh, "begins to care for man at the cradle, follows him with his ministry through all the phases and vicissitudes of life, and does not abandon him even when the last sod is put on his grave. He follows him into the eternal world by his blessed ministrations, praying and offering sacrifices for his departed soul. Like his Divine Master, he goes about doing good, reclaiming the sinner, reconciling neighbors, bringing peace into families torn by dissensions, instructing the ignorant, visiting the sick, comforting the afflicted, helping the poor, protecting the widow and the orphan; in a word, giving glory to God in the highest and bringing peace and happiness to men of good will."

To none could this language be applied more fittingly than to the young priest who now had charge of the Niagara parish. At this date, from the mouth of the Niagara River to the Detroit Narrows, and in the whole north-western part of Ontario, there were but three priests. The parish of Niagara included the Niagara peninsula, taking in also Dundas, Adjala, Tecumseh and the adjoining townships; and, in truth, after the return of Bishop Macdonell from his western visit, stretched to St. Thomas and London. To appreciate the labors, sufferings and hardships of the solitary pastor of Niagara in his journeyings to these remote points in his mission, we must remember that, except occasional settlements, the land was a wilderness, and that in many of the townships *blazed* paths alone existed. Nor was his life socially enviable, for the traditions of other days were in the minds of his Protestant fellow-citizens, associated with any but a favorable opinion of the *Romish* priest.

Many of the United Empire Loyalists who fled to Canada after the American Revolution, brought with them most exaggerated ideas about the Catholic Church and her priests. They were sturdy, honest people, loyal to the British Crown, and hating Pope and Popery with an honesty and sincerity that there was no disputing. The Catholic Church was to them the abomination of desolation seated on the high places, the Pope was anti-Christ, and the priests his obedient slaves. The repeated and time-worn calumnies of blood, poison and daggers associated with the priests, and woven into the fireside literature of the day, struck terror into the boldest hearts. The priest was a familiar and terrible figure—a dark, mysterious, unreliable spectre, with ten tricks at hand and ten times ten in a bag. The enlightened intelligence of our cities and towns has long ago banished this apparition, but the ghost still haunts some farming inland districts, where a priest is a curiosity if not an object of fear. Just before the stage drove out one morning on its way from Queenston to Niagara, a worthy, comely, well-fed and well-intentioned dame entered it, followed by a quiet, ministerial-looking, middle-aged gentleman, with a meek aspect and a benevolent smile. The two, as the stage progressed, entered into an animated conversation, and being each prepossessed with the other's appearance and sentiments, they formed what may be termed a stage acquaintance. The lady talked much, as ladies of that age are apt to do, of the wickedness of the times. "And then those Papists," said she; "those wicked, Popish Papists—they are worse than all put together. Whatever shall we come to if they settle amongst us?"

" Papists, ma'am?" said the gentleman. "What are they, and what wickedness do they commit?"

" Is it possible, sir," said the lady, "that you never

heard of those Papists that are turning the world upside down ? "

The meek gentleman admitted that he had heard of such people, but that he did not know a great deal about them, and as for turning the world upside down, the lady had just admitted that she did not see much good in the side which was now uppermost.

" Do you know," said she, speaking confidentially, in a low, solemn voice, and laying her hand upon his arm; " do you know that priest Campion himself sacrifices a lamb every Sunday ? "

" Nonsense, my dear madam," said he, deprecatingly, " I am priest Campion, and I never sacrificed a lamb in my life ; I have not the heart to do it, and I don't know how to kill it, either ! "

The air in the stage grew colder, and became so frosty that all conversation ceased in a short time.

Father Campion remained pastor of Niagara for six years, leaving for Glengarry in 1830, to act as secretary to his Lordship, Bishop Macdonell. He died in 1841, after a noble life passed in the service of God and his fellow-man. During the second year of his incumbency, Bishop Macdonell visited the parish, and in the baptismal register for that year I find the following entry :

" *The* 12*th August*, 1827.—By the Right Rev. Alex. Macdonell has been baptized Mary Harris, born the 11th July, 1827, of the lawful marriage of John Harris and Margaret Grey, who is not a Roman Catholic ;

13

the sponsors being Patrick McArdle and Mary Fegan, also McArdle.

"✝ ALEX. MACDONELL, R. Ep."

The extraordinary care with which the Catholic Church has always sought to protect the sacrament of marriage from profanation, and the conscientious character of her early priests, are well illustrated by the entries in the marriage register of these days. Here is an interesting extract from the register of 1827 :

"*The 8th day of October*, 1827.—Cornelius Calahan and Mary Carrol, both from Ireland, having solemnly declared and given a certificate of their not being married or contracted before with any person, and not being able to discover any impediment to prevent them from getting married, I, the undersigned Roman Catholic missionary for Niagara, Dundas, etc., etc., have received their mutual consent of marriage, and have given the benediction according to the rules of the Holy Roman Catholic Church, in presence of Patrick Cullen, Patrick Handy, Andrew Boylan, Patrick Flynn and Mary Kelley.

"JAMES W. CAMPION, M. Pt."

VICAR-GENERAL GORDON.

CHAPTER XI.

FATHER GORDON.

Appointed to Niagara—The Baptismal Register—Building of the First Church—Announcing a "Station"—Arrival of the Priest—The "Station"—Edward Keating—Churches Built—Baptism of "Vanus" —Following a "Blaze"—With the Early Settlers—A Night at Michael Spilling's—Extraordinary "Sick Call"—Marshall's Conversion—The Church Builder—Sylvester Doran—Jerry Finnegan and the Priest— Tom, the Orangeman—Father Gordon and the Tipperary Lad—A Tilt with Colonel Kingsmill—Letters to the Colonel—D'Arcy McGee— Death of the Priest—Growth of Liberality.

> " What though he standeth at no earthly altar,
> Yet in white raiment, on the golden floor,
> Where love is perfect and no step can falter,
> He serveth as a priest for evermore.
> He is not dead, but only lieth sleeping
> In the sweet refuge of the Master's breast,
> And far away from sorrow, toil and weeping
> He is not dead, but only taking rest."

AFTER the departure of Father Campion, the Rev. Michael Lalor, whose name was for forty years identified with the growth and development of Catholicism in Western Canada, held the parish until the appointment of a permanent pastor. In 1830 there was ordained to the priesthood by Bishop Macdonell, at St. Raphael's Seminary, Glengarry, a young man whose name afterward became a household word among the scattered Catholics living in the upper part of this province. This priest was commissioned by his Ordinary, four years after his ordination, to proceed to Niagara and take permanent charge of that territorially extensive parish. He played a conspicuous part in the early ecclesiastical history of this province for nearly a half a century, and has left his name indelibly written on our Catholic annals. On April 27th, 1834, in clean, easily legible and well-drawn characters, he makes his first entry in the Baptismal Register for that year:

"*April 27th.*—Was baptized by me, the undersigned priest, John, aged four weeks, son of William Kay and Elizabeth Shean. Sponsors, Edward McCann and Margaret O'Connor.

"EDW'D GORDON, M. Ap."

Father Gordon was a man endowed with all the gifts of mind and body necessary for a great and onerous duty; of strong physical powers, much austerity of life, indomitable will and shrewd mental qualities. No difficulties daunted him; no slight or rebuff discouraged him, and in the presence of danger he was a man. He put his hand to the plough, walked the furrow to the end, sowed the good seed, the harvest of which we are now reaping. On the 3rd of May, 1832, on block 24, of the town of Niagara, four acres were cut off from the military reserve and deeded to Bishop Macdonell by the Crown. This extraordinary prelate, in recognition of his loyalty and patriotism, was granted blocks of land for church purposes in Toronto, Kingston, Hamilton, and, indeed, wherever there was a Catholic settlement. The young priest signalized the beginning of his pastorship by the erection of the first Catholic church on this peninsula. In three months, with the co-operation of his people, his ceaseless energy overcame all obstacles, and for the first time in the history of the Catholics of Niagara, they worshipped in a temple of their own— every stick of timber of which was paid for by their contributions.

After the completion of his church, Father Gordon entered upon a tour of his vast parish; he visited Niagara Falls, Dundas, Trafalgar, Toronto Gore and Adjala, saying mass, hearing confessions, and preaching in barns and log huts. In less than ten years he built the first Catholic churches in these places; and, indeed, was the only priest that many of the Catholic settlers had seen since they moved into the clearings. In those days these pastoral visits were known as " Stations," and when, during the Lenten and Advent seasons, the priest began his visitations, announcement was made on Sunday that on the following Wednesday he would say mass at a particular place. This notice was conveyed to the congregation in words to the following effect: " If there be anyone here living in the neighborhood of Edward Keating, of the Twenty-mile Creek, send word to him that a ' Station ' will be given at his house next Wednesday, and tell him to be sure to let all of his Catholic neighbors know it. I will be there on Tuesday night." The priest, after mass, took particular care to ascertain if there was any neighbor of Keating's present, and if not, he commissioned some one to bear a message to him. On the following Tuesday, carrying with him the vestments, altar stone, wine and altar breads, he left home on horse-back, and through the clearings and forest held his way till he reached Keating's house, where he was greeted warmly by the stalwart settler and his family. That night a few of the neighbors dropped in, and after desultory remarks about the weather and crops, the conversation flowed into the subjects of Ireland and the Catholic Church. The following morning the priest rose early, placed a table on four chairs, put the altar stone thereon, covering it with the three linen altar-cloths. He then nailed a crucifix to the wall, arranged the altar cards, opened the missal or mass-book, with the mass of the day marked, and after hearing the confessions of the people, blessed the house, and offered up the Holy Sacrifice. In many of the settlers' log shanties the ground floor was but one room, forming the kitchen, dining and living apartment, and the ceiling was often so low that a tall priest was obliged to offer up the Holy Sacrifice in a bending position. After mass he instructed them in the teachings of the Catholic Church, encouraged them to lead good lives, to hold fast to the faith, and bring up their children in the fear and love of God. During this time the good woman of the house was preparing dinner, and from the blazing hearth, upon which the dinner was being cooked, there came forth a heat that made the room almost unbearable. Before finishing his exhortation, the priest announced another "Station," fourteen or fifteen miles farther west; and thus, from week to week, in the pelting rains, over swollen streams, across fallen timber, he pursued his journey for months, till the man of God had completed his biannual visitations. Such was the life of the pioneer priests of Western Canada, and such is to-day their lives in Algoma and the townships north-west of Lake Nipissing.

Edward Keating, at whose house the Station was held, came to this country from King's County, Ireland, when a young man, and in 1823 married Maria Elizabeth, the daughter of Mr. George Ball, a representative United Empire Loyalist, who settled in this district as early as 1783. Mrs. Keating, at the time of her marriage, was a Protestant, and remained such for some years. Her husband was a man remarkable for his uprightness and honesty of purpose, and when Mr. Ball opened his extensive mills, in 1824, Edward Keating was appointed manager of his interests. Notwithstanding a difference of religion, Mrs. Keating received and entertained the priest with a courtesy and urbanity characteristic of the Ball family. Like

EDWARD KEATING'S HOUSE, 1834.

many another of those days, she inherited peculiar ideas touching the nature of the priesthood and the Catholic religion, but as she became more intimately acquainted with the one and instructed in the other, her prejudices gradually disappeared, and she finally entered the Catholic fold. The unostentatious piety of her husband, his charity and kindly nature were greatly influential in changing her religious convictions. M. Y. Keating, of St. Catharines, is the only surviving son, and as the infant Church in pioneer days had no more manly or honest adherent than Edward Keating, neither has the Church at the present day in this section of the country a more sincere and representative supporter than his son Michael.

Father Gordon built churches at Niagara, Niagara Falls, Trafalgar, Toronto Gore and Adjala, and many are the amusing stories told of him in association with his labors on these missions. A laughable incident occurred at Toronto Gore in connection with the baptism of a child of a young man named Sweeney, who, with his wife, was living at his father's house. When the priest asked what name he would give his child, the young man replied, "Vanus, your Reverence."

"What!" said Father Gordon; "why, you blackguard I'll never give a Catholic child the name of a heathen goddess, and the worst of them at that."

"Well, your Reverence," replied Sweeney, "that's my father's name."

" You lie, you scoundrel," replied the priest. " No Catholic priest, particularly an Irish one, would give her name to any child, male or female; so go and get your father, before a drop of water goes on the head of this helpless infant."

When the father entered the house his first greeting from the priest was, " What's your baptismal name, Sweeney?" " Vanus, yer Reverence," replied the man.

" Why, blame it all," retorted the priest; "sure you never got that name at baptism?"

" No, sir," answered Sweeney. " I was baptized Sylvanus, but the neighbors always call me Vanus for short."

Father Gordon spent half his time in the saddle, and though he spared neither himself nor his horse, it was impossible for him to visit the more distant portions of his mission more than once or twice a year. In those early days the entrance to a clearing in the great forests was marked by a "blaze"—that is, a chip chopped out of the trees which led to the settlement. Frequently in the dusk of the evening the " blaze " was lost, and the wearied and travel-worn priest, after hours of wandering, often lost himself in the dense woods.

When Father Gordon first entered the townships of Adjala and Tecumseh, there were not more than thirty Catholic families settled in these districts, and as he could only visit them once or twice a year, he

was welcomed with a warmth and cordiality characteristic of the generous-hearted settlers. In his latter
days he longed to dwell on the memories of the past,
and repeat with enthusiasm the kindness which he
always received from these large-hearted people.
Here is one of the stories which he loved to relate :
" I arrived one evening at the house of a well-to-do
settler, named Spilling, and, as I was jaded and worn-
out, I made up my mind to go to bed early. I soon
fell asleep, but was suddenly awakened by Spilling.
' What's the matter, Michael ?' I said. ' Why, then,
your Reverence, it's a strange matter—the strangest
matter I ever heard of. Young Marshall has brought
his dying father to you, since you wouldn't be allowed
to come to him.' ' Why, man,' I replied, ' you're joking.
The son could never bring his father on his back all
the way from his house to yours.' ' Faith,' replied
Spilling, ' the matter is too serious to be joking
about, for the man may die before morning.' It was,
nevertheless, the literal truth. Marshall, who was a
Protestant, and was seriously ill, learning that I was
staying at Spilling's house, desired to see me. His
good wife, hearing him giving instructions to the son,
entered a protest, stating that no member of her
family ever died a Papist, and she wasn't going to
be disgraced now by her own husband. She further
threatened to brain any Popish priest that would dare
to stick his head inside her door. But the dying man
was inconsolable, and he moaned and wept in a

manner to touch the heart of one of his sons, to whom he addressed the most earnest entreaties that he might be allowed to die as he wished to die. Moved alike by the tears and importunities of his father, the son at length yielded. But what was to be done? The priest could not enter the house—his mother would not allow that—how, then, could his father's wish be accomplished? There was only one way of doing it, and that was quickly resolved upon and adopted. Carefully wrapping the dying man in the clothes in which he lay, the son raised him gently on his back, and, stealing softly with his precious burden, he crossed the threshold with noiseless step, and bore his father a mile through the dark forest to Spilling's house. Whether it was that nature rallied her failing resources, or that the spirit rose superior to the frailty of the body, it may be difficult to say; but the father preserved strength enough to be received into the Church and prepared for death, and to be brought back to his own home, in which he shortly afterwards breathed his last. For several years, or as long as his mother lived, the son did not separate from her communion; but he afterwards became a Catholic, and is now the wealthy head of a large Catholic family, all good and religious, and full of worldly prosperity."*

* Michael Spilling was the father of Spilling Brothers, Michael and John, manufacturers, Toronto. The grandsons of Marshall were well known to the writer when he was pastor of Adjala and Tecumseh, in 1870, and the incident above recorded still lives as a tradition among the Catholics of these townships.

A PIONEER RESIDENCE, ADJALA, 1831.

In 1836, Father Gordon took the census of Niagara, Niagara Falls, Queenston and Chippewa, and registered a population of 817 Catholics; and on the 25th of August of this year he records the visit of Right Reverend Remigius Gaulin, the Coadjutor Bishop of Kingston, who confirmed twenty-five candidates.

One of the earliest pioneers of Catholicity in the western portion of the County of Lincoln was Sylvester Doran, who, with his wife and young family, emigrated in 1821 from Ireland, and settled on land close to the present village of Grimsby. Sylvester Doran was, at this time, the only Catholic settler in the neighborhood, and as the Catholic Church and her doctrines were the subject of frequent discussion at " bees " and " barn raisings," Doran was repeatedly put on his defence. It was in vain that he protested that Catholics were not idolaters, that they did not pay the priest for forgiving their sins, adore the blessed Virgin, buy indulgences to commit crimes, or pay hard cash for the release of souls from purgatory. All his protestations were laughed at, and the poor man was frequently overwhelmed with sarcasm and ridicule.

" Why, man," said a neighbor to him one day, " didn't my own father tell me that when Jerry Finnegan last went to confession to the priest, he was asked by him, after he had retailed a story of sin as long as your arm :

" ' Did you never do anything good at all since your last confession, Jerry ? '

"'Oh! yes, your Reverence; I shot an Orangeman.'

"'Thanks be to God,' replied the priest, heaving a sigh of relief; 'that wipes out all your other crimes.'"

Doran would offset this by the story of an old Orangeman in the County of Down, who, when asked:

"Are times as good now, Tom, as when you were a boy?" replied,

"Faith, they are not; for they take you up now for shooting a Papist."

Still Sylvester held his own in the community, and his large heart and straightforward conduct won for him the esteem and friendship of his neighbors. He was the first man to bring a load of stone for the Catholic church built in St. Catharines in 1835, and at his house the priest was always a welcome guest. His son James still resides in Grimsby, and five more of his sons occupy respectable positions in Hamilton and in the County of Brant.

As Father Gordon was often obliged to go to Toronto to consult his bishop, he became a familiar figure to all the hackmen. He arrived one day in a snowstorm, wet and wretched enough, and anxious to get to the bishop's residence as soon as possible; he was on the look-out as he touched the wharf, and was delighted to hear a voice melodiously bawl out:

"O! blur' an' oons, boys, if here isn't Father Gordon!"

The planks were shoved over, and, at the same moment, half a dozen voices greeted him with the accustomed:

" Here's a hack, Father Gordon ! "

" Och ! sure your Reverence 'll go wid me this turn for luck ! "

" You're welcome, Father Gordon ; long life to yez ! It's I've the carriage 'll whip you up to the palace, snug and dry, in no time."

In the midst of this din, whilst he was yet on the gangway, he perceived a tall, raw-boned, Tipperary lad, who had evidently decided on appropriating him, making his way most unceremoniously through the crowd, shouting out in a tone that drowned all competitors :

" Och ! thin, will yez stop yer bawling, and don't bother his Reverence, when his *own* carriage has been waiting for him here these two hours ! "

An appeal like this was not to be resisted ; he therefore accompanied the driver to *his own* carriage, and whatever doubts he entertained as to this part of his statement, the fact of its having been in waiting for " two hours " he could readily credit, for he found it half-full of snow.　He remarked upon its condition, saying that, as he was expected, *his* carriage might have been better looked after.

" Wasn't I below looking afther ye're Reverence, and that's the way the snow got in without my seein' it ; indeed, we're not a dale used to snow at this time of the year, but I'll have it out and turn the cushions and powdher you up to the palace in a minute."　All this was said and done in an accent and with a manner that made him forget the annoyance, and in a few minutes he was at the palace enjoying the generous hospitality of Bishop Power.

For some years, during Father Gordon's stay in Niagara, the 3rd Battalion P.I. Militia, commanded by Colonel Kingsmill, was stationed at the Fort. Kingsmill was a bit of a military martinet, and if we may be allowed to use the expression, a temperance "crank." In his battalion were a number of Catholic non-commissioned officers and privates who were unable to attend mass, as the colonel claimed that at the hour mass began the regimental doctor made his examinations. Father Gordon, who was himself a strict disciplinarian, espoused the cause of the Catholic soldiers and wrote the subjoined letter to the Commander of the Battalion :

"Saturday Morning, *April* 13*th*, 1839.

" Sir,—I regret to find that the Catholic soldiers of your regiment do not attend Divine service on the Sunday mornings. They have not been in the church in the forenoon of Sunday but once since the time I first had the honor to speak to you in their behalf. Divine service commences on Sunday mornings at eleven o'clock, precisely, at which hour you will have the kindness to allow them in future to attend.

" I have the honor to be, sir,

" Your most obedient and humble servant,

" Edward Gordon,
" Catholic Pastor of Niagara.

" Colonel Kingsmill, 3rd B., P.I. Militia, etc., etc., Niagara."

14

For a few Sundays the soldiers were permitted to attend mass, when, to the surprise of the pastor, they again absented themselves. When he met a few of them the following day, they said they were all desirous to attend, but the colonel insisted upon detaining them. Father Gordon returned to his house, and sent by a messenger to the Colonel the following letter:

"NIAGARA, *June 3rd*, 1839.

"SIR,—Having observed with regret and surprise that the Catholic non-commissioned officers and privates belonging to the regiment under your command, now stationed at Niagara, continue to absent themselves from their church during Divine service on Sundays, I beg again to call your attention to this subject, and to request you will be pleased to take steps to insure their attendance for the future on those days at not a later hour than eleven o'clock, as according to the discipline of their Church, as I have already stated to you, all Catholics are obliged, in conscience, to give their attendance during the celebration of the Holy Sacrifice of the Mass, which is always offered up to God only in the forenoon. In again calling your attention to this subject, I beg to remark that should this communication fail in having the desired effect, I should feel that in omitting any longer to bring the matter before his Excellency the Major-General commanding, I should be guilty of a very reprehensible neglect in the performance of a sacred duty devolving upon me as the resident Catholic clergyman of this town.

"I have the honor to be, sir,

"Your most obedient and humble servant,

"E. GORDON, *Ptr*.

"To Lieut.-Colonel Kingsmill, commanding 3rd Battalion, Inl'd Militia, etc., etc., Niagara."

Failing in his repeated appeals on behalf of the Catholic soldiers, Father Gordon now addressed himself to the Major-General commanding the forces in Canada. With the characteristic sense of justice and equity which belonged to the English officer, Colonel Kingsmill was commanded to allow his Catholic soldiers to attend divine service at whatever hour suited their chaplain. This venerable priest, after twelve years of faithful priestly labor, removed to Hamilton, which was then becoming an important centre; and when the Diocese of Toronto was divided and Hamilton erected into a separate See, Father Gordon was appointed Vicar-General. He discharged the duties of his exalted office with the thoroughness and conscientious sense of responsibility which marked his whole priestly life. He was on friendly terms with many of the leading men of the Province, and among a host of warm and generous friends was Thomas D'Arcy McGee, who, before leaving on his last trip to Europe, addressed him the following letter :

" MONTREAL, *Sunday morning.*

" MY DEAR AND VENERABLE FRIEND,—The same day I got your note recommending Mr. Shea, I wrote as strongly as I could to Mr. Howland, then and now at Toronto. I have been awaiting his answer to enclose it to you, but lest it should not reach me before leaving for Ireland, *via* Portland (which I shall, please God), on Thursday next at latest, I write to assure you I did not neglect your request. Begging your pious prayers for a safe and useful journey.

"I remain, dear Vicar-General, yours always,

"T. D. McGee.

"P.S.—Please present my dutiful respects to his Lordship, and my kind regards to John McKeown, Fitzpatrick, Dr. O'Dea, etc. Our friend Devany is well.

"Very Rev. V.-G. Gordon, Hamilton, Ont."

This venerable priest died at the Episcopal residence, Hamilton, in 1870. He died as he lived, a Christian with the meekness of the lamb and the fortitude of a hero.

> "And, to add greater honors to his age
> Than man could give him, he died,
> Fearing God."

He supported the tedious infirmities of age, the languors of sickness, and the pains of dissolution with Christian resignation, and his death, like his life, was an edification and an instruction. One of the most consoling features in association with the lives of these early priests was the spirit of friendship and kindly cordiality that existed between them and the clergymen of the different Protestant denominations. The records and letters that remain testify to their goodwill for one another, and from these letters we glean that not only did they interchange social visits, but alternately dined at each other's table. This example of kindly feeling extended to the laity, and if the religious asperities that existed in Great Britain and Ireland in other days have almost disappeared in this section of the Province, we owe it to the example established by these educated and sensible men. With them began the hope of the realization of the poet's vision, and it remains for us and our immediate successors to actualize it in deeds.

> " Then let us pray, that come it may—
>   As come it will for a' that—
> That sense and worth, o'er a' the earth,
>   May bear the gree, and a' that,
> For a' that, and a' that,
>   It's comin' yet, for a' that,
> That man to man, the warld o'er,
>   Shall brothers be for a' that!"

Father Gordon was succeeded in Niagara by the Rev. John Carroll, who continued in charge until January, 1850. This venerable priest was appointed administrator of the Diocese after Bishop Power, in 1847, was struck into the grave in the fever sheds of Toronto. He was a distant relation of the Maryland Carrolls—one of whom signed the Declaration of Independence, and another was the companion of Franklin on his journey to Lower Canada, in an effort to detach the people of that province from their allegiance to Great Britain. Father Carroll died in Chicago in 1891, having reached the patriarchal age of 93 years.

CHAPTER XII.

A PERIOD OF GLOOM.

The Irish on the Continent—Irish Valor—Flight of the Nobility—In the Barbadoes—Exodus to Nova Scotia—A Stream of Emigration—Mr. Davin—The Scotch Crofters—Lament of the Scottish Exiles—The Struggle for the Land—The Reformation—The Eighth Henry—Penal Laws in Spain and Austria—In the Low Country—Settlement of Ulster—Buoyancy of the Celt—The Penal Code—Ruthless Laws— Summary of the Penal Code—The Mountain Mass—Penal Laws of Nova Scotia—Of Newfoundland—Blue Laws of Connecticut.

> " I'm bidding you a long farewell,
>   My Mary, kind and true ;
> But I'll not forget you, darling,
>   In the land I'm going to—
> They say there's bread and work for all,
>   And the sun shines always there :
> But I'll not forget old Ireland
>   Were it fifty times as fair."

IN the record of deeds preserved in the Registry Office, St. Catharines, is written the name of James Black, Esq., who, for the sum of sixty-two pounds, ten shillings, deeded April 13th, 1832, to the Right Rev. Father in God Alexander Macdonell, Bishop of Regiopolis ; the Very Rev. John O'Grady, Vicar-General ; the Rev. John Cullen, parish priest of St. Catharines ; James Fitzgerald, of the same place, merchant; John McDade, of the same place, grocer; and Edward Keating, of the township of Louth, yeoman—church wardens—one acre and sixteen perches. This is the first official mention we find recording the existence of the office of pastor for St. Catharines. The Rev. John Cullen, acting on instructions received from Bishop Macdonell, visited St. Catharines, and in compliance with the wish of his Lordship, purchased the above-mentioned property. Previous to this, and for some time afterwards, the few Catholics residing here were attended to from Niagara.

Until 1834, the registers of the parish of Niagara record the baptisms and marriages of the St. Catharines Catholics. In that year the Rev. J. M. Burke took up his residence in this city, and built the first Catholic church, a small frame structure. The population of the village was, at this time, according to the census, 1,034, including about 200 Catholics. The appointment of Father Burke carried with it practically the establishment of St. Catharines parish, which stretched from lake to lake, along the line of the Welland Canal, and extending on the west to Burlington Bay.

The reverend gentleman remained here but a short time, and was succeeded by Father Cassidy, who, in 1841, resigned the pastorate and returned to Ireland. We now come to the building of the Welland Canal, and the beginning of the most important era in the history of the peninsula, and in some respects in that of the Province. Before dealing, however, with this important period, and the large number of Irish Catholics employed in the construction of the canal, it is expedient that we should have a comprehensive knowledge of the causes which conspired to lead up to the extraordinary emigration of Irishmen which, for fifty years before, set in towards this country. "In a political, as well as in an economical point of view," writes Goldwin Smith in his "Irish Character," "the Irish people may be considered as having been arrested at a certain stage of development, and prevented by a series of calamities from advancing in the ordinary course."

The Abbe McGoghegan, in his "History of Ireland," which he dedicated to the Irish Brigade in France, records the almost incredible statement that, "from calculations and researches made in the French War Office, it was found, from the arrival of the Irish troops in France in 1691, up to the year of the battle of Fontenoy, 1745, more than 450,000 Irishmen perished in the service of France," and Newenham, in his "Statistics on Irish Population," states that though the numbers stagger belief, it is not incredible. The flight of the "wild geese," as the Irish exiles were called, began after the civil war of James II., and the stream of emigration flowed on till, in 1848, it was swollen into a river. The Irish gave to France, Austria, Spain and Russia, generals and marshals. The O'Donnells, Taffs, O'Briens and MacMahons rose to be grandees of Spain and magnates of the French Empire. At

Pondicherry, under Lally, and at Fontenoy, under Clare, the Irish troops turned the fate of battle against England. At Ramillies, Almanza and Lawfeld the valor of the Irish troops was conspicuous.

The flight of the Irish Catholics practically originated with the Reformation. It began with the departure of a few of the nobility in the reign of Henry VIII.; their number was increased under Elizabeth, and grew to larger proportions still under James I.; but a far greater number, sufficient to make a very sensible diminution in the population of the country, was doomed to exile by Cromwell and the Long Parliament. The next following movement on a large scale occurred after the surrender of Kilkenny. The details of this first exodus are recorded by many modern writers, particularly by Mr. Prendergast, in his " Cromwellian Settlement." It is hardly necessary to remind the reader of the ruthless banishment under Cromwell of more than twenty thousand women and children to the Barbadoes, Jamaica and the West India islands; nor is this the place to dwell on the number of the so-called convicts who were transported to Virginia and the New England States, and there held as *quasi* slaves. Taking no account of the members of the disbanded Irish Brigade who settled in Canada at the dawn of the 17th century, the first Irish emigration to this country of any importance occurred in 1761, when two hundred Irish emigrants reached Nova Scotia. After the peace of 1763, a large number emigrated to the same colony, where, under the distinguished Bishop Burke, the diocese of Halifax was formed. The troubles of 1798 were followed by a large exodus of the Irish people. "From Ireland," says McMullen, "where the troubles of 1798 had left many a hearth desolate and many a heart seared and crushed with sorrow, came most of the Old Country people. Better a free land, even though it were the rudest shanty of the backwoodsman in the sad and sombre forests of Canada, than the cottage in old Erin, where any moment the Whiteboy might cruelly thrust the crackling turf into the thatch, or the minions of Castlereagh level its walls to the ground. And thus settlements gradually spread on every side."

From 1815 to 1845 the stream of emigration flowed rapidly, and went on swelling in volume and widening in extent from year to year. According to Mr. Rolph, in his "Statistics of Emigration," it amounted to thirty thousand. The records of emigration having been accurately kept since 1815, it is easy to ascertain the number of Irish people who landed in Canada from this period till 1848. While a certain number pushed on immediately or soon after to the United States, still a large proportion settled in the Dominion. It is now ascertained that within ten years—from 1839 to 1849—428,000 Irish people arrived in Canada.

Now, what were the causes that led up to this

unparalleled exodus of Irish Catholics to these shores?
Remember, we take no note of those who fled to the
United States and other countries. "Whoever,"
writes Nicholas Flood Davin, in his "Irishman in
Canada," "studies the history of Ireland, not in what
are called popular histories and students' manuals,
but in contemporary documents, will learn that the
great bone of contention, from age to age, was not
religion nor form of government, but the land."

The brilliant author but re-echoed the conclusion of
Mr. Prendergast, the fair and impartial writer of the
"Cromwellian Settlement," who was of the opinion
that the ultimate object of the Code was the robbing
the Irish of their lands and securing what chattels
were in their possession. That this undoubtedly was
one of the great aims always kept in view we are not
disposed to contest, for the history of Protestant Scotland furnishes, alas, too many melancholy examples
of the extremes to which avaricious men will push
their covetousness. "I have seen," writes the author
of " Destitution in Sutherlandshire," " calamity upon
calamity overtake the Scotch crofters. For five suc-
cessive years, on or about the term day, has scarcely
anything been seen but removing the inhabitants in
the most cruel and unfeeling manner, and burning the
houses which they and their forefathers had occupied
from time immemorial. The country was darkened
by the smoke of the burnings, and the descendants of
those who drew their swords at Bannockburn, Sheriff-

muir and Killicrankie, the children and nearest relations of those who sustained the honor of the British name in many a bloody field, the heroes of Egypt, Corunna, Toulouse, Salamanca and Waterloo, were ruined, trampled upon, dispersed and compelled to seek an asylum across the Atlantic; while those who remained, from inability to emigrate, deprived of all the comforts of life, became paupers, beggars—a disgrace to the nation whose freedom and honor many of them had maintained by their valor and cemented with their blood." In the ruthless process of extermination there was no sympathy or consideration for the starving people, and, driven at last to extremity, the Scotch crofters, aided by English generosity, abandoned the lands that by the laws of clanship and by divine right were theirs.

In the lament of the " Highland Emigrants," the poet McKay gave expression to the sentiments and feelings of indignation and sorrow which these unfortunate people carried with them to foreign shores :

I.

"Come away ! far away ! from the hills of bonnie Scotland ;
  Here no more may we linger on the mountain—in the glen—
  Come away ! why delay ! far away from bonnie Scotland,
    Land of grouse, and not of heroes ! Land of sheep, and not of men !
      Mighty hunters, for their pastime,
      Needing deserts in our shires,
      Turn to waste our pleasant places,
      Quench the smoke of cottage fires.
  Come away ! why delay ! Let us seek a home denied us,
  O'er the oceans that divide us from the country of our sires.

II.

" Come away ! far away ! from the river, from the wildwood,
From the soil where our fathers lifted Freedom's broad claymore,
From the paths in the straths that were dear to us in childhood,
From the Kirk where love was plighted in the happy days of yore.
Men and women have no value
Where the Bruce and Wallace grew,
And where stood the clansman's shieling
There the red-deer laps the dew.
Come away ! far away ! But to thee, oh bonnie Scotland,
Wheresoever we may wander shall our hearts be ever true.

It would be a consolation and a soothing reflection to the descendants of the Irish people if the facts of history supported Mr. Davin's contention. The struggle for the possession of the land was, indeed, so fierce, bitter and prolonged that it is yet unsettled, after three hundred years of disputation. That the struggle was mainly for the possession of land, and that this was one of the great objects always kept in view, no intelligent student of Irish history will contest, but that it was the only one we may be allowed to deny. The Reformation in Switzerland and Northern Germany had from the first struck at the doctrine as well as the supremacy of Rome. In England it was for a long time a social and political, rather than a religious, revolution. The Eighth Henry burned those who asserted the Pope's supremacy, but he also burned those who denied the doctrine of the Real Presence, or who affirmed justification by faith. In Ireland, however, from the establishment of the State Church, the contest became agrarian and religious. How could it be otherwise than religious, when the homilies of the New Church proclaimed to the Irish Catholics that "in the pit of damnable idolatry, all the world as it were drowned, continued until our age (that is, the Reformation), by the space of over eight hundred years, so that laity and clergy, learned and unlearned, all ages, sects and decrees of men, women and children of whole Christendom have been at once drowned in abominable idolatry, of all other vices most detested of God, and most damnable to men?" Nor do we wish to conceal the fact that at this time a persecuting spirit stalked through Europe.

In Spain, Austria, and the Netherlands the Protestants were subjected to laws as severe as those which oppressed Catholic subjects under Protestant rulers. The penal laws of the Low Country ordained that whosoever should be convicted of having taught heretical doctrines, or of having been present at religious meetings of heretics, should be put to death by the sword. Tortures and the flames were used indiscriminately by Catholic and Protestant princes in those days; but every impartial writer of history is disposed to admit that the penal laws against Protestants, introduced chiefly for political reasons, were but passing waves, atrocious, no doubt, in their effects, while Ireland was submerged for nearly three hundred years under the awful waters of purification. These atrocious outbursts of religious and political fanaticism are deplorable incidents in the history of our race, and prove to us, who have outlived the spirit of those times, the wisdom of cultivating charity and brotherly feeling. The acquisition of landed property is in civil society a great stimulus to exertion. After the settlement of Ulster and the confiscations of James, the Irish were barred by carefully-worded enactments from purchasing even a grave for their dead in their native land. "The prohibition," says Prendergast, "has been already extended to the whole nation by the Commonwealth Government, and when the lands forfeited by the wars of 1690 came to be sold, in 1703, the Irish were declared by the English Parliament incapable of purchasing at auction, or of taking a lease of more than two acres." The object of this enactment was to reduce the Irish to actual pauperism. Nor was there any loophole whereby they could escape this degradation. Pauperism became a necessary misfortune; yet, if millions of Irishmen have lived and died paupers, owing to the barbarous laws enacted for that purpose, every enlightened man will agree with Thebaud, that few indeed among them have been reduced, even by hard necessity and the extreme of misery, to manifest a pauper's spirit or a miserly bent. The proverbial buoyancy of the Celtic nature survived the degradation which the English wished to fasten upon it, and rose superior to the dark designs of most ingenious opponents. Nevertheless, the condition of the people was at times unutterable,

and too frequently the victims of these cruel enactments were reduced to famine and starvation.

" The Code," writes Goldwin Smith, " in truth
stands in need of all palliations which the largest and
calmest view of history can afford; and when all those
palliations have been exhausted, its memory will still
remain a reproach to human nature, and a terrible
monument of the vileness into which nations may be
led when their religion has been turned into hatred,
and they have been taught to believe that the indul-
gence of the most malignant passions of man is an
acceptable offering to God."

For it was a code of degradation and proscription,
not only religious and political, but social. It denied
to the persecuted sect the power of educating their
children at home, and at the same time, with an
almost maniacal cruelty, it prohibited them from
seeking education abroad; it disabled them from
acquiring freehold property; it subjected their estates
to an exceptional rule of succession—a reproduction,
in fact, of that very custom of gavelkind which had
been abolished as barbarous, with a view to break
them into fragments, and thus destroy the territorial
powers of the Catholic proprietors; it excluded them
from the liberal and influential professions; it took
from them the guardianship of their own children;
it endeavored to set child against parent, and parent
against child, by the truly diabolical enactment
that the son of a Papist, on turning Protestant, should

dispossess his father of the fee simple of his estate ; the father's estate, even in that which he had himself acquired, being reduced to a life-interest, while the reversion rested absolutely on the son, as a reward for his conversion to the true religion. It would not be difficult to point to persecuting laws more sanguinary than these. Spain, France and Austria will at once supply signal examples. But it would be difficult to point to any more insulting to the best feelings of man, or more degrading to religion.

The infamous enactments which disgraced the statute books of England, and which were enforced with a ruthlessness surpassing belief, though chiefly directed against the religion of the Irish people, were, in reality, instruments for their annihilation. That the Irish emigrant, the victim of the Code, retained his manhood, to say nothing of his religion, is a mystery enclosing the providential protection of the Irish Celt. If the descendant of the Irish emigrant wishes to learn what his Catholic ancestors endured for their religion and nationality, he will do well to read and re-read this summary of the Penal Code, which is epitomised for his benefit.

SUMMARY OF THE PENAL LAWS.

1. Catholics could not sit in either House of Parliament.

2. Catholics were excluded from all State offices.

3. Catholics were excluded from all municipal offices.

15

4. Catholics were excluded from the bar.

5. Catholics were excluded from the Universities.

6. Catholics were excluded from the army.

7. Catholics were excluded from the navy.

8. Catholics were deprived of the franchise.

9. Catholics were not permitted to possess swords or firearms.

10. Catholics were not permitted to possess a horse worth more than £5.

11. Catholics were (except sailors, fishermen and day laborers) banished from Limerick and Galway.

12. Catholics in business were subject to a special tax, called quarterage.

13. Catholics' houses could be appropriated by the militia.

14 Catholics were bound to make good damage done by robbers and hostile privateers.

15. Catholics (except in the linen trade,) could not have more than two apprentices.

16. Catholics were not allowed to buy land from a Protestant, to inherit from one, or to receive it as a gift.

17. Catholics could not lease a farm for life; utmost thirty-one years.

18. Catholics' net profits on leased farms restricted to one-third, and if more was earned and not declared, the farm passed to the first Protestant who denounced the Catholic tenant.

19. Catholic land-owners could not bequeath pro-

perty ; must be divided equally among all the children ; but if the eldest son joined the Anglican Church, he became entitled to the whole estate.

20. No Protestant woman worth £500 might marry a Catholic without forfeiting her estate to nearest Protestant heir.

21. Priests celebrating a marriage between a Catholic and Protestant were liable to death.

22. Marriage of Catholics to Protestants declared null and void.

23. No Catholic to act as guardian of a child.

24. Catholic orphans to have Protestant guardians, and to be brought up in the Protestant faith.

25. Catholics forbidden to open schools or teach in a school.

26. Catholic parents sending children to the Continent to be educated to forfeit their estates.

27. Catholic chapels not to have steeples or bells.

28. Observance of religious festivals not sanctioned by the State punished by heavy fine.

29. Any person converting an Anglican to Catholicism to forfeit his estate.

30. Catholic priests, on joining the English Church, made pensioners.

31. Catholic priests to sign a register and to take the oath of abjuration (abjuring the authority of the Pope).

32. Catholic bishops, deans and heads of religious orders banished, and a price offered for disclosure of

retreat of those who disobeyed the law and of unregistered priests.

33. Irish cattle trade with England suppressed.

34. Irish trade with British colonies suppressed.

35. Irish woollen trade with the Continent suppressed.

It was in execration of these infamous enactments that Thomas Davis, the poet of Young Ireland, wrote his famous song, "The Penal Days," in which he emphasized the fact that—

> "They bribed the flock, they bribed the son
> To sell the priest and rob the sire ;
> Their dogs were taught alike to run
> Upon the scent of wolf and friar."

In the *Gentleman's Magazine*, for April, 1748, there is this piece of news from Ireland : "One George Williams was convicted at Wexford Assizes for being perverted from the Protestant to the Popish religion, and sentenced to be out of the King's protection, his lands and tenements, goods and chattels to be forfeited to the King, and his body to remain at the King's pleasure." This punishment was incurred under the following provision of the Penal Code :

"If any person shall seduce a Protestant to renounce the Protestant and profess the Popish religion, the seducer and the seduced shall incur the penalty of Præmunire, mentioned in " 16th Richard II.," chap. 5 ; that is, they shall be put off the King's protection, their lands and goods forfeited to the King's use, and they shall be attached, by their bodies, to answer to the King and his Council.*

" Henceforth," writes Nicholas Flood Davin, " the Irish Catholics were the victims of an oppression more awful than has ever been dealt out to any people, or any portion of a people. Many of those Catholics were of Saxon and Norman descent, though a majority were, perhaps, pure Celts; and that they should have emerged from such persecution so little damaged by all this brutalizing tyranny, is one of the strongest evidences of the greatness of the race. Education was denied them, but they gathered by the hedgeside and learned from the page of Virgil the immortal tongue of Rome. Wealth and honor, freedom from shame and sorrow were offered them if they forsook their faith; but no bribe an empire had to give could make them abandon the despised religion they believed. The priest said mass when and where he could—in the lonely glen, on the desolate mountain-side, in the mud hovel, in the caves of the earth, he celebrated the rites of the proscribed Church; and, in his faded clothes, was armed with a talisman for the hearts of an enthusiastic people, such as no crozier of an endowed church could equal. He proved every hour his self-denial, his devotion, his sympathy; and while the rector drove to the squire's domain to enjoy his luxurious dinner, the priest shared the potato and cake of his miserable flock. The peasantry courtesy low

* " Macnevin's Irish History," p. 157.

when they meet a priest, however familiar they may
be with him, even when he is their own brother or son.
The reason has often been misunderstood. It is a
custom which has survived a time when the priest
carried the consecrated elements constantly on his
person, and when at a favorable moment, he would
make the mountain his altar; and while the language
of Tiber mingled with Gaelic prayers and the murmur
of wild rills, the host would rise like a moon against
the sky, now bright as the hopes of heaven and dreams
of the past, and now dark as the fate of a people for
whose wrongs its recesses seemed to hoard no vengeance. The son was tempted to turn against the
father, but the Irish people have remained to this day
examples of strong family affection."

When the Irish Catholic left his native land and
crossed the Atlantic Ocean, with the delusive hope that
in the wilderness of Canada he would escape the awful
consequences of these terrible laws, he found to his
horror that the ghost of the Penal Code still pursued
him. In 1758, the Government at Halifax passed an
Act to confirm titles in land. The second section of
this Act reads as follows: "Provided that no Papist
hereafter shall have any right or title to hold, possess
or enjoy any lands or tenements, other than by virtue
of any grant or grants from the Crown, but that all
deeds or wills, hereafter made, conveying lands or
tenements to any Papist, or in trust for any Papist,
shall be utterly null and void.* Having thus made it

* "Laws of Nova Scotia," Vol. I.

the law of the land that no Papist could even own
his mother's grave, the Government passed an "Act
for the establishment of religious public worship in the
Province, and for suppressing Popery." It was decreed
that "every Popish person exercising any ecclesiastical
jurisdiction, and every Popish priest or person exercising
the functions of a Popish priest, shall depart out of this
Province on or before the 25th March, 1759."* It was
furthermore decreed that if any person should harbor
or relieve any Popish priest, he should be fined fifty
pounds and exposed in the pillory; so that if a hunted,
famishing priest should apply to his Protestant neighbor for a night's lodging, the law stepped in and barred
the door against the starving man. We have seen
that in Ireland all hope of educating a child, unless at
the sacrifice of its faith, was abandoned, and that in
those days ignorance of reading or writing was among
the Irish people a patent of nobility. When the Irish
emigrant reached the Maritime Provinces, with the
hope that here at least he could educate his children,
he was confronted with this enactment: "If any
Popish recusant, Papist or person professing the Popish
religion, shall be so presumptuous as to set up any
school within the Province, and be detected therein,
such offender shall, for every such offence, suffer three
months' imprisonment, without bail or main prize, and
shall pay fine to the King of £10."† If crushed and
broken-hearted, the unfortunate man fled from Nova

* "Laws of Nova Scotia," Vol. I.   † Ibid.

Scotia to Newfoundland, the same dark and gloomy spectre met him. In 1762, Hugh Palliser, Governor of Newfoundland, issued a proclamation to the following effect :

1. Popish servants are not to be permitted to remain in any place but where they served the previous summer.

2. No more than two Papists are allowed to live in one house unless in the house of a Protestant.

3. No Papist to be allowed to keep a public-house or sell liquors by retail.

For every Catholic that was buried on the island an infamous payment of twelve shillings was exacted from the relatives.*

If, despairing of any future for his family in Nova Scotia or Newfoundland, the Irish Catholic sailed away for the Eastern States, the "Blue Laws" of Connecticut and Massachusetts made his existence a hell. During all this long and dark night of suffering, persecution and sorrow, what was it that sustained this wonderful race? How, with this hollow agony devouring their physical and spiritual life for centuries, did they live on? Thebaud, in his "Irish Race," claims for the Irish, as for the Jew in the days before the Messiah, a special providence; and, indeed, no one can rise from a study of a history of the race without realizing that God sustained them for some divine reason. The Spirit of God, speaking by the prophet

* Howley's "Newfoundland," p. 271.

Zacharias, makes this promise to the descendants of Abraham : " I will bring the third part through the fire, and will refine them as silver is refined, and will try them as gold is tried. They shall call on my name and I shall hear them. I will say thou art my people, and they will answer, the Lord is my God." And truly, if a people were ever tried and refined, the Irish can fairly lay claim to the distinction. How they clung to their religion is a mystery ; but, beyond question, their faith sustained them physically and spiritually. It was a power to multiply the widow's handful of meal and cruse of oil to an abundance. It is an honor and a dignity to descend from such a race. If our Irish fathers and mothers, when they landed on the shores of America, could neither read nor write, it was to their everlasting honor ; and if they reached our shores in destitution, the men brought with them a magnificent manhood, and the women a purity that has passed into a proverb.

Up to 1834, there were no schools in Ireland open to the children of the peasantry or the working-classes. Whatever of instruction they received was from the hedge schoolmaster or at the hands of their hunted priests under the shadow of the " Mass-rock." That the people were not reduced to savagery was due to the sign of the Cross, their love for the blessed Virgin, and the purity she symbolized. Let us close this chapter, reiterating what now should be an aphorism : It is an honor to descend from such a people.

CHAPTER XIII.

THE IRISH HEGIRA.

A Land of Fertility—The Harbors of Ireland—The Famine of 1741—
Appalling Records—"High Farming"—Deportation Contracts—Lord
Devon's Report—Opinion of Lord Brougham—The Famine of 1845
and 1846—Opinion of John Mitchell—Foreign Sympathy—Magna-
nimity of the English People—Flight of the Irish People—Floating
Coffins—Account of an English Emigrant—The "Julius Cæsar"—Hor-
rors of Ship Fever—In Quarantine—Appeal of the Irish Mother—
The Irish Emigrant—Address of Henry Giles—Heroism of the
French-Canadian Priests—Descendants of the Irish Emigrants in
Quebec.

"That which the palmerworm hath left, the locust hath eaten ; and that
which the locust hath left, the bruchus hath eaten ; and that which the bruchus
hath left, the mildew hath destroyed."   (Joel i. 4.)

DEATH on the field of battle, though in a foreign
cause, carries with it glory and honor, but the
countless multitudes that famine and plague sweep
into their graves excite but a passing commiseration.
History does not record the name of any people who,
blessed with a land teeming with fertility and verdure,
have suffered such frequent and appalling visitations of
famine and pestilence as have the Irish. According to
all trustworthy authorities, Ireland is eminently fitted
for grazing and agriculture. The herbaceous vegeta-
tion of Ireland is admirable, and it is not without

reason that the shamrock has become the heraldic emblem of the "Green Isle." The vast Atlantic clouds, which soften the hues and outlines of the scenery, drop fertility on the lands and clothe the mountains with the brightest verdure. That country's grazing and dairy farms, if owned by the people, ought to supply with their produce the population of England.

As a commercial country, Ireland is furnished with excellent harbors, and with a superabundance of internal water communication. It is to-day admitted, even by the enemies of the Irish people, that Irishmen in every country but their own are industrious, frugal and prosperous; and there is no reason to doubt that, under favorable conditions in their own country, they would have attained to a position of prosperity equal to that of any other people. That the young Irish-Canadian may have some idea of what his ancestors suffered, we will hurriedly review a gloomy chapter in the history of the Irish people. In 1741, the author of the "Groans of Ireland" wrote as follows: "Having been absent from this country for some years, on my return to it last summer I found it the most miserable scene of distress that I ever read of in history. Want and misery on every face; the rich unable to relieve the poor; the roads spread with dead and dying bodies; mankind the color of the docks and nettles which they feed on; two or three, sometimes more, on a car going to the grave for want of bearers to carry them; and many buried in the fields and ditches where they perished. Universal scarcity was followed by fluxes and malignant fevers, which swept off multitudes of all sorts, so that whole villages were laid waste." The writer adds, that 400,000 perished in this famine; and Berkeley, in his address to the " Catholic clergy," speaks of this terrible famine as a calamity for which the Land Laws and landlords of Ireland must ever be held responsible.

About the time of the Clare elections, when O'Connell and Richard Lalor Shiel were arousing the Irish peasantry to a sense of their importance as men who, by their votes, could send independent representatives to Parliament, it happened that new theories of farming became fashionable. The object of " High farming " was to bring about more grazing, more green cropping, abolish the small holdings, and, by steam and horses, cultivate larger farms. Practically, then, the clearance system began in 1829, the year of Emancipation. Whole communities were frequently thrown on the highways, and the houseless creatures compelled to live on the charity of their neighbors. Crowbar brigades were organized all through the south and west of Ireland, and, protected by the police and local magistrates, made short work of the ejectments. The tenants were remorselessly thrown out, and, if they offered any opposition, their cabins were either burned or levelled to the ground by the "brigade." Landlords, to rid themselves forever of the shocking spectacle presented by the wretched outcasts, contracted with emigration companies to deport them to America for a lump sum; others, more hardened and ruthless, did not care what became of the ejected, and hundreds perished during the winter from exposure. Workhouses, erected under the new Poor Law, received many of the unhappy people; "but it is a strangely significant fact," remarks John Mitchell, in his "History of Ireland," "that the deaths by starvation increased rapidly from the first year of the Poor Law."

In 1844, the Landlord and Tenant Commission was ordered by the Government to begin enquiry into the state of affairs. The Chairman, Lord Devon, was an Irish absentee landlord, and the other members of the Commission likewise belonged to the landed gentry. The Irish people had no confidence in the Board, and were satisfied that, whatever report would be made to Parliament, it would not ameliorate the condition of affairs. "You might as well," said O'Connell, "consult butchers about keeping Lent as consult these men about the rights of farmers." The Commission reported that as there was a surplus population in Ireland, the best thing the English Government could do would be to encourage emigration, and to this end Sir Robert Peel began to bend his energies. But a most efficacious ally now stepped in, and, in a couple of years, did more to remove the surplus population than could Mr. Peel and the British House of Commons. An interesting history might be written relating how the famine helped Sir Robert Peel, and how Sir Robert Peel helped the famine. It is yet a debatable subject whether Sir Walter Raleigh brought a blessing or a curse upon Ireland when he introduced the potato. The failure of the potato crop in 1844 and 1845 brought ruin and desolation to thousands. The horrors of the famine that ensued have never been, and never will be, catalogued. Lord Brougham was aghast when he heard the awful condition of affairs, "surpassing anything in the page of Thucydides, on the canvas of Poussin, or in the dismal chant of Dante."

A month after the blight had fallen on the crop of potatoes, on which five millions of the Irish people had been reduced to depend for existence, there came from all the counties of Ireland a cry of terror and alarm. The famine and the fever raged, and the verdict, "Death by starvation," became so common that the newspapers often omitted to record it. In the eventful years of 1845 and 1846, hundreds of famished wretches died every day from extremity of suffering. By the ditch where they had fallen, on the public roads where they sank from sheer exhaustion, or in the cabins to which they had crawled, they drew their last breath alone and in silence. Englishmen, who were compelled by pressure of business or serious necessity to visit the western coast of Ireland, were appalled when they came upon some lonely village where the houses were tenantless, save for the skeletons of men, women and children that lay upon the hearths. Men looked on in dumb despair, wondering if the Almighty had doomed the Irish people to annihilation. "All this while," writes John Mitchell, "until after the meeting of Parliament, there was no hint as to the intentions of Government; and all this while the new Irish harvest of 1845 (which was particularly abundant), with immense herds of cattle, sheep and hogs, quite as usual, was floating off on every tide out of every one of our thirteen seaports, bound for England, and the landlords were receiving their rents and going to England to spend them, and many poor people had lain down and died on the road-sides for want of food, even before Christmas."

And thus it went on, till the nation became almost panic-stricken, and a deep and pervading anxiety to fly anywhere took possession of the people. It is an instinct that forms a part of our nature, that when we are pursued by wild beasts we will fly even into the sea; and if a country be made too hot to hold its inhabitants, there remains for them but flight, the last refuge of the hunted man.

And so the hegira began. Before going further, however, three facts mentioned by Mitchell should be borne in mind.

1st. That by a careful census of the agricultural produce of Ireland for the year 1847, made by Captain Larcom, as a Government Commissioner, the total value of that produce was $224,790,600, which would have amply sustained *double* the entire people of the island. This return is given in detail, and agrees generally with another estimate of the same prepared by John Martin, of Loughorn, in the County Down.

2nd. That at least five hundred thousand human beings perished this year of famine and of famine-typhus ; and two hundred thousand more fled beyond the sea to escape famine and fever.

3rd. That the loans for relief given to the Public Works and Public Commissariat Departments, to be laid out as they should think proper, and to be repaid by rates on Irish property, went, in the first place, to maintain ten thousand greedy officials, and that the greater part of these funds never reached the people at all, or reached them in such a way as to ruin and exterminate them."

From the doomed land there rose up an agonizing cry so prolonged and pitiful that it was heard across the English Channel, and the nations of Europe became appalled. Even the heart of the Turk was touched, and through the Golden Gate there sailed away for Ireland a vessel freighted with provisions for the starving people. France, Germany, Sardinia and the Papal States sent liberal contributions. From the ports of New York and Philadelphia ships sailed bearing the sympathies and offerings of the American people. But, alas! it was now too late. "Ireland," said John Martin, in 1846, " is one vast charnel-house, in which all is hastening to decay and decomposition."

The English people, to their eternal honor be it

written, had, from the beginning of the famine, contributed most generously to the relief of the Irish people ; and, from meetings convened all over England, there rose up indignant protests, demanding, in tones of thunder, that the English Parliament should give up discussion and take action, and that at once, or the members of that Parliament would have to answer with their political lives to the people of England. In the meantime thousands had fled from the famine-stricken land. Into those floating coffins, the " emigrant ships," they poured themselves, where death under another and no less awful aspect confronted them. Only an inspired writer may record the sufferings of the unhappy people when the dread scourge of ship-fever rioted among them. He alone may tell of the crushed hopes and ruined prospects of the full-grown man, of the sorrows of the delicate Irish mother,

> " Bent o'er her babe, her eyes dissolved in dew,
> The big tears mingling with the milk it drew,"

and the thousands of brave and loving hearts who found forgetfulness of their miseries in the repose of the deep.

And lest we might be charged with exaggeration in describing the horrors of an Atlantic voyage in these rotten emigrant ships, we append the account of one who made the passage in those trying days :

"On each side of the vessel, 'between decks,' were two rows of bunks, one above the other. These were

16

made of boards; each bunk held two persons, and the division between bunks was nothing but a narrow strip of lumber. They might properly be described as an upper and a lower bunk running all round the ship. On these mattresses were laid, which we ourselves bought in Liverpool. The second cabin differed from the steerage only in this, it was the after part of the ship, while the steerage was the forward part. There were no first cabin passengers on this ship. The whole was simply a large floating dungeon or cellar. There was no light or ventilation whatever, except what we got from two hatchways—one forward, the other aft. Each emigrant was allowed by law thirty-three inches of room in width; but we didn't get it. Into this dark cellar were crowded, in the month of July, 1847, four hundred emigrants—men, women and children. We had to furnish and cook our own provisions, grates for cooking being provided by the ship. To prevent starvation, each ship was required to carry hard bread sufficient to give each passenger a pound per day; and had the bread been eatable it would have saved us— but it was not; it was a black substance, made of rye and beans, stale and worm-eaten. You could break it with a hammer, but in the teeth it was gritty, like brick-dust, and not any more nutritious. The infernal cruelty and cupidity of the men who owned the ship, and the criminal neglect of the Government which permitted their extortions and deceptions, were exhibited in other ways. They lied to the emigrants with

malice aforethought. When the officers and agents of
the vessel were asked how long the voyage would
probably be, they flippantly answered that they
expected to make the run in twenty-one days, but
they might have bad luck and head-winds, in which
case it might take them twenty-eight days. They
also amused us with fabulous accounts of fast-sailing
exploits performed on former voyages by this decayed
old humbug called the *Julius Cæsar*. The poor
emigrants laid in their provisions in accordance with
these lies. The wicked imposture was made worse by
delay. The vessel did not sail at the time appointed
—not for ten days afterwards—and all this time the
emigrants were consuming the food that should sub-
sist them on the voyage. At length the day of sailing
came. A surgeon visited the ship and examined all
the emigrants ; he pronounced us sound and healthy,
every one ; as, indeed, we were. Then a search was
made for *stowaways*, poor wretches who seek to steal a
passage without paying for it. A couple of these were
found and turned over to the police.

"What a satire on the British Government was this,
that there should be in the British Empire gaunt men
so starved and stricken as to steal into this ghostly
coffin to escape from England ! Four hundred men,
women and children, huddled together in this black
hole, soon filled the atmosphere with poison, and there
the foul god Typhus held high festival ! Decency
was a luxury only had by stealth, and cleanliness was

of necessity neglected. For a time people stole into bed with as much modesty as they could; but at last undressing was abandoned, and they lay in their bunks with their clothes on. Let it be borne in mind that there were no separate apartments for women. A man in one bunk might have a woman for his neighbor in the next bunk—it was a matter of accident altogether; and the division between bunks was simply nothing. So long as the emigrants were well, they kept themselves on deck in the open air as much as possible, but when sick, and also at night, they had to go below. Vermin literally swarmed all over us. What food we had was poorly cooked; and at last we had no food at all.

" When the weather was rough, the old ship actually groaned and shrieked as if in pain; the creaking of her old, rheumatic timbers made weird and hideous sounds. Most of the emigrants were Irish peasant farmers; there were some Scotch and a few English, of which last number I was one. When the winds blew our old hulk went along lazily enough, and in calm weather she lay restless on the sea. When little more than a week out we had a fearful storm; it pounded the *Julius Cæsar*, and threatened to send her to the bottom; but though somewhat damaged, she lived it through. The moral effect of this hurricane was bad; it broke the spirits of many of the emigrants, and made them easier victims for old Typhus, who was even then hatching pestilence in the

heated vapor of that plague-stricken ship. He had
not long to wait for victims, plenty of them were at
hand.

" We were just two weeks out from Liverpool when
the first of our number died. It was a calm, hot
night. There was not a breath of air to wrinkle the
face of the sea; our sails hung dead against the
masts; the moon shone clear and bright. The ocean
was like glass, and absolutely motionless, except that
breathing pulsation which seems as necessary to earth
as to man. The victim was a stout, well-made young
fellow of 20 years of age. He and his uncle were
emigrating together. They were from a place in
Ireland called Skull (the very name was ominous). I
saw him die. He had been sick in his bunk but a
few hours, and had risen to get a drink of water; he
was on his way back, but sat on his trunk to rest
himself. Shortly after he lay back and died. I can
see him now lying there; his legs hanging over the
trunk and his feet resting on the floor, the blue signs
of mortification painting his lips and brow, his eyes
wide open, staring at the dirty dungeon roof; and
there was none to close them—not one. Fear and
superstition had taken possession of all his countrymen; they were actually stunned by the catastrophe.
All fell on their knees to pray, but no one touched the
dead man, not even his own uncle. There he lay for
hours, until myself and Jack Fisher, an English shoe-
maker from Liverpool, went to the captain and told

him it was his duty to have the dead man buried. He was a Scotchman, named Fleming—a cold, brave man, utterly destitute of sentiment. He said: 'No; I'm a heretic. They won't like it if I touch him. Let his own people bury him. Let them sew him up in canvas, tie a weight to his feet, say a prayer over him, and bury him like a Christian.'

"He would not do anything, so Jack and I, with a couple of other English chaps from London, took the dead man, laid him as he was upon the hatch covering, placed one end of it upon the bulwarks, then tilted up the other end, and slid our poor fellow-emigrant into the sea. He did not sink, and would not leave the ship. The moon shone full upon his upturned face, and I thought then, and I think now, that I could read upon his lips a curse for the Government and the system that had murdered him. At length he floated away from us, and we saw no more of him.

"Death gave us a respite for three days. On the fourth day a woman in the 'second cabin' died. She belonged to what is called the 'better class'; her family were with her, and she had a Christian burial. The death panic had subsided. She was sewed up in a piece of sail-cloth, heavy weights were put at her feet, the emigrants all gathered at the funeral, somebody read the burial service of the Roman Catholic Church, tenderly the body was laid in its watery grave, and it sank at once into the 'bosom of the deep.' Our captain looked on with calm indifference; our sufferings were none of his business. His duty was to command the ship, to land what might be left of his cargo at the port of Quebec, and to bring a load of timber back to Liverpool. He never once came down below to visit us.

"From this time forth the deaths were frequent and sudden. Sometimes we would go a couple of days without any deaths at all, and sometimes we would bury two or three a day. One day, six people died, and we threw them overboard. Those whose friends had money got a better funeral than the others. They were sewed up in cloth by the sailors, who got pay for doing it, and they had weights to sink them. Those who could not afford this luxury were thrown overboard to the sharks, with their clothes on, exactly as they died.

"There was a very decent family from Wexford, who were all very much attached to me because of little kindnesses which I had shown the children, of whom there were five. The eldest was a beautiful, bright boy about ten years old ; he was my playmate. The fever struck him, and we laid him on the floor underneath the hatchway, that he might have what chance there was of air. The grief of his father, as he knelt beside him watching his young life go, was something terrible to see. I knelt beside him, too ; I held his hand until he died, and my own grief remains with me to this day. We buried him lovingly and tenderly, but our sorrow was not yet full. One by one the other children died ; and, when we landed, I saw the father and mother swung ashore in baskets— they were both stricken with the fever. Whether they lived or died I never knew. I hope they died. The grief of that ship would have been a memory too burdensome to carry through a lifetime.

"There was a Cornwall miner on the ship making his way to Pennsylvania, where he had some friends. His mother was with him—a kind old English dame. She was always doing something for the sick—making tea or gruel for them, bathing their foreheads or their hands. She was very brave, but the fever struck her and she died. When we buried her the stout Cornish-man, her son, went mad, and when we landed he was hopelessly insane. There was a young Irishman on board from the neighborhood of Dublin, who was home-sick, or rather, I should say, mother-sick. He was always talking of his mother. He belonged to the richer class of farmers, for his clothes were all of good quality, and quite new. He was a model of physical manhood, six feet high and proportioned like Adonis. His health was perfect, but the horrors that surrounded him were more than he could bear. One night he and I stood on the deck together talking until very late, and then we went below. His bunk was exactly opposite mine. In the morning I got up ; I saw him lying in his bunk, and I crossed over to wake him ; he was dead. There was nothing the matter with him ; he had died from sheer despair or from a wish to die. If ten thousand doctors should tell me this could not be I would not believe them. I am certain that he just wished to die, and died. In the next bunk was a young woman, whose name I have forgotten. She shared her mattress with a young girl about her own age. One morning I woke up, and looking at my neighbor, saw that she was dead. I jumped up to rouse her companion, when I saw that a young woman who occupied the bunk below was also dead.

"These were not the worst horrors that I witnessed on that ship. When the 'twenty-one days' had passed, the provisions of many began to run short, and hunger was now added to our other miseries. Those who had plenty shared with their less fortunate companions as long as the provisions lasted, and then all starved together. We got nothing from the ship's stores except water and the black, impossible bread that I spoke of before. To the help of Typhus came his deputy plague, Dysentery, and between them killed or wounded nearly every person on that ship. I don't think that twenty of those four hundred emigrants landed in good health. Even the crew were on short rations before the voyage ended. How the weary days dragged on! The 'twenty-eight days' were passed, and yet we saw no signs of the promised land. Forty days went by, and still we starved and died. Forty-five days were gone, and yet the dreary voyage was not ended. At last, on the fiftieth day out from Liverpool, we cast anchor at Grosse Isle, the quarantine ground, a few miles below Quebec.

"Of the four hundred emigrants who started well and sound on board the *Julius Cæsar*, sixty-two had died and were buried at sea. All of us yet alive were landed at Grosse Isle, the quarantine station. This lovely island, in the St. Lawrence River, must ever bear the reproach of being the plague-spot of the world in the year of our Lord 1847, the shame of the civilization of that era. Those of our cargo who had the fever were taken to the fever sheds; those of us who had it not were taken to other sheds, where good soup and bread were given to us, and where we feasted like famished wolves on the good fresh beef which was supplied to us by the humanity of the Canadian Government.

"Well would it be for Britain if the waters of the St. Lawrence could disintegrate Grosse Isle, and carry it as mud and sand far away to sea, for as long as it remains it will bear witness of her deep disgrace, her unpardonable sin. These sheds I speak of were long, narrow buildings, made of boards; beds were ranged along each side with their heads against the wall, thus leaving narrow aisles the whole length of the buildings—avenues of death. Often I stood at the doors and gazed with stupid curiosity down the ghastly streets of beds, upon the black and swollen faces of the emigrants that filled them, and wondering whether what I saw was real or a phantasy of nightmare. Every morning the doctors would come to our quarters and examine us; all who showed fever symptoms were ordered to the fever sheds. The pitiable appeals of relatives to the doctors not to send their loved ones to the fever sheds, and thus separate them, perhaps for ever, makes me sad and sorrowful even now, although thirty-four years have come and gone since then. And there, upon that lovely island, with the rippling waters of the St. Lawrence murmuring their everlasting requiem, sleep a hundred martyrs of humanity, the sainted heroes of the poor; brave doctors who perilled their lives, and gave them without flinching, in the service of those wretched people; priests and ministers of all denominations, who sucked death into their bosoms as they shrived and comforted the dying penitents; nurses, men and women, from Quebec and all the country round about; Sisters of Charity, whose gentle hand upon the burning foreheads cured like the touch of a new Redeemer; fearlessly, by night and day, they walked like blessed angels through those corridors of death. Many of them were stricken with the plague and died, and if ever the sin of that great suffering will be forgiven it will be through their intercession and because of them. How many of our cargo died at Grosse Isle I cannot say.

"After some days, those of us who were considered

well enough to go were put on board a steamboat and ordered to Quebec. When we reached that city we were not allowed to land; the authorities forbade it; they were overcrowded now; they had more emigrants than they could manage; so they sent us up the river to Montreal, and there upon the levee we were flung like damaged goods. Some took the fever even after that, and died in the sheds of that city. Estimating the deaths among our party at Grosse Isle, at Montreal and other places, and adding them to the sixty-two thrown overboard, I am sure that of the 400 emigrants that sailed from Liverpool on board the *Julius Cæsar*, July, 1847, at least 100 died of the ship fever; of the remainder, another hundred were dangerously attacked, and nearly all the rest were more or less afflicted.

"No battle of modern times can show such mortality as this. In proportion, it is twice as great as the loss of the English at Waterloo, and four times greater than their loss at the battle of Trafalgar. It may be thought that the case of the *Julius Cæsar* was exceptional, but it was not. It was a fair average of the suffering endured on English emigrant ships in 1847. We may have suffered more than some, but I know we suffered less than others. One ship had such great mortality among the emigrants and crew that she could not reach her destination, and was compelled to put into the port of Miramichi, New Brunswick;

and many of her dead were still lying in their bunks when she arrived. Besides, the records of Grosse Isle will prove that our case was not exceptional. In the sheds of Grosse Isle there died, in the summer of 1847, no less than 7,000 emigrants, an average of fifty a day. How many died that year in the sheds of Quebec, Montreal and other places I have never learned, but I know that the mortality was very great. This proves that the condition of the ships was very much alike. Let it be borne in mind that these emigrants were not paupers, they were passengers; they had paid their money for decent treatment and accommodation. They were defrauded and murdered. As I read this story over I am ashamed to see how feebly it portrays the life and death and sufferings on board an English emigrant ship in 1847; but no pen and no language could picture the reality."

There are those still living in our midst who remember when the emigrant ships discharged their cargoes of human freight quivering in the throes of infectious disease. Melancholy and sublime was the spectacle which the Irish emigrants offered to the world in these memorable days of 1847; when, crawling from the foul and fetid atmosphere of the plague-stricken ships, they died, gasping for breath like fish out of water. For months the very air was tainted with the exhalations of death that arose from the quarantine island, where our ill-fated countrymen were shedded indiscriminately together. There was to be met with the young maiden, with the hectic flush of fever on her cheeks, calling to memory in her delirium the familiar friends of other days, the green valley, the sparkling brook, the Catholic chapel of her native land; there, also, was to be seen the once strong man, whispering into the ear of the priest his last confession upon earth, and the sorrows and misfortunes of a broken heart.

Terrible beyond conception were the sufferings of our countrymen in those days, when, in the language of Holy Writ, "there was no light, but all was darkness." The Eternal Father Himself seemed to have turned away His face from His own, and to have decreed, as He did the Canaanites of old, the whole race to extermination.

During all this long night of misfortune, amid the appalling sufferings of human beings calmly awaiting death, there was no murmuring against the will of God; no cry of despair arose; nothing was heard but the sob of repentance and the voice of resignation. Often, indeed, they returned in fancy to the land that gave them birth. They were bound by a thousand nameless associations to its hospitable shores, and the dying mother expressed but the wish of their hearts when. with a withered shamrock clasped in her hand, she called the young priest to her side and, in a voice of unutterable pathos, asked him if her soul would pass through Ireland on its way to its God. How

beautifully has the Irish poet caught and expressed
the aspiration :

> "Oh, Soggarth Aroon !* sure I know life is fleeting,
>   Soon, soon in the cold earth my poor bones will lie ;
>   I have said my last prayer and received my last blessing,
>   And if the Lord's willing, I am ready to die.
>   But, Soggarth Aroon ! will I never again see
>   The valleys and hills of my own native land ?
>   When my soul takes its flight from this world of sorrow
>   Will it pass through old Ireland to join the bless'd band ?
>
> "Oh, Soggarth Aroon ! sure I know that in heaven
>   The loved ones are waiting and watching for me,
>   And the Lord knows how anxious I am to be with them
>   In those realms of bliss 'mid souls pure and free.
>   But, Soggarth Aroon ! ere you leave me forever,
>   Relieve the last doubt of a poor dying soul,
>   Whose hope, next to God, is to know that when parting
>   'Twill pass through old Ireland on its way to its goal.
>
> "Oh, Soggarth Aroon ! I have kept through all changes
>   The thrice-blessed shamrock to lay o'er my clay,
>   And oh ! it has minded me often and often
>   Of that bright smiling valley so far, far away.
>   But, Soggarth Aroon, will I never again see
>   The place where it grew on my own native sod ?
>   When my body lies low in the land of the stranger
>   Will my soul pass through Ireland on its way to its God ?"

"Do you find it hard to die?" asked a priest in
Montreal, as he stood by the side of a dying emigrant.
The green valleys, the mountain side, his father's

* Soggarth Aroon—"Priest dear." A term of endearment used by the Irish
peasantry dating back to the penal days, when the priest, defying the laws,
emerged from his hiding-place, anointed the dying, and, in the darkness of
night, at the grave-side said the prayers for the dead.

cabin, the mother's love, her soft musical voice came before his fading fancy. His eyes brightened for a moment, and then were drowned in one large tearful wave.

" I do," said the dying man, "but not half so hard as I found it to leave Ireland."

The dying expression of this poor fellow summarized the sentiment and feeling of every Irish Celt that left his native land for foreign shores. Physical suffering will ever excite the sympathy of civilized man, for it appeals through the senses to the heart with a tenderness peculiarly its own, but the agony of the emotions and feelings is known but to God alone. The Irish Celt is and was a man of strong sympathy and strangely pathetic ; of an imagination keen and sensitive, and possessed of a heart loving and lovable. Twenty years after he had left the shores of Ireland, Henry Giles thus calls his native land back to his memory : " I see her through the mists of memory ; I see her with the mists of ocean resting on her hills, with mists of time resting on her towers ; I hear, as afar off, the eternal music of the waves around her coast ; I hear in her valleys and her caves the songs of the winds soft as the sounds of harps ; I recall her in many a vision of lonely beauty, brightened by the sunshine on river, lake and dell ; in many a vision, too, of sombre glory in the battle of the tempests against her mountain summits and her rock-bound shores. I bring her *national* life back to my mind in heroic story, in saintly legend, in tales passionate and wild, in the grand old poetry of the supernatural and solemn imagination which people love, to whose spirits the soul of the immortal whispers, on whose ears there linger the voices of the mighty *past*. I bring her *domestic* life back to my heart in her gracious old affections which so sweeten earthly care; in her gracious old phrases into which these old affections breathe; for never did fondness deepen into richer melody of love than in ' *Cuishla Machree*'; and never did the welcome of hospitality sound in more generous eloquence than that of ' *Cead mille failthe.*'"

In the middle of the St. Lawrence, about forty miles below Quebec, is a small island whose consecrated clay shrouds the ashes of 10,000 Irish victims of the murderous typhus of 1846 and 1847. Quebec, Montreal, Kingston and Toronto yet record the sorrowful story of the harrowing scenes which fifty years ago they witnessed, whilst all along the river St. Lawrence the very banks are honeycombed with the unmarked graves of thousands of our unfortunate countrymen. Nor when recording these sorrowful scenes should we forget the gallant conduct of the French-Canadian priests, who, in those days, moved among the dead and the dying, breathing the fetid atmosphere of the fever-shed, and inhaling the odors of decomposition. In that most trying of ordeals, Cardinal Taschereau, then in the morning of his young manhood, was to be seen at his post of duty, bending over the dying

17

penitent, preparing the parting soul for its passage to eternity, and soothing, as only the priest can soothe, the last moments of the Irish emigrant. On the banks of the St. Lawrence, near the scene of his labors, is the grave of a French priest, a good man, a warm-hearted, unselfish man, who passed the first days of his young priesthood in the fever sheds, whose aspect, changeless and death-like, alone met his eyes. For weeks he moved among the haggard forms of the dying, helping all, as it was written of St. Charles Borromeo, with hand and main and purse, full of compassion where pity had been crushed out of other breasts; relieving the distressed, encouraging the faint-hearted, standing by the sick, when, mad with the instinct of self-preservation, the friend deserted the friend, and the brother turned away from the sister, while her pleadings were still wailing in his ears. For days and nights this man of God scarcely closed his eyes in sleep, and when at last he himself was stricken down, the boots had to be cut from off his feet. When carried to his bed, his hair was dark as that of a Spaniard, and when at the end of three weeks he was able to sit up, it was as white as the snows that cover the neighboring plains in winter. If his life be ever written, it will serve for the lives of his brother priests who went down to their graves in those days, the saddest to us in the annals of Canadian history. Of the twenty-five priests who were attacked with the fever, seven paid with their lives the penalty of their devotion. Not a few of these men were professors in colleges; but at the appeal of the Archbishop they left their classes and their studies for the horrors and perils of the fever sheds.

The descendants of the Irish emigrants owe an eternal debt of gratitude to the brave and generous priests and people of Lower Canada. From the breasts of the dead mothers, from the straw pallets of the dying fathers, Vicar-General Cazeau, Cardinal Taschereau and Father Proulx gathered the helpless infants and orphans, and placed them under the affectionate care of the Sisters of Charity. These tender children were adopted by the French-Canadian farmers, in whose homes they took their places as wards of Christ, and were placed on an equality with the sons and daughters of the large-hearted and hospitable *habitants*. When the time came for dividing the property and chattels they received their share, and to-day, in the remote parishes, these children, now grown to man's estate, may be recognized by their blue eyes, light complexion and fair hair.

CHAPTER XIV.

"THE TOILERS OF THE DEEP."

Proclamation of Baron Sydenham—Election of Mr. Merritt—The Welland
Canal—The Call for Men—The Bread Riots—Rev. Dr. Lee—Letter
to the Governor—Appeal of Dr. Lee—Liberal Response—The Sick
Call—Wm. Hamilton Merritt—His Character—The Toilers on the
Canal—Dignity of Labor—Opinion of the London *Times*—Fever
and Ague—The Deadly Miasma—The Laborers' Friend—An Apostolic
Mission—Death of Dr. Lee—Father McDonagh—St. Catharines'
Church--An Interesting Inscription—Patriarchal Men.

BY proclamation of the Governor-General, the
Right Honorable Baron Sydenham, dated at
Montreal, 10th day of February, 1841, the two provinces of Upper and Lower Canada were reunited,
after a separation of fifty years. The first general
election under the Union opened on the 8th of March,
and William Hamilton Merritt was elected for this
county. The polling under the then Election Act
continued for six days, and as his opponent, Mr. Geo.
Rykert, was an influential and popular man, the
contest at the polls was keen and ably sustained. In
the following June, the first Parliament of Canada
opened at Kingston, and in the Speech from the
Throne, Lord Sydenham foreshadowed, among other
public works, the enlargement of the Welland Canal.

DANIEL McGUIRE, ESQ.

In addition he sent a message to the members in session, recommending the completion of the canal and the opening of communication for schooners and steamboats between Kingston and Montreal. By advertisement, dated 8th of October, 1841, it was proclaimed that tenders would be received for the widening and deepening of the " Feeder " to the Welland Canal. This "Feeder" was twenty-two miles long, extending from the Grand River Dam at Dunnville to its junction with the present canal at the town of Welland. For this work an appropriation of £4,500 sterling was made by Parliament, and soon after the contracts were let. Notices were now published in the press of Canada and the United States calling for laborers to work on the contracts. The Erie Canal was already completed, and as there were no other important works under contract in the States or Canada, a large body of unemployed men, far in excess of the number required, made application for work. The destitution and suffering that followed from this condition of affairs led up to what was known as the " Bread Riots," and considerable disturbance ensued along the " Feeder," and at Marshville and Broad Creek. The timely arrival, however, of the Rev. Dr. Constantine Lee prevented any serious outbreak.

In the month of May, 1842, it was proclaimed that the Home Government would guarantee abundant means for the enlargement of the whole canal and the constructing of stone locks. On the 12th of this month there appeared in the St. Catharines *Journal* an advertisement, calling for tenders for the excavation of a branch to connect the Feeder with the Grand River, the building of an entrance lock to the same, and six locks between St. Catharines and Thorold. The tenders were opened on the 15th of June, the contracts let, and advertisements inserted in the newspapers calling for laborers. Four thousand men, a large number having families with them, answered the call, but for reasons now hard to explain, most of the contractors were not ready to go on with the work. As a result great suffering ensued, and gangs of men who, with their families, were perishing with hunger, began to threaten serious attacks on the provision stores and mills in St. Catharines and along the canal. The authorities in vain reasoned with them. They contended that in the face of starvation provisions became common property. To the number of two thousand, these hungry men marched into St. Catharines, and after breaking open one or two stores, seized thirteen barrels of pork from a schooner discharging at Mittleberger's mills. The next day there was great excitement among the villagers, for the starving men menaced the peace of the place. At this crisis Father Lee stepped into the breach, and, says the *Journal*, "through his untiring exertions and eloquent appeals they were restrained from executing their avowed purpose." Meanwhile the following petition was sent to the Governor-General, Father Lee having pledged himself to go in person if necessary, and plead their cause before the Governor:

"*To His Excellency the Right Honorable Sir Charles Bagot, G.C.B., etc., etc., Governor-General of British North America, etc., etc.:*

"We, the undersigned, being clergymen in the village of St. Catharines, Canada West, humbly petition your Excellency on behalf of a sober, industrious multitude of operatives, who have been induced by advertisement and otherwise to assemble here and along the line of the Welland Canal, from all parts of the British Empire, to seek expected employment on the Government works now projected on this line. From causes which we do not profess to understand, the works are not proceeding immediately; and, consequently, a multitude of well-disposed persons are reduced to a state of absolute starvation. To satisfy the cravings of hunger, some acts of violence have already been committed, which we exceedingly deplore. We have reason, also, to fear that further acts of depredation will be committed unless some measures are speedily devised for their relief. The number of laborers, amounting to several hundreds, would render individual efforts for their relief unavailing. We, therefore, most earnestly and humbly beseech your Excellency to take into consideration the agonizing cries of infant children and starving but industrious parents, and we shall ever pray, etc.

"CONSTANTINE LEE, D.D.,
"*Catholic Pastor.*

"JOHN WM. BAYNES, A.M.,
"*Presbyterian Minister.*"

Dr. Lee now drew up and circulated a petition, soliciting subscriptions on behalf of the starving people, the Hon. William H. Merritt heading it with a subscription of £10. The merchants and business men of the city contributed proportionately, and after the list was closed the priest publicly thanked his Protestant fellow-citizens for the courtesy and kindness with which they received him, and their charity towards the suffering laborers and their families.

Father Lee was a distinguished scholar, an eloquent speaker, and is said by those who remember him to have been a man of tenderness and much refinement of character. As most of the men working on the canal were Catholics, his influence with them was paramount. As was to be expected, a good portion of his pastoral time was given to the members of his flock who were working on the " Feeder."

He lived, however, but a short time after his appointment to this parish. He was summoned one night from St. Catharines to attend a dying man on the works near Broad Creek; and as he responded to the call of duty in a drenching storm of rain, he contracted pneumonia, and died in a few weeks, at the comparatively early age of 45. It is this constant readiness of the Catholic priest to answer to a call of duty, at all hours of the night, and under all circumstances, that, in a measure, wins for him the reverence and respect of his people. He ventures, when summoned to a sick call, into the foulest, most pestilential atmosphere. His health, his comfort, his time, his very existence are all laid down as full ungrudging gifts on the altar of his sacred calling; and, when he applies the consecrated oil to brows damp with the moisture of imminent dissolution, the heart of the dying man and the hearts of his children go out in love and reverence towards him.

> " Who, in the winter's night,
> Soggarth Aroon,
> When the cold blast did bite,
> Soggarth Aroon,
> Came to my cabin door,
> And on my earthen floor
> Knelt by me, sick and poor ?
> Soggarth Aroon."

Truly may it be said of Father Lee, as Grattan said of Kirwan, " In feeding the lamp of charity he exhausted the lamp of life." He was buried under the main altar of St. Catharines church, and his funeral was, if we may use the term, an ovation. When the head of the funeral procession had reached St. Catharines, the rear portion was leaving Thorold. Perhaps no greater compliment could be paid to his eloquence and kindly spirit of liberality than that which he received from his separated brethren of Chippewa, who, to the number of 150, invited him to address them.

The contractors were soon in a position to give employment to all the men, and the great work of deepening and widening the historic canal practically began.   The Hon. William Hamilton Merritt, the projector and originator of this great water-way, connecting Lakes Erie and Ontario, deserves more than a passing notice in these pages.   He was a man of much intellectual power, great force of character, and of a largeness of heart that won him a high place in the affections of the Irish Catholics employed on the works.   There are those yet living in this city who speak of his charity and liberality with warmth and enthusiasm.

"What is the matter, Ahern," he said one morning to the section boss, "with this man immediately to the right of us ?   He doesn't appear to be able to do his work."

"His wife and two children," answered Ahern, "have been down with the fever and ague for two weeks, and I think this poor man, instead of sleeping, has been sitting up at nights caring for them."

" What's his name ? "

" His name is Dolan," spoke back Ahern.

Mr. Merritt called Dolan to him, and, after speaking with him for some time, told him to go home.   Then turning to Ahern, he thus addressed him :

" Now, William, when you go to St. Catharines to-night, send a doctor up to Dolan's at my expense, and no matter how long this poor man Dolan may be away from the works, remember his pay goes on till his wife recovers."

HON. W. H. MERRITT.

In January, 1847, Mr. Merritt called a public meeting in St. Catharines to raise subscriptions for the famine-stricken people of Ireland. At this meeting, in his capacity of chairman, he made an eloquent and pathetic appeal on behalf of the suffering people. He headed the subscription list with a generous donation, and forwarded to the Roman Catholic Archbishop of Dublin, in his own name and that of the people of St. Catharines, a handsome sum of money.

At last we find the Irish people at work. De Tocqueville could not pay a more just or more beautiful tribute of praise to the genius of the American people than when, in 1825, he said that every honest occupation in the United States was honorable. The same may be said of Canada. The honest, industrious man is honored with us whether he works with his hands or with his brains, because he is indispensable to the progress of the Dominion. Labor contributes to the advancement of the country, and whatever conduces to a nation's welfare is most worthy of commendation.

> " Honor and fame from no condition rise ;
> Act well thy part, there all true honor lies."

Our blessed Lord and His foster father, by working at the carpenter's bench for their support, made labor honorable. Cincinnatus lent dignity to agriculture by working at the plough; while Caligula and Nero, by their infamous lives, degraded the royal crown and imperial purple. The laboring man is the bee in the social hive and the benefactor of his race, because he is always producing something for the common-weal.

The London *Times*, during the famine of 1846, charged the Irish with laziness and shiftlessness, but if the English reader of those days could be transported to this peninsula and look upon the thousands of fine fellows laboring here under the burning rays of a July sun, he would give the lie direct to the London editor. Here were men subsisting on the coarsest fare, holding their lives as uncertain as those of the leaders of a forlorn hope. Men excluded from all the advantages of civilization, often at the mercy of a hard contractor, who wrung his profits from their blood—blasting rocks, digging in the hard clay, uprooting trees, clearing the ground of briars—and doing all this for a pittance that merely enabled them to exist. The fetid exhalations arising from the pestilential swamps in which they were working produced diseases unknown and unheard of in their own country. The Irish laborers of those days stood in trenches up to the knees in water and mire, and the putrid exhalations rising from the earth consumed them with fever or set their teeth chattering as with cold, while the sweat rolled from their foreheads. They waded knee deep in black muck, wheeled, dug, hewed, bore heavy burdens on their shoulders, exposed at all times to every change of temperature, till stricken down with fever, they took refuge in the shanties, and in narrow bunks trembled with disease.

" Along the line of the works," writes the author of the " Life of William Hamilton Merritt," " on the Feeder the fever and ague was raging; strong men were wasted to skeletons, and the general feeling of despondency and discontent, which all these vicissitudes bring in their train, was felt in the ranks of the workmen who were there employed. To stir them up and to cheer forward the work was a duty which devolved on him (W. H. Merritt), and none who now read these pages can form any idea of the pain and annoyances which a sensitive mind like his often felt under the circumstances. The season had been a dry one, and consequently the miasma from the stirred-up earth was more severe in this section than usual; so severe had it been that the work was delayed in consequence." This was the work that attracted large numbers of Irish laborers. They had left their country, crossed the ocean under circumstances already detailed, and this was the occupation for which they came three thousand miles. We can picture the shanties in which they lived, the innumerable extortions to which they were subjected, the mutations and changes of a climate to which they were unaccustomed, the close swamp, the stagnant air which they were doomed to breathe; their labor of fourteen hours a day, with spades and picks, in a blazing sun.

Deprived of education at home and pauperized by stern laws, the Irish laborer found himself, when he reached this country, with few resources save his bodily strength and his cheerful habits. His character was spread before the public by journal, tract and magazine as that of a lazy, thriftless, drunken creature. Public references to him were accumulations of falsehood. His brogue was detested, his honest' face was caricatured, his word was doubted, and his religion hated as a thing absurd and idolatrous. Yet his indomitable spirit was not broken, he was sustained in all his trials with the strength of his imperishable faith and the cheerful advice and comforting words of the Catholic priest.

It was only their religion, with its beauteous promise of reward hereafter and its comforting assurances, that enabled them to bear their hard lot and the scorn and contumely of men. Hidden from them and from the eyes of all were the great purposes of God in regard to them; they were a portion of the beginning of an *apostolic mission* on the part of a whole people—" A mission," writes Thebaud, " which will form one of the most moving and significant pages of the ecclesiastical history of the nineteenth century." Many of these men and their families formed centres of Catholic parishes from end to end of the Welland Canal and in other parts of the Province. The "shanty chapels," which were built from their limited means, have disappeared, and on their sites have been erected stone and brick churches, whose crosses, piercing the clouds, proclaim to passing man that " Christ reigns," " Christ rules,"

"Christ conquers." Their children have become an educative power in the country, and have built, beside these churches, schools and convents, that are now imparting to the young Irish-Canadian a finished education. The walls of prejudice are broken down, and the sons of these Irish emigrants, merged into the social life of the country, are the firmest upholders of the Dominion. On Ascension Sunday, 1843, the corner-stone of St. Catharines church was laid by the Rev. W. P. McDonagh, who succeeded Dr. Lee as pastor of this parish.

In the *Journal* of May 25th, 1843, there appeared the following notice of the laying of the corner-stone: "On Thursday, the 25th inst., the ceremony of laying the corner-stone of the new Catholic church, now erecting in this village, on the site where the old one was burned last season, was performed by the dignitaries of that Church in their usual formal and impressive manner. The address of the reverend gentleman officiating on that occasion is spoken of in the highest terms by all present, as being given in a liberal and truly Christian spirit of toleration towards all denominations professing the cardinal principles promulgated by the Saviour of mankind."

On the 10th of June, 1845, the church was opened for Divine worship, and, as the men working on the canal had crowded into town to be present at the dedication, over two thousand, unable to gain admission, were packed in the graveyard, and heard mass through the open windows. During the seven years that Father McDonagh acted as pastor, he visited every section of his large parish, wherever a few Catholics were gathered together. Such was his intimate acquaintance with the men working on the canal, that he could call almost everyone of them by name. In 1851, he was recalled to Toronto, and becoming afterwards associated with the diocese of Kingston, was appointed pastor of Douro, near Peterborough, where he died in 1863.

Father McDonagh was a ripe scholar, of commanding presence, and familiar with the language and habits of the Irish emigrant. He was untiring in his devotion to the interests of those employed on the canal, and did much to allay the asperity of feeling that sometimes manifested itself between men from different parts of the Old Country.

As the work on the church advanced, a large stone tablet was imbedded in the *façade*, immediately over the front entrance, bearing this inscription: * (See opposite page.)

* "D. O. M."—To God, the Greatest and the Best, and under the invocation of the Blessed Catharine, Virgin and Martyr, the Irish working on the Welland Canal built this monument of faith and piety.

"I. H. S."—Contraction for the Greek name of Jesus.

☧—Monogram of Christ. This monogram may almost invariably be discerned upon the greater part of the monuments of Christian antiquity which have descended to us. Its appearance upon the marbles, mortuary tiles and lamps extracted from the catacombs, and exhibiting the sepulchral inscriptions of the martyrs and early believers in the Gospel, who were buried there, must be familiar to everyone who is at all conversant with Christian archæology. It is composed of the two Greek characters, X and P—the two letters with which the name of Christ commences in Greek, Χριστος.

IHS
D.O.M.

Et Svbinvocatione Beatæ Catharinæ
Virg, et Mart
Hoc fidei ac pietatis monvmentvm
Erexervnt.
Hibernici in Canal Velland laborantes
MDCCCXLIV.

Of the men who contributed to the erection of the new church, four only are now living. Two of these, R. D. Dunn and Daniel McGuire, are residents of St. Catharines. Mr. McGuire was born 85 years ago, in the city of Cork, within hearing of the Shandon bells

> " Whose sounds, so wild, would
> In the days of childhood,
> Fling 'round *his* cradle
> Their magic spells."

He has always been a liberal supporter not only of his Church, but of every charity that appealed to him for assistance. He has been intimately identified with the growth and development of St. Catharines for more than fifty years, and to-day deservedly enjoys the respect and esteem of his fellow-citizens. By his energy and devotion to business he has acquired a large amount of property, which assures him an honorable competence in his declining years. He is held in reverential affection by his sons and daughters, who emulate each other in their love and veneration for him.

The historian of the progress and development of the Catholic Church in this section of the peninsula would omit an important duty if he failed to make mention of one whose unostentatious charity and conscientious Christianity evoke the respect of his friends and acquaintances. For almost seventy years, Mr. R. D. Dunn has lived and moved among the

R. D. DUNN, ESQ.

people of this section of the country. He was for many years paymaster on the Welland Canal, and there is yet to be heard a man who speaks otherwise than respectfully and kindly of him. While he enjoys an assured revenue for the balance of his life, his kindly nature and large generous heart prevented him from acquiring the fortune which his ability and commercial integrity warranted. The writer has been honored with his friendship for many years, and it is for him a privilege and a pleasure to record this expression of his admiration of the splendid qualities of head and heart that have won for Mr. Dunn the confidence and esteem of his fellow-citizens.

CHAPTER XV.

A TYPICAL SOGGARTH AROON.

The French Professor—The Seal of the Fisherman—A Providential
Meeting—The Curé of Tourville—Arrival of Father Grattan—From
Pleasant Normandy—Foreign Opinion of Canada—Father Conway—
A Large Mission—Irish Wit and Humor—The Baptism—A Brilliant
Passage—Collecting for the Church—The First Separate School—A
Close-Fisted Parishioner—Church in Smithville—Martin Lally—His
Unselfish Character—Death of Father Grattan—A Tribute to His
Memory.

> " Whose remembrance yet
> Lives in men's eyes ; and will to ears and tongues
> Be theme and hearing ever."—" Cym.," Act III., Sc. 1.

ON April 18th, 1850, a French priest, a member
of the Sulpician Order, was instructing in the
Seminary of Aix thirty or forty young men, who were
completing their theological studies for the priesthood.
Presently the door of the class-room opened, and the
Superior of the Seminary, a venerable man, on whose
countenance was stamped the impress of gravity and
piety, walked towards the teacher, and placing in his
hand a large envelope, having on it the Seal of the
Fisherman, courteously remarked that he would take
charge of the class while the professor retired to his
room to read the letter. This Sulpician teacher was

DEAN GRATTAN.

(From Photograph taken in 1858.)

Armand Francis Marie de Charbonnel, the son of
Count de Charbonnel, Baron of Saussac, Lord of Bets
and Camblaire. The letter, which he held in his
hand, was a Papal bull, informing him that he was
preconized Bishop of Toronto, Canada. Six years
before, the Archbishop of New Orleans had asked this
same priest to become his assistant bishop, with the
right of succession, and he had courteously but firmly
declined. He now hastened to Rome to plead before
the Sovereign Pontiff his unworthiness for the exalted
office, representing in his humility his unfitness for
the position. Pius the IX. would, however, take no
refusal, and Armand de Charbonnel was, on the 26th
of May, 1850, in the Sistine Chapel, consecrated
Bishop of Toronto, in succession to the lamented
Dr. Power. In a few days he quitted Rome, and
on his return journey was detained at Tourville, in
the Province of Normandy. Here he was waited upon
by the curé or pastor of the parish. The Bishop,
after a short conversation, learned, to his surprise and
pleasure, that the priest was an Irishman, and as he
was most favorably impressed with his simplicity and
honesty, pleaded with him to resign his parish and
come to Canada. The Bishop argued that the priest
could accomplish more good among the Irish settlers
in Upper Canada than he could in his present position,
adding, moreover, that in the Diocese of Toronto
there was a great scarcity of priests. The Irish
ecclesiastic replied, that if the bishop thought it was

the will of God for him to go to Canada, he was prepared to make the sacrifice. Bishop Charbonnel embraced him affectionately, and, bidding him farewell, expressed the hope that he would meet him again in Toronto. In six weeks this priest, then in the flower of his manhood, resigned his parish, stayed a short while with his friends in Ireland, and, on the 23rd of September, greeted Bishop Charbonnel in his Episcopal residence, Toronto. Almost immediately he was appointed to the parish of St. Catharines, and for fourteen years Father Grattan—the curé of Tourville—devoted himself heart and soul to the spiritual and material welfare of the Catholics of this parish.

Bartholomew Grattan was a man of plain and simple tastes, full of sound sense and playful amiability—a true pastor, "who knew his flock" intimately, and was not above taking an interest in the smallest domestic affairs of the humblest among them. To appreciate the great sacrifice he made in surrendering his parish in pleasant Normandy, it is necessary to bear in mind, that in those days Upper Canada was regarded by the most of Europe as a frozen solitude. It was to the priests of France what Labrador is to us—a desolation of forest and rock and snow-covered waste; and yet, when this saintly priest learned that there were numbers of his fellow-countrymen settled in this province, he bade good-bye forever to the pleasant vineyards of sunny France, and sailed away for a land which he believed offered him but years of suffering and self-denial.

In 1853 he was joined by his nephew, Father Conway, who, after his education in Ireland and France was completed, took an additional course of theology and canon law in the Sulpician Seminary, Baltimore. As we will have occasion to refer frequently to this large-hearted and genial priest, it may be as well to now state, that Father Conway is still living, and with his wonted energy laboring for the salvation of souls in the Diocese of Peterborough. The parish of St. Catharines, at the period of which we write, included the present missions of Smithville, Dunnville, Port Colborne, Thorold and Merritton, and entailed an amount of labor and exposure known only to the priest who, twenty-five or thirty years ago, ministered to scattered flocks in remote places. There were no railroads in the peninsula in those days, and when a dying Catholic from Port Colborne or Smithville asked for the services of his priest, the "sick call," particularly if the roads were bad, entailed considerable suffering. It is hardly necessary to explain to the Catholic reader, that the privilege of saying two masses on a Sunday is a dispensation granted by the Holy See on behalf of the people, and only conceded when two or more missions are served by the same clergyman. At the period of which we write, the Holy Sacrifice was offered up on Sundays at Port Colborne, Welland and Thorold, and when the priest said mass at either of these places, he drove fasting, in all seasons, to offer up another mass in St. Catharines.

Nothing but an iron constitution could stand the wear and tear that was attached to the exercise of the priesthood in those days. Father Grattan, who was blessed with a splendid physique and an admirable personality, never omitted to say mass at the appointed places and on the appointed Sundays.

Notwithstanding his long residence in France, he lost nothing of the *bonhomie* and wit characteristic of the Irish people.

"What name are you going to give this child, Maurice?" he asked a father who had brought his child to be baptized. Maurice hadn't contributed anything to the support of the priest for some years, and was known to be a man who seldom paid a debt if he could avoid it.

"What name is it, your Reverence? I was thinking of calling the boy Owen, after an uncle of mine in the Old Country."

"Well, Maurice," said the priest, with a twinkle in his eye; "you may as well call him that as anything else, for if he follows in the footsteps of his father, he will be *owin'* till he dies."

Father Grattan seldom preached a prepared sermon —his addresses to his congregation were generally free and easy talks. As a consequence, the burden of preaching fell on the shoulders of his nephew, Father Conway. Sometimes, when warmed up to his subject, the young priest detained the congregation beyond the allotted half-hour, and as his uncle, who said the mass, was fasting, and compelled to remain in the sanctuary till the preacher had concluded, he at times manifested considerable restlessness. On one occasion, when Father Conway had written out his sermon, memorized it, and delivered it to his own satisfaction, he asked his uncle, after mass, what he thought about it, no doubt expecting an expression of flattering appreciation.

"The sermon was very good," said Father Grattan, "if it were only original."

"What! do you mean to say I took that sermon out of a book?"

"I mean to say," retorted the other, "that I read every word of it before."

This bold assertion irritated his nephew, and he offered to give ten dollars to any charity if his uncle could make good his statement.

"I don't want to rob you of your ten dollars, but I tell you I read every word of it long ago, answered the other."

This repeated charge of plagiarism annoyed Father Conway, and in a burst of irritability he demanded to know the name of the book.

Father Grattan took a step or two towards his nephew, and in a confidential whisper, said: "If you promise me to say nothing about it, I will tell you the name of the book."

"I promise," replied the other.

"Well," said Father Grattan, in a low voice, "I read every word of it in 'Webster's Dictionary.'"

" Well, there was one splendid passage in your sermon to day," said Father Grattan at another time, as he entered the sacristy from the sanctuary, while Father Conway was walking up and down cooling off after a sustained effort of three-quarters of an hour.

The young priest paused, delighted that his uncle was pleased with his discourse.

" I flatter myself," he said, " that the whole sermon was brilliant; but what was the particular passage that pleased you most?"

Quick as a flash the uncle answered back: " The passage from the pulpit to the sacristy was the best part of the whole sermon."

On the 21st of January, 1857, Father Grattan called a meeting of the representative Catholics of St. Catharines and made provision for the opening of the first Separate School in that city. At a meeting convened on the 29th of January, this year, presided over by Mr. Hugh McKeown, sr., the following gentlemen were elected as trustees: Joseph Kelly, Hugh McKeown and Daniel McGuire; and on the following morning this notice was addressed to the Chairman of the Board of Common School Trustees for the town of St. Catharines :

" Sir,—We, the undersigned Roman Catholics, inhabitants of the town of St Catharines, beg leave to give notice that, in accordance with the Roman Catholic Separate School Act, 18th Victoria, chapter 131, being desirous to establish a Roman Catholic Separate School, we have convened a meeting and elected the undersigned gentlemen as trustees for the establishment and direction of said Separate School.

" Trustees of R. C. Separate School:

> " JOSEPH KELLY,
> " HUGH McKEOWN,
>> "*Gentlemen.*
>
> " DANIEL McGUIRE,
>> "*Merchant.*

(Signed) " Rev. B. Grattan, John Callaghan, Thos. J. O'Brine, Richard Tuite, Daniel O'Donnell, John Fitzgerald, Maurice Ellis, James Bulger, John McCarry, Patrick Corrigan, Thomas Butler, Patrick Hennigan, Patrick Carey, Patrick Kenny, Matthew Battle.

" A copy of the above notice was this day deposited with James G. Currie, Esq., chairman of the Board of Common School Trustees of St. Catharines."

A building was now rented on Geneva Street, and on the 3rd of February of this year, the first Separate School in the peninsula was opened.

In 1859 Father Grattan began the enlargement of the church by the building of the east wing. The methods of collecting for church purposes in those days were somewhat crude, and meant much labor and anxiety on the part of the pastor. As the day approached for paying an instalment to the contractor, the parish priest and his assistant, with book and pencil, went from house to house or man to man soliciting subscriptions. The most of the collecting for the new wing was done by Father Conway, but occasionally Father Grattan himself would take a hand in with gratifying success.

" Michael," said he one day to a member of his congregation who was notoriously close-fisted, and rather shiftless in his habits, " for what will I put you down for the new wing ? "

" Put me down for nothing," replied Michael, " for I havn't anything."

" Well, give me a dollar or two, anyway, so that I won't go home and say you are the only man that refused me."

" Didn't I tell you," retorted Michael, " that I haven't anything ; and how can a man give what he hasn't got ? "

" Faith, Michael, my *bouchal*, you're the only one in the parish that can do that same, for you could give your neighbor, Ned Hennessy, a good character, which is something that no living man could give you."

With the proverbial hospitality of his countrymen, he was never more pleased than when surrounded by his friends at his own table. On these occasions he was bubbling over with wit and humor, and loved to call up the memories of the past. His *brogue*, when recounting the reminiscences of other days, was inimitable. Carleton himself could not surpass him in imparting to a story a flavor racy of the Irish soil.

"I remember," he said to his guests on one occasion, " a wordy altercation that took place between two

hedge-schoolmasters about the administration of a
Ribbonman's oath; after a warm exchange of words
one of them remarked :

" ' I'll read yez that part of the oath which binds
us all,' etc.

" ' I condimn *that*,' observed the other master; 'I
condimn it as being too latitudinarian in the principle, and containing a paradogma ; besides, 'tis bad
grammar.'

" ' You're rather airly in the morning wid your bad
grammar,' replied the other; ' I'll grant the paradogma, but I'll stand up for the grammar of it.'

" ' Faith, if you rise to stand up for *that*,' replied his
friend, 'and doesn't choose to sit down till you prove
it to be good grammar, you'll be a standing joke all
your life.'

" ' I believe it's pretty conspicuous in the parish that
I have often, in our disputations about grammar, left
you without a leg to stand upon at all,' replied the
other.

" ' I would be glad to know,' the other inquired, ' by
what beautiful invention a man could contrive to
strike another in his absence ?   Have you good grammar for that ? '

" ' And did you never hear of detraction ? ' replied
his opponent. ' Does that confound you ? Where's
your logic and grammar to meet proper ratiocination
like what I'm displaying ? '

" ' Faith,' replied the other, ' you may have had logic

and grammar, but I'll take my oath it must have been
in your younger years, for both have been absent ever
since I knew you. They didn't like, you see, to be
keeping bad company.'

" ' Why, you poor cratur',' said his antagonist, ' if
I let myself out I could make a hare of you.'

" ' And an ass of yourself,' retorted the other.

" ' Hut ; you poor Jamaica-headed castigator,'
bawled the opponent, ' sure you never had more nor
a thimbleful of sense on any subject.'

" ' Faith, and the thimble that measured yours was a
tailor's one, without a bottom to it ; and good measure
you got, you miserable flagellator.' "

Among many of his warmest friends he counted a
number of Protestant gentlemen, at whose tables he
was frequently a welcome guest. The conversation
turning one day on the relations of Protestants and
Catholics in Ireland, he contended that, apart from
the ebullition of feeling produced by enthusiasm gener-
ated by the Twelfth of July and St. Patrick's Day,
there was a kindlier feeling existing between the two
parties in the Old Country than in the New. " I have
known," he added, " the most intimate cordialities to
exist between Catholics and Protestants in Ireland,
and doubts of one as to the ultimate salvation of the
other have often seemed to me to mingle, in a strange
sort of a manner, the mirthful with the serious. I
recollect, when I was a boy, hearing some extraordinary opinions ventured upon by my Catholic neighbors :

" ' I wonder,' says Rafferty to Regan, 'that Catholics here in this Ireland of ours are so poorly off, and that so many of us true believers go to the bad ? '

" ' Well,' says Regan, ' if you don't know the reason, it's small blame to you. Nature, you see, didn't give you the gumption. I'll excogitate it for you, you spalpeen. Being mimbers of the thrue docthrine, you obsarve, we're persecuted, like Lazarus and Melchizedek. The ould boy is always a timptin' of us, and he niver laves us aisy; but as for thim Protestants, you see, they're well-behaved, because the ould boy lets them alone ; and he lets them alone because he's always sure of them.'

" There was, however, one Protestant whom Rafferty did not like to consider within the power of the ancient sinner. ' Regan, asthore,' said Rafferty, ' do you think that the ould dark vagabone can ever catch a howld of the dacent man Jack Hayden ? '

" ' Jack Hayden, forsooth ! He's had howld of better men, and I don't see what should make a differ for Jack Hayden.'

" ' I'm sorry for him,' said Rafferty; ' a better neighbor than Jack Hayden niver smoked out of the same pipe with. He was always ready in a fight to help a friend with his stick, and on the rint-day he was quite as ready to help with his money. Ah, Jack agrah ! what shall I do if I haven't you near me in the next world ? for a good fellow you were to me in this. But I have comfort for you, Jack, my brother.   When all the clothing and blankets which you gave every winter to the poor will be wet and wrapped about your sowl, the niver a blast of the bad fire can come near you, though Satan and all his sarvints were bursting their cheeks in blowing of it.' "

Soon after the completion of the new wing, Father Conway built the Catholic church in Smithville, where a number of Catholics had settled, chiefly on the invitation of Mr. Martin Lally.   In this gentleman's house was said the first mass ever offered up in Smithville.   Martin Lally was a genial, enterprising Irishman who, in 1832, crossed the Atlantic in the good ship *Constantine*, of Sunderland.   As early as 1840 he settled in Smithville, where he opened a general store and also engaged in manufacturing.   He gave employment to a large number of men, and invited Father McDonagh to say mass once a month in one of his vacant buildings.   When, in 1855, the Catholics of Smithville were in circumstances that would justify them in building a church, Mr. Lally donated a large piece of ground for the church and cemetery.   He practically built the church, for when the contractor failed before the building was half completed, Martin Lally instructed the workmen to finish the church and he would see that they were paid.   It is to be presumed that a compliment was intended to be conferred on the generous benefactor, when the temple of worship was dedicated to God in honor of St. Martin.

Mr. Lally was distinguished for his hospitality and

generosity. He was the descendant of a respectable well-to-do family in Galway, and retained till his death the manners of the Irish gentleman. His faith was as strong and sincere as his heart was large and open, and during his long residence in Smithville he won and retained the good-will of his neighbors in every part of the country. He died a few years ago, mourned and regretted by a large number of friends in St. Catharines and the township of Grimsby. In 1862, the late Archbishop Lynch, in recognition of the labors and ability of Father Grattan, appointed him Dean of the Niagara peninsula, and two years afterwards he began the erection of the Catholic Church in Grimsby. The contract was let for a stone building, but owing to uncontrollable circumstances, it cost much more than the accepted tender warranted. The Dean, who was well and favorably known in Albany and Troy, visited his friends and relatives in these cities soliciting contributions for the Grimsby church. As he was a man well advanced in years, and never spared himself when the work of the holy ministry called for his services, the tax he imposed upon himself was more than his constitution could bear. Returning one night after collecting the whole day, he retired immediately to his room, and never again left his bed. He died three days afterwards, at the age of 68, and in the consecrated earth of the Catholic cemetery of Troy, all that is mortal of the good-natured priest lies buried, awaiting the " resurrection of the dead." His death was, to his people of St. Catharines, a dramatic calamity, for by his devotion to duty, and his innumerable little acts of kindness and charity, he was loved by all as a father. With his neighbors of every creed, and every shade of opinion, he lived on terms of unreserved and familiar intercourse. While ardently attached to his religion, and filled with the conviction of the sanctity of its precepts, and the Divine authority of its teachings, he aimed to extend its influence among all—not by disputatious criticism, nor by uncourteous reference to the religious opinions of others, but by the rectitude of his life, and the exercise of all the manly but unobtrusive virtues which should adorn the character of the priest. The affectionate warmth of his heart, the benevolence of his disposition, and the simplicity of his manner, did much to establish and perpetuate the friendly spirit of liberality that exists among all classes in that city.

He ended his days in peace and quietness, and the end came while he was working for the people of his parish. "Greater love than this hath no man, that a man lay down his life for his friend." The large and splendid memorial window over the main altar in St. Catharines church commemorates his death and his virtues. It was the monument of his people's love for him, proclaiming while the church exists their affection and attachment to one who, through good report and evil, yielded unstinted service on their behalf.

CHAPTER XVI.

THE NEW-BORN PARISHES.

Parish of Thorold—A Contrast—An Early Pioneer—The First Bible—
Growth of Catholicity—An Enterprising Priest—John Battle—Sketch
of His Career—Port Colborne—Its First Church—Peter Gibbons—
Welland—An Unselfish Priest—Church of Niagara Falls—A Retro-
spect—" Our Lady of Peace "—The First Mass in the Peninsula—
Wintering Near Dunnville—A Zealous Priest—Fort Erie—Its Early
History—The Church in Merritton—Loss of Faith—Causes of the
Defection—Ignorance of Catholic Doctrine—A Hopeful Outlook.

AS far back as 1834, it will be remembered that
there was only one church and one priest in
the whole Niagara peninsula. While in sixty years
the growth and development of religion has been slow,
compared with other parts of the Province, it has,
nevertheless, been steady, progressive and satisfactory.
There are now fifteen churches and fourteen priests,
with a Catholic population numbering over five thousand. In 1841 the first mass ever offered up in
Thorold was said by the Rev. Dr. Lee, in the house of
Thomas O'Brien. This sturdy Irishman was born in
Cork in 1788, and died in Dunnville, at the wonderful
age of 101 years. He settled in Thorold in 1830, and
when the first Catholic church was built by Father

McDonagh, in 1843, Thomas O'Brien, who was a carpenter, took the contract, and finished the building. O'Brien, like many of the early settlers, was often called upon to defend his religion, and when the charge that Catholics were not allowed to read the Bible was flung into his face by some of his neighbors, he sent to New York for a copy of the Holy Scriptures, and one morning triumphantly produced the book as a substantial refutation of the accusation.

This history would be imperfect should it allow the names of the old pioneers—the patriarchs of the church in Thorold—to remain in oblivion. The following meagre items concerning them have been gleaned from tradition, principally from their surviving descendants:

The brothers John and William Heenan, who were employed on the canal, the one in 1832 and the other in 1842, were prominently identified with the early growth of the Church in this locality. William was a friendly, sociable man, whose physical development excited the admiration of his neighbors. John is still living in Thorold, at the ripe old age of 82 years, having filled many responsible positions in the town. The names of Patrick Donahoe, Amantus Schwaller and James Boyle, who, with others, were liberal contributors toward the support of the infant church in this parish, live in affectionate remembrance; and if the cup of cold water given in charity receives its reward, the unselfish generosity of these men on behalf of religion has assuredly been remembered before the throne of the Almighty.

In 1853 Thorold was erected into a parish, and placed in charge of the Rev. Michael McLaughlin; and since then, with one or two breaks in the succession of pastors, it has always had its own parish priest. In 1871 Father Sullivan was appointed to the spiritual care of this mission, and from that date the spiritual and material progress has, for the population of the parish, been phenomenal.

In twenty-three years over $60,000 has been expended in the construction of buildings. Its schools, church, convent, and presbytery are splendid material proofs of the generosity of the people and the unflagging zeal of the pastor. If one should require convincing evidence of what may be accomplished by a zealous and enterprising priest, supported by a generous and appreciative people, he will here find it abundantly and amply.

In the archives of this parish the name of John Battle frequently occurs as a liberal contributor to the support of religion. In the history of the County of Sligo, the Battle family occupies a representative place. Two members of this family—John and Mathew—came to this country in 1842. Mathew Battle settled in Quebec, where he resided until 1870, when he removed with his family to Ottawa, where his son is now Collector of Inland Revenue. John Battle settled in Thorold in 1842, where he lived until his death, which occurred on February 26th, 1891.

The career of Mr. Battle is an interesting study for the young men of this generation. He began here as a day laborer, but, notwithstanding the handicap, he rose by sobriety, industry, and indomitable energy, step by step till he became one of the most wealthy and influential men in the peninsula. He was an enthusiastic Irishman, and when he had accumulated a fortune, his first period of rest was spent in a visit to Ireland. As he approached the green hills of his native land, the memories of the past crowded upon him, and he hailed it with the warmth and generosity of the Irish exile :

> " Now fuller and truer the shore-line shows !
>   Was ever a scene more splendid ?
> I feel the breath of the Munster breeze !
>   Thank God that my exile's ended.
> Old scenes, old songs, old friends again,
>   The vale and cot I was born in !
> Oh, Ireland ! up from my heart of hearts
>   I bid you the top o' the mornin'!"

The vote of condolence passed by the Thorold Council to the wife and family of Mr. Battle, the expression of admiration embodied in the resolution, and the recognition of the loss the town had sustained in his death, were splendid and consoling tributes to his memory, coming from the representatives of the people.

THE LATE JOHN BATTLE.

Port Colborne and Welland.

The prosperous and flourishing village of Port Colborne, picturesquely situated on Lake Erie, at the mouth of the Welland Canal, was attended from St Catharines as early as 1844. As the Catholic population increased, it became necessary to provide suitable accommodation, and, in 1856, a good-sized lot was purchased by Father Conway, and a frame building erected thereon. In this humble church the Irish Catholics who had remained in the neighborhood after the canal was built, assembled on occasional Sundays; and, after assisting at the Holy Sacrifice, listened with eagerness to the instructions given them by their priest.

Conspicuous among the names of the early contributors is that of Mr. Peter Gibbons. Mr. Gibbons settled in Port Colborne in the forties, and, as he was a man of considerable education, active and energetic, his influence with his Catholic neighbors was great. When a meeting was convened for the building of the church, he was appointed secretary-treasurer, and throwing himself into the work with characteristic Celtic warmth, he superintended the work, solicited subscriptions, and by his persistency met all obligations. Mr. Gibbons is still living in full possession of his mental and physical faculties, though moving towards his 80th year.

In 1859, the mission was formed into a separate

parish, with Father Voisard as pastor. Since then its religious growth has been steady; a handsome brick church and presbytery have been built, and a Separate school opened. In the annals of this parish the names of Fathers Kilcullen and McEntee occupy a conspicuous place. The former for eighteen years held the parish, and during his incumbency were erected the buildings that to-day reflect favorably on the generosity of the Catholics of Port Colborne. When leaving for a larger sphere of labor, Father Kilcullen carried with him the respect and best wishes of all classes. Father McEntee expended some $5,000 in improvements during his rectorship of five years; so that to-day, owing to the energy of these reverend gentlemen, the parish of Port Colborne has a group of very creditable buildings—free from all en- cumbrances.

As the town of Welland has been for many years ecclesiastically wedded to Port Colborne, it forms with it practically one parish. The church in Welland was built by Father Wardy in 1864, on land purchased some years before by Dean Grattan. Father Wardy was a man of much holiness and purity of life; he was born at Ardeche, France, and was ordained to the priesthood in Lyons. His mind was well stored with classic and ecclesiastical lore, but his scholarly attainments better qualified him for a professor's chair than for the rough, hard work of the mission. Wanting in

CHURCH AND PRESBYTERY, PORT COLBORNE.

practical knowledge of men and methods of doing business, he was continually involved in trouble. Dean Grattan, jocosely, was accustomed to say of him that he was "*too holy*, was always praying, and would not *take any money*." The latter weakness was undoubtedly a serious one, and quite a disqualifier. This good priest died at Cleveland in 1883.

The Catholics of Welland have always been liberal supporters of the Church, and are spoken of by the priests who served the mission with warmth and affection. One of the early pioneers of this parish was John Brown, father of the Brown Brothers who settled in Welland when it was known as Burgess. He acted as secretary and treasurer when Father Wardy was building the church, and by his encouragement and support relieved the parish priest of much worry and anxiety. He died some years ago, leaving to his sons the inheritance of an untarnished name.

NIAGARA FALLS.

This interesting and picturesque parish was visited in 1826 by Father Campion, from Niagara, who twice a year gave a "Station" to the handful of Catholics who were settled in the neighborhood of the "Falls."

The quaint old church, now known as "Our Lady of Peace," was built in 1837, by Father Gordon. At its altar knelt the early pioneers of the Catholic religion, and here, also, the venerable priests of the historic past offered up the Holy Sacrifice. In the consecrated clay of the ancient graveyard are returning to dust the bones of the old pioneers, who, in their rugged simplicity, worshipped God with loving hearts. Beside them in the grave repose the partners of their joys and sorrows, and when the " Awake, ye dead, and come to judgment " of the angel of the resurrection rouses them from their slumbers, they will have no reason to fear the terrors of the great day. The mission of " Our Lady of Peace " was erected into a parish in 1858, with the saintly Father Juhel as its first pastor. This holy priest, like so many of the early and hard-working consecrated men of Upper Canada, was born in France, and died a voluntary exile in his parish, January, 1862. The present Bishop of Peterborough, Right Rev. Dr. O'Connor, was parish priest here for three years. In 1875, the Carmelite Fathers were invited by Archbishop Lynch to take charge of this parish and Clifton. Its interests henceforth became identified with the Carmelite Order —a brief history of which will be found elsewhere.

CLIFTON.

The parish of Clifton, also known as Niagara Falls, was under the care of the pastor of Niagara Falls South until the coming of the Carmelite Fathers, when they appointed one of their number to its exclusive charge. Since then this parish ranks amongst the first in the diocese. Its present pastor, Father O'Malley, has built a school at a cost of $5,000, and is now engaged in the erection of a church, estimated to cost $20,000. A third church, St. Joseph's, stands at the intersection of the roads leading from Stevensville, Chippewa, Black Creek and Netherby, whose congregation, composed of Germans, is also served by the Carmelites.

DUNNVILLE.

Two hundred and twenty-five years ago two priests of the Catholic Church, Francois Dollier de Casson and René de Brehart de Galineé, offered up, in the neighborhood of Dunnville, the first mass ever said on the Niagara peninsula. This was on the 22nd of October, 1669. They were on their way to the great West to preach the Gospel to the tribes in that region. On the first of October, at the village of Otinaouataoua, on the Grand River, they separated from La Salle, who had accompanied them, and in fourteen days reached the mouth of the river and encamped on the shore of Lake Erie, which they described as "a vast sea, tossed by tempestuous winds." Selecting a convenient spot a mile inland, they built a cabin, in one end of which they raised the first altar dedicated to Christian worship in this peninsula.* Here they passed the winter, and when leaving on the 23rd of March, 1670, erected a cross, to which they attached the arms of Louis XIV., and took formal possession of the country in the name of the French king. Not

---

* The first mass celebrated in Canada, according to Le Clercq, was said at Quebec, by the Franciscan priest D'Olbeau, on the 25th June, 1615.

until 1848 was the Holy Sacrifice again offered up in this locality.

Nothing has been written, and consequently very little is known with accuracy, of the early Catholic history of Dunnville. An examination of the registers at Caledonia, to which parish the mission of Dunnville was, until 1886, attached, shows the births, deaths, and marriages, but no incident of a historic value. According to Daniel Barry, one of the early pioneers now living in Canboro' township, the first mass celebrated in Dunnville was said by Father McIntosh in 1848. Up to this time and for many subsequent years the few scattered Catholics settled in this district brought their children to Buffalo to be baptized. In 1852 Dunnville was visited by Dean Grattan, who served the parish until it was affiliated to the Diocese of Hamilton. Then the mission was attended by the Rev. John McNulty, who resided at Caledonia, where he built the present brick church, and had in his spiritual charge the united missions of Caledonia, Walpole, Indiana, Binbrook, and Dunnville. On a site donated by Thomas Carroll it was intended to build a church in 1859, but owing to some flaw in the title deeds, another lot was purchased from Mr. Thomas Street, of Niagara Falls, and a frame church erected. In 1886, Dunnville was constituted into a separate parish and committed to the care of its present pastor, Father Crinnon. During his pastorate the reverend gentleman has labored with untiring energy. With his customary enterprise, he began, soon after his installation, the building of the present handsome brick church. This building is well furnished, and is equipped with all necessary ecclesiastical requirements. Father Crinnon next built the presbytery, and to-day, owing to his energy and zeal, supported by an approving people, his parish is materially and spiritually in splendid condition.

FORT ERIE.

Fort Erie was originally built by Colonel Bradstreet on the east side of the river, while on an expedition against the Western Indians in 1764. From this fort, which was held by the British until 1796, and not from the Canadian Fort Erie which, with Fort George, was built after the Revolutionary war, the present town derived its name. Bradstreet states in a letter to General Amherst, quoted by Orsamus H. Marshall, in his historical sketches, "That when he arrived at the locality he found no harbor. That vessels were compelled to lie at anchor in the open lake, exposed to every storm and liable to be lost. In addition to this they were obliged to send more than twenty miles for their loading; that on examining the north shore he found a suitable place to secure the vessels by the help of a wharf just above the rapids. A post," he adds, " is now building there, and all that can will be done toward finishing it this season." Its Indian name signifies "The Place of Hats." The Duke of

Liancourt says that when he visited the place, in 1795, the fort was a cluster of buildings surrounded with rough, crazy palisades. Outside of the fort was a few log-houses for the officers, soldiers and workmen. In the summer of 1687, Baron La Hontan stayed here for a short time on his way to the West, and on the map, which illustrates his journal, he marks both banks of the river at this point. From this fort the present village derives its name. There is here a fair sized Catholic congregation, presided over by the Rev. P. McColl ; owing, however, to its proximity to Buffalo, the Catholics of Fort Erie are never in spiritually destitute circumstances.

MERRITTON.

Merritton was separated from Thorold in 1883, and Father Finan, who built the presbytery, was commissioned as the first pastor. Its very handsome and commodious school was built by Father Allain a few years ago. Its present pastor, the Rev. Felix Smyth, was appointed in 1894, and is now actively contemplating the erection of a fine brick church. The people of Merritton are proverbial for their large-heartedness and attachment to their religion. There is no congregation of its size in Ontario that contributes more liberally for Church purposes ; and as soon as the present pastor is prepared to enter upon the erection of his new church, we feel satisfied that he will be ably supported by his people.

SMITHVILLE.

Perhaps in no part of the Niagara peninsula has the Catholic Church suffered such serious loss in numbers as in the townships of Caistor and Gainsboro', and in North and South Grimsby. The early Catholics themselves, we are satisfied, never lost the faith, although living for years without any religious support, receiving no instruction or advice, and deprived of the Holy Sacrifice—frequently, indeed, of the sacraments—yet the faith which they brought with them from the Old Country was so deeply rooted in their hearts that it could not be eradicated. Doubtless they did everything in their power to transmit their religion to their children, but all they could do was to teach them a few prayers, warn them of the dangers around them, and give them the example of a blameless life. There was no priest to instruct and console them, and no books to teach and edify them, for Catholic literature, in the modern sense, did not yet exist. When their children were of an age to go to school, they were called " Paddies " by their playmates Cyrus, Darius, Wesley or Calvin, and when they asked for an explanation from their parents, the poor people were scarcely able to give them satisfactory answers. As a result, the children became ashamed of the nationality of their parents, and began gradually to take on the habits and manners of their Protestant companions.

When the epithet of Papist was applied to them, it carried to their young minds superstition and idolatry. The shameful "Revelations of Maria Monk," the lectures of Achilli, and the fabrications of Baron De Gammon were circulated from house to house, and frequently loaned to the Catholic children. Traditions of nursery stories, school stories, tavern stories, platform and pulpit stories, treating of the horrible doctrines of the Romish Church, lived in every household. The newspapers, magazines, reviews, pamphlets, romances, novels, poems, and light literature of all kinds, were in those days saturated with misrepresentations of the Catholic Church, her doctrines and traditions. Moreover, the non-Catholic neighbors were civil, friendly and hospitable, and in all sincerity, believed the Church of Rome to be the "Abomination of desolation seated on the high places." They were a people well off in this world's goods, fairly educated for those days, and kindly disposed to their Catholic neighbors, while they hated their religion. In fact, public opinion was anti-Catholic, and it was a powerful agent in destroying Catholicity in isolated country places. When the young Catholic reached marriageable years, his faith was already shaken, and it required only a marriage alliance with some Protestant to eradicate it almost entirely. Still, it would not be right to conclude that all this was an unmitigated loss to the Church of Christ. Those who, in after life, remembered that they "ought to be Catholics," would not accept all the absurd calumnies spread against the Church throughout the townships. Even their children had heard, by a kind of tradition, of what their ancestors had formerly suffered, and all of them were not inclined to join in the universal denunciation of a creed, germs of which still remained in their blood. However, when on September, 1866, Father Laboreau was appointed first pastor of Smithville and Grimsby, the defection from the Church practically ceased, and to-day the Catholics of the Grimsby townships are as well instructed, and as devoted to their religion, as those of any parish in the peninsula.

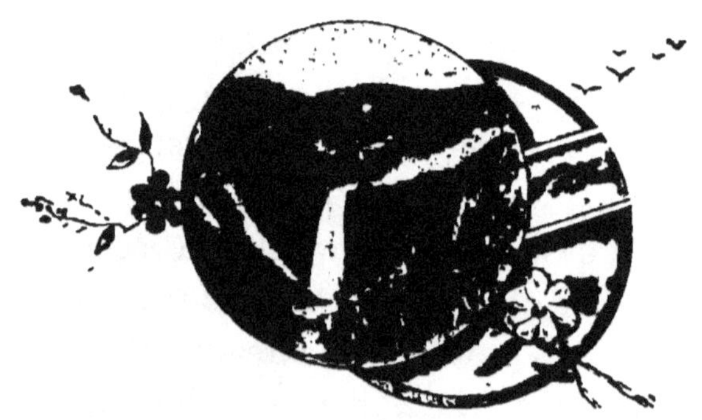

CHAPTER XVII.

THE RELIGIOUS COMMUNITIES OF THE PENINSULA.

Sisters of St. Joseph—Arrival in St. Catharines—A Courteous Intro-
duction—Founding of the Community—Dispersion—Condemned to
Death—Arrive in America—Introduction to Toronto—The House of
Providence—Heroism and Self-denial—Sisters of Loretto—Their
Foundation—Their English Home—Rathfarnham—Their Diffusion—
Introduced to Toronto—Their Methods of Teaching—Christian
Brothers—A Great Bishop—Opinion of the Duke of Wellington—
Founding of the Order—The Venerable de La Salle—The First
Public School—Methods of Teaching—Manner of Life—The Vin-
centian Fathers—Founder of the Order—St. Vincent de Paul—
Sketch of His Life—Establishment of the College of the Holy
Angels—Chartered as a University—Dr. McHale—Order of the
Carmelites—Antiquity of the Order—Origin of the Name—Elias the
Prophet—Sketch of the Order—Coming of the Carmelites—Their
Prospective Building—The Canadian Superior.

"There are some in whose minds convents and monasteries are associated
only with dark ages. Dark ages there are certainly in the history of the
Church, but they are such to those only who are in the dark about them and
their spirit and their institutions. If the dark ages must be stretched so
far back as to take in all monks and monasteries, and nuns and nunneries,
then all the general councils and the greatest fathers of the Church, and the
very dawn of the divine religion of Christ, must likewise be included in the
ages of darkness."—Montalembert.

ANY work of the nature we are now engaged on
would be incomplete if the religious communities settled in this peninsula received but a passing
notice. The members of these communities are
enrolled in the militia of Jesus Christ, and are distinguished for the devotion and fidelity with which

they carry on the work of God. In December, 1856, at the request of Dean Grattan, there arrived in St. Catharines, to take charge of the Parochial Schools, three ladies, members of the community of St. Joseph.

The Sisters were introduced to the people by the Dean in language characteristically tender and courteous. He foreshadowed the great benefit their presence would be to the people, and the lasting influence for good their instructions would leave on the minds of the children. In prophetic language he outlined the growth and development of the community in this parish. As the population of the town increased, additional members were added to the society, and to-day there are eighteen Sisters teaching in Merritton, St. Catharines, and in their own imposing convent. A brief history of the community will be of interest to the Catholic reader. The beginning of the " Congregation of the Sisters of St. Joseph " goes back to the year 1650, when Bishop de Maupas, of Le Puy, France, established the Order. In this year the bishop, after exhorting the pious novices in the love of God and of their neighbor, invested them with the religious habit, placed them under the protection of St. Joseph, and confided to their care the Female Orphan Asylum in his Episcopal city. These ladies bound themselves with the vows of chastity, obedience and poverty. From this humble beginning the Order spread, and several houses of the congregation were founded in the diocese. Gradually the community extended to the adjoining parts of France. Up to the time of the French Revolution, the ladies of this Order were employed in the education of the young, in the visitation of the poor, and in attending to the wants of the orphan, the sick and the aged. During the reign of terror, the revolutionary avalanche in France destroyed their convents and dispersed the members. The Superior retired to her father's house, where she was joined by two other Sisters, but being discovered, they were imprisoned in the fortress of St. Didier, and, with other members of the community, condemned to death. The night before the day appointed for their execution, Robespierre was guillotined, and the sentence of execution was annulled.

After the Napoleonic Concordat was signed by Cardinal Consalve, on behalf of the Pope, the community was re-established, and in 1812 we find new foundations, not only in France, but also in other European countries. In 1836, the Sisters of St. Joseph were introduced to America by Bishop Rosati, and opened their first house in St. Louis, Missouri. In 1851, Bishop de Charbonnel visited the States and prevailed upon Mother Delphine Fontbonne to take up her residence in Toronto, with some of the members of her community. The bishop's father, Count de Charbonnel, gave valuable assistance to this lady when she was re-organizing the community after the French Revolution, and in gratitude for his services she now offered to take charge of the poor and orphan children of the bishop's diocese. She **was** accompanied by three of her *religieus*, one of whom, the venerable Mother Bernard, still survives as Superior of the Sacred Heart Orphan Asylum, Toronto. For more than forty years this estimable lady has devoted herself to the unremitting care of the orphan, the poor and the helpless.

In 1852, the Separate Schools of Toronto were intrusted to their care, and since then this " Congregation of Religious " has diffused itself through the cities and towns of Ontario. The unselfish and heroic labors of the Sisters of St. Joseph in the House of Providence, St. Michael's Hospital, and the Sunnyside Orphanage have brought a benediction on the diocese. Even in the Catholic Church, so fruitful in examples of self-sacrifice and self-denial, there is nothing superior to the heroism manifested by these ladies in their solicitude and care for the unfortunate of our race sheltered in the House of Providence, Toronto. In this great institution of charity the refined and educated daughters of many of our best families minister with a tenderness of mothers from day to day to five hundred of the poor and suffering of this large diocese. This is a marvel of Christian charity—a charity that lifts these Sisters into a sublime region not far from the kingdom of God. Wherever possible the Separate Schools have been committed to their charge, and their methods of teaching have met with the highest approval on the part of the governmental inspectors and of those whose children are confided to their educational care. In their convents they impart a refined and finished education, and give to their graduates a tone and culture worthy of admiration.

SISTERS OF LORETTO.

On the 5th of November, 1686, Sir Thomas Gascoigne, of York, England, purchased a house and garden at a place known as Micklegate Bar, and deeded it to some English ladies, who were then living in Munich, Bavaria. They were voluntary exiles, who, influenced by a spirit of zeal and self-sacrifice, quitted England during the troublesome reign of James I. and sought a home on the Continent, in order to enjoy the exercise of their religion in peace and quietness. At Munich they opened a school for the education of English girls; and, forming themselves into an organization known as the Institute of the Blessed Virgin Mary, they drew up a code of rules for the government of their society, which, at the request of the Duke of Bavaria, was confirmed by the then reigning Pontiff, Clement XI. From this institute came the ladies who opened their first convent in England at Micklegate Bar.

This convent—either through a providential interposition or the influence of some one near the throne—escaped confiscation and suppression during the penal days, and, unostentatiously and quietly, the ladies at its head imparted to the daughters of English Catholic gentlemen a secular and religious education. From this educational centre there radiated rays of light that illuminated the dark period covering the penal days; and, if time would permit, it would be an interesting study to measure the influence of this institute in preserving the faith in England.

With the unobtrusiveness and quiet sanctity still so characteristic of the ladies of Loretto, they continued their noble work till, in 1821, Archbishop Murray, of Dublin, invited the Order to establish a convent at Rathfarnham, in his diocese. In conformity with his wishes, Frances Ball, a distinguished woman, accompanied by three others, established Loretto Abbey, near Dublin. It was named after the famous Italian shrine of Loretto, and from this house the title has, by common consent and by a mysterious law of application, become identified with the Order, whose members are now known wherever the English language is spoken as " Loretto nuns."

From the dawn of Christianity until the present day a mysterious and apparently insoluble problem invites the attention of thoughtful men. Every religious organization of a progressive and permanent nature began in humbleness and almost in solitude; then, like the sacred oil of Isaiah, it diffused itself throughout the world, and penetrating into the solitary places, is touched with the burning Spirit of God, and darkness becomes light. From the humble tree planted in 1686 at Micklegate Bar have been taken grafts that, bedded in foreign soils, have produced wonderful fruit. In Australia, South Africa, the Mauritius, in Austria, Prussia, Hungary and Italy, in the colonies of Great Britain, in Turkey and Spain, are over 150 branches of the Loretto Order.

Almost fifty years ago, on the invitation of Dr. Power, the first Bishop of Toronto, the nuns of Loretto opened a convent in his Episcopal city. On their arrival they were met at the wharf by the Hon. John Elmsley and Mr. Samuel G. Lynn, and conducted to the humble house rented for their temporary accommodation. On the vicissitudes and trials which confronted them during the first years of their residence in Toronto we need not now dwell. They began in poverty, suffered trials with a commendable resignation, endured with heroism the severity of our Canadian winters; and, of the five who came to Canada, two died the first year. From this infant colony permanent institutions have grown up in Stratford, Guelph, Hamilton, Belleville, Joliet and in other places. In 1861 they opened their convent at Niagara Falls, and such was their success that in nine years they began the erection of a building which to-day represents an expenditure of $70,000.

The work accomplished by the Loretto nuns in Toronto and elsewhere in the Province, calls for no expression of approval or admiration in these pages. In every city and town of this progressive country are to be met with the graduates of Loretto convents, whose refinement and culture appeal to the appreciation of enlightened minds. Like the Sisters of St. Joseph, they impart in their academies all the amenities and accomplishments of a higher female education ; and, like them also, they give to the children in our Separate Schools a practical training, blended with an admirable self-possession that serves them in good stead throughout their lives.

THE CHRISTIAN BROTHERS.

Bishop de Charbonnel was a man cast in a physically heroic mould, and his spiritual and mental endowments were in harmony with his commanding presence and striking personality. While his confidence in Divine assistance was boundless, his devotion to and zeal for Catholic interests were only limited by the exigencies of time and the possibilities of his environment. When he had completed a visitation of his diocese his observant and acute intellect grasped and solved a problem that, for thirty years, had been puzzling the minds of the American bishops. He was practically twenty years in advance of his time, for he saw, like the great Duke of Wellington,* that education divorced from religion

* The Duke had decided views on education. "Take care what you are about," he said, "for unless you base all this education on religion, you are only making so many clever devils." Lord Stanhope's "Notes of Conversations with the Duke of Wellington," p. 131.

BISHOP DE CHARBONNEL.

would inevitably lead to infidelity. He fought and defeated the late distinguished Dr. Ryerson on this question ; and, with the assistance of his brother bishops, wrung from the Parliament of Canada the right of Catholic parents to educate their children as they thought best. While he was still grappling with the educational problem, and uncertain of its solution, he invited the Brothers of the Christian Schools to establish themselves in Toronto. His intention was, if Parliament refused his just demands for parental control in the education of the child, to appeal to his people for assistance to support the Christian Brothers.

This remarkable community was founded by the Blessed John Baptist de La Salle, a priest and canon of the Cathedral of Rheims, France. He was of an honorable French family, identified with the magistracy of his native city. La Salle was a man modest and collected, and of a charitable and saintly tenderness that commiserated every form of human suffering. At the time of his birth, 1651, Europe was desolated with wars and in a state of transition. The education of the masses was, for reasons which space will not permit us to consider, wofully forgotten and neglected. La Salle, deploring the almost universal indifference to the development of the minds of the poorer classes, gathered thirty ragged boys from the slums and back streets of

Rheims into a small house he had rented, and day after day instructed them in the rudiments of a Christian education. This was practically the first Public School ever opened at Rheims. It was maintained at his own expense, and the scholars very often fed from his own table. Gradually he affiliated to himself other pious men, and in 1682 he practically established the Institute of the Christian Brothers. The holy priest announced to the assembled Brothers that he had broken with the past, and that henceforth he would devote his life to the education of the masses. "We'll place ourselves under the protection of God," he said; "we will devote eight days to communion with God, and then, together, we will frame rules for the government of ourselves and the education of the children confided to our care." After the completion of their eight days' retreat the Brothers, on their knees, invoked the assistance of the Blessed Virgin, inviting her to be the patron and guide of their schools. This was the beginning of the Christian organization of popular education, 150 years before the State had dreamed of taking up the great work.

From Rheims the Order spread to Paris, and here, for the preparation and training of his teaching staff, he founded the first Normal School in Europe. Since his death, which took place in 1719, the community of the Christian Brothers has increased marvellously, till to-day it numbers six thousand professors, engaged in teaching over four hundred thousand scholars.

In 1876, on invitation of the late Dean Mulligan, they established a branch of their Order in St. Catharines, and from that year until now the Brothers have been permanently identified with the education of our children. It is hardly necessary to dwell at any length on the advantages that must accrue to any Catholic community from the continuous presence of a body of devoted men, who have bound themselves by serious vows to the profession of education. For more than two hundred years, with unbroken continuity, the members of this Order have yielded themselves to the complex study of the child's nature, and the experience acquired from habitual observation and diverse methods of instruction has been to them of untold advantage in their present system of teaching.

Their rule of government for their community life is rigorous; obliging them in all seasons to rise at half-past four in the morning, to devote three-quarters of an hour to prayer and meditation, assist at the Holy Sacrifice of the mass, and give three hours every day to the preparatory work of teaching. In their class-rooms they wear the habit of the Order, and regard the children committed to their care as sacred wards, for whose morals the Eternal Father will hold them in a measure responsible.

THE VINCENTIAN FATHERS.

We would fail in a most important duty if we neglected to publicly acknowledge the debt of gratitude which the pastors and Catholic people of this peninsula owe to the Fathers of the congregation of the Mission of the Niagara University. Situated on the eastern banks of the Niagara River, the College of the Holy Angels always offered a hospitable welcome to the priests of this diocese. As the river only divided them from the peninsula, the Lazarist Fathers most cheerfully responded to any call for assistance that was made upon them by us; and so intimately identified have they been with the spiritual and educational interests of the Catholics of this section of Ontario, that we may claim them in a sense as our own.

The Congregation of the Mission—commonly called the Order of Lazarists, from the name of its first principal house, that of St. Lazare, Paris—was founded by the great St. Vincent de Paul, in 1632. St. Vincent de Paul was born on the 24th of April, 1576. His father was a French peasant, and had no higher ambition than to train his son for a quiet pastoral life; but God had ordained otherwise. Lifting him from the humble and lowly calling of a shepherd into the exalted ranks of the priesthood, He dowered him with a wealth of sanctity, of tenderness and commiseration for every form of human suffering that won for

Vincent de Paul a foremost place in the calendar of the saints of the Catholic Church.

This marvellous and providential man for sixty years labored with an unselfish and saintly heroism that makes his name to-day, after a period of two hundred years, venerated and revered in the Christian world. Among the works of benevolence with which his name is more immediately and personally associated, are the establishment of the distinguished Lazarist Order, a hospital for galley slaves at Marseilles, the organization of the Sisters of Charity, and of two establishments for foundlings at Paris.

To enumerate his other and extraordinary works of charity is beyond the scope of this review. His name will ever remain in the annals of the Catholic Church as a providential and saintly man, whom God called from the humblest walks of life, *de stercore erigens*, and appointed to do a magnificent work, whose wondrous influence remains for all time. When St. Vincent founded the Lazarists, or Congregation of Priests of the Mission, his intention was that the Fathers would preach the Gospel to the poor country people of the villages of France, give retreats to the clergy, and train young students for the holy priesthood.

As the Order increased in influence and numbers, missionaries were sent by its zealous founder to other countries, even those beyond the pale of civilization, to China, Persia, Madagascar—in the two former of which the society still supports two prosperous and thriving missions. In 1874, their establishments throughout the Turkish Empire numbered sixteen, and in the same year they had fourteen institutions in the United States. Their total number throughout the world is computed at from three to four thousand members.

The introduction of the Priests of the Mission into America took place in 1819. Bishop Dubourg, shortly after his consecration as Bishop of New Orleans, brought a colony from Rome, where the Vincentians (as they love to be called) had been established from the days of their venerated founder. About 1820, the "Barrens," Perry County, Missouri, was taken possession of by the Vincentian Fathers, and conducted as a diocesan seminary. From the "Barrens," the homestead of the Congregation of the Mission in America, colonies of missionaries were sent to various States throughout the Union. Their introduction into New York State was due to Bishop Timon, C.M., of Buffalo, who was a member of the congregation. In 1856, he and his confreres established a college on the outskirts of Buffalo, near the lake shore. In 1857, a more desirable site was selected, that at present occupied by the college and seminary of Our Lady of Angels, on the New York bank of the Niagara River, about midway between Suspension Bridge and the village of Lewiston, N.Y. Its founder and first president was the Rev. John Joseph Lynch, C.M., afterwards Archbishop of Toronto. He was succeeded in the presidency by the amiable and saintly Father Rice, whose holy influence still lingers around the institution he loved so well. After his death the Very Rev. P. V. Kavanagh was chosen rector, and for eighteen years presided over the college and university with a courtesy and ability that won him the approbation of the American priesthood.

The institution was chartered in 1863 as a college, and in 1883 was erected into a university by Act of the Legislature of New York State. Affiliated with the university are colleges of medicine, art, philosophy and divinity. The proverbial courtesy and hospitality of the faculty of the university, presided over by the Very Rev. Dr. McHale, C.M., has won for the institution a large and influential number of friends and admirers. Throughout the American States and Canada the priests and members of the learned professions, educated at the Niagara University, retain the urbanity and hospitality acquired from association with its courteous president and learned professional staff.

ORDER OF THE CARMELITES.

In a picturesque grove on the banks of the Niagara River, in sight and hearing of the Imperial cataract and the Niagara Falls, there nestles an unpretentious building, the home of the Fathers of the Carmelite Order, and glorified with the name of Monastery. It is the dwelling of a small family of consecrated

21

monks, members of the great and illustrious Order of Mount Carmel. The Order derives its name from Mount Carmel in Palestine, a mountain famous in the history of the Jewish people, and sanctified by the miracles of Elias and his successor, Eliseus. Here these prophets of the Lord dwelt; here they communed with God, and wrought the prodigies and wonders that have won for them immortality. The name is a mystical jewel, sanctified by holy memories, and imperishably associated with the inspired poetry of the Hebrew prophets. To add greater honor and glory to this historic mount, the "new-born Church" revering it for its antiquity and sanctity, consecrated it anew, by building on its sacred summit an altar for Christian worship. To the care of saintly men she committed this mount and altar, and thus Carmel becomes the spiritual heirloom of a religious Order, illustrious by the brilliancy of its monastic glory, the continuity of its name and the excellence of its deeds.

St. Athanasius, in his epistle on "Virginity," and St. Jerome, in his "Pauline" epistle, give to this Order priority of foundation in the Christian Church, and trace back its origin to the great prophet, Elias, thus ante-dating Christianity. In the IV. Book of Kings, the disciples and followers of the patriarch and prophet are dignified with the title of "Sons of the Prophets." Nor is Papal authority wanting to add assurance to its Elian origin, for Sixtus IV., in a Pontifical bull, affectionately refers to it as the

" Sacred Order of the Blessed Virgin Mary of Mount Carmel, which now flourishes in the Church of God, and whose members are the lawful successors of the Holy Prophets, Elias and Eliseus." To still further confirm its place of honor among the great Orders of the Catholic Church, the statue of the Hebrew prophet in the group of marble representations of the founders of religious orders, takes the foremost rank in the Basilica of St. Peter's at Rome.

After the ascension of our Divine Lord, the Carmelite hermits built a church in honor of the Virgin Mother of Christ. This was the first temple ever erected in memory of Our Lady. Four hundred years after the ascension of our Blessed Lord, John, Bishop of Jerusalem, framed a code of rules for the government of the hermits, and this code, Aymeric, patriarch of Antioch, translated from Greek into Latin for the direction and guidance of the Western members who accompanied the Crusaders to the Holy Land. In 1171 St. Albert, patriarch of Jerusalem, revised, at the request of St. Brocard, the first General of the Order of the Latin Rite, the rule governing the monastic observances of the West, which remains in force until this day. When the Saracens swept like a whirlwind into Palestine, the remnant of the Order that escaped massacre fled to Europe, and settled in England, France and the island of Cyprus. The now famous Carmelite monastery, known as " Des Carmes," in Paris, was the gift of St. Louis, King of France, to six members of the Order, who accompanied him on his return from the Holy Land.

The Sixth General of the Order of the Latin Rite was St. Simon Stock, who, in 1251, dwelt in his monastery at Cambridge. In the chapel of this convent took place, on the 16th of July, 1251, the apparition of the Blessed Virgin to the saint, and here from her hands he received the miraculous scapular, now universally known as the brown scapular. In England the Fathers were called the White Friars, from the white cloak worn over the brown habit.

The first house of the Carmelite Order in North America was founded in Leavenworth, Kansas, in 1864, by two Bavarian Fathers, commissioned by the Superior General at Rome. In October, 1874, Archbishop Lynch, with holy persistency, succeeded in inducing the Order to establish a branch in his diocese. In a small house on a shaded bluff, overlooking Niagara Falls, three Fathers, in May, 1875, took up their residence, having at their head the Rev. Pius. R. Mayer, now Provincial Superior of the Order in North America. From this secluded retreat the Fathers from time to time emerged to give missions to the various parts of the Province with gratifying success. The humble and unpretentious monastery at the Falls is soon to be superseded by an imposing and costly structure in stone ; the wing of the new building intended for a monastery, hospic and home for aged priests, worn out in the service of God, is now in course of erection, and the entire building when completed will cost about $160,000. The institution will undoubtedly rank among the finest ecclesiastical buildings in America, in harmony with its sublime surroundings, and a splendid monument to the holy and inspired conception of the late Archbishop Lynch.

The present Superior or Prior, Very Rev. Anastasius Kreidt, is a man remarkable for his scholarly attainments, his religious zeal and indomitable energy. Trusting in the providence of God and in the generosity of the people, he began this great building, confronted with obstacles and difficulties that would have disheartened a lesse nergetic and enterprising man. Overcoming all discouragements he has succeeded beyond the expectations of his friends, and will undoubtedly carry his great work to a successful finish. This exceptionally talented and large-hearted priest established a few years ago the *Carmelite Review*, a well-edited monthly magazine, which has already reached a circulation of four thousand, and is slowly and steadily widening its circle of readers. The *Review* is the only Catholic periodical published in Ontario, and merits a generous encouragement.

CHAPTER XVIII.

DEAN MULLIGAN.

His Early Days—Ordination to the Priesthood—The Bishop's Letter—
Pastor of St. Catharines—His Zeal and Energy—A Priest's Life—
Mortality of the Priesthood—The Confessional—The Midnight Sum-
mons—Zeal for Temperance—The Total Abstinence Society—The
Poor Man's Friend—Patrick Marren—The New Churches—St. Vin-
cent de Paul Society—The Wasted Frame—The Dean Leaves for
Ireland—Death of Dean Mulligan.

> "Gentle was he, wise, pure, and lowly-hearted ;
>   Sober and modest, ever foe to strife ;
>   While in his frame there flowed as yet unparted
>   Currents of life."
>
> —Office of Confessor, Roman Breviary.

THE Reverend Patrick Mulligan was born in the
County of Longford, Ireland, in 1831. His
parents were respectable, well-to-do farmers, and
when their son was of an age to attend college they
sent him to the Seminary of All-Hallows. He was a
plodding, industrious boy, hardly equal in ability to
many in his class, but endowed with practical common-
sense, and a habit of conforming with strict regularity
to the severe rules of the institution.

When about to enter upon his second year's theology he came to Toronto, on the invitation of Bishop

DEAN MULLIGAN.

Charbonnel, and entering the Grand Seminary, Montreal, completed his theological studies, and was ordained to the priesthood, September 14th, 1856. Soon after his ordination he was commissioned to take charge of the Toronto Gore Mission, including the townships of King, Caledon, and Albion.

His next appointment was Niagara-on-the-Lake, and after a year or two of missionary work here, he was nominated parish priest of Niagara Falls, taking in Clifton, Chippewa, and the surrounding country. Here he labored for some years with commendable energy, built the church at Clifton, and was seriously thinking of erecting another at the Falls, when, one evening after returning from Clifton, he received the following letter :

"St. Michael's Palace,

"Toronto, Oct. 11th, 1866.

"My Dear Father Mulligan,—I have much pleasure in appointing you parish priest of St. Catharines. This important parish has been vacant since the death of the lamented Dean Grattan. You will make arrangements to be there a week from Sunday. I will take the earliest opportunity of visiting St. Catharines, when I will publicly appoint you Dean.

"I remain,

"My dear Father Mulligan,

"Yours in Christ,

"†John Joseph Lynch."

For ten years Father Mulligan had labored in scattered missions with fidelity and unobtrusive piety.

During these years the observant eyes of his bishop were upon him, and when one of the most important parishes of his vast diocese became vacant, he chose from among his priests the one whom he deemed most entitled to the honor.

When, in obedience to the wish of his Ordinary, he took charge of the parish of St. Catharines, the zealous priest was in the prime of his manhood. In fulfilment of his promise, the bishop visited the parish the following Sunday, when he publicly inducted Father Mulligan as pastor of St. Catharines and Dean of the Niagara peninsula. In his address to the congregation his Lordship spoke most approvingly of the dean's labors in the various parishes committed to his care; he feelingly referred to the unexpected death of Dean Grattan, and while he mourned with them in the great loss they had sustained, he, at the same time, congratulated them on the new appointment.

At the very threshold of his pastorate Dean Mulligan began a renewed life of intense energy and application. He entered upon a house to house visitation, became in a short time personally acquainted with his flock, and with unflagging zeal made provision for their spiritual needs. His parish at the time of which we write embraced Port Dalhousie, Smithville, Grimsby, Jordan and St. Catharines. Nothing but a herculean constitution could stand the wear and tear of such an extensive mission. His indefatigable devotion induced the dean to duplicate every Sunday, and undertake

ST. CATHARINES' CHURCH.

more than his strength could bear. The bishop noticed that his health was failing, and, on questioning him as to the cause, was startled when he learned of the hardships and the difficulties associated with his mission. At the earliest opportunity he sent him an assistant.

Here it may be permitted us to dwell for a while on the daily routine of a priest's life. Of the seventeen assistant priests who were here with Dean Mulligan from January, 1867, to July, 1884, ten are in their graves. When some American priests applied a few years ago to the insurance companies to insure their lives in favor of churches which they had built, and were at the time heavily in debt, the companies, before issuing policies, deemed it prudent to make enquiries as to the number of years Catholic priests in the United States lived after their ordination. Their actuaries made a report, based on a period of forty years, and the figures were startling. From this report it was shown that the average life of the priest after his ordination—say when twenty-four years of age—was fifteen years. And if it should be asked, " What is the cause of this alarming mortality? " we will not have to go far for the answer. When the young man enters the priesthood, after passing fourteen or fifteen years in college and seminary, he is scarcely fitted for the rough, hard work of missionary life. All aglow with fervor and zeal, his piety prompts him to undertake more than very often his strength warrants; or he is assigned as assistant to a large parish, where his labors are more than his young constitution can bear. After a year or two he is appointed to the charge of a scattered parish, where on Sundays he is compelled to rise early, hear confessions, say mass, and drive eight or nine miles to another church, where he again offers up the Holy Sacrifice, and, while he is still fasting, address his people.

If his parish, as is very often the case, be territorially large, he is compelled in the most trying seasons of the year—Lent and Advent—to give " Stations " in the remoter parts of his mission. Returning some afternoon from one of these Stations, he finds when he reaches home that perhaps a " sick-call " awaits him in another part of his parish. A call of this nature is imperative, and cannot be neglected under pain of mortal sin, whether it comes at night or day, in a pelting storm of rain or the severest frosts of winter. Nor can he excuse himself on the plea that the dying man is stricken with small-pox or diphtheria. The Catholic Church holds that the salvation of a soul counts for more than the life of a priest, and she commands, that under all circumstances where possible, the dying man must receive the sacraments. The young priest, scarcely giving himself time to snatch a morsel of food, leaves to attend the sick man, and returning that night he takes to his bed, and may never again rise from it. The already enfeebled constitution is not equal to the strain, and in a few days all is over.

Let us take another case. The newly-ordained priest is appointed by his bishop as assistant in a large city parish, where three priests are trying to do the work of six. The pastor is engaged in building or (what is perhaps more onerous) fighting a heavy debt on a church already built. The repeated calls upon his time as the responsible head of the parish, throw upon the shoulders of his assistants the visitation of the sick, and much of the labor which under more favorable circumstances would devolve on the parish priest.

For seven hours on Saturday the priests in large parishes are morally chained to the Confessional; and no one but a priest can conceive what this trying ordeal means. The following day brings severe work, and more severe responsibilities. The young curate must be on the altar at seven o'clock saying his mass, in which he administers Holy Communion to 150 or 200 people. After mass he drives to some Catholic institution and again offers up the Holy Sacrifice. In the afternoon he superintends the catechism classes, attends the meetings of religious societies, and in the evening is expected to deliver an excellent sermon.

He retires to bed at ten or eleven o'clock, anticipating a fair night's sleep, when at about one o'clock the door-bell rings. When he opens the door a man tells him that one of the parishioners has been taken suddenly ill, and wishes to see a priest immediately.

The messenger is unable to give any clear account as to the nature of the attack, the extent of the danger, or the opinion of the doctor—for no doctor has as yet been called in. The tired priest may hesitate for a moment, and be tempted to argue with himself that the case is not so urgent as to call for immediate attendance. Frequently before he had been summoned at night to attend the sick, and found that he might have remained in bed without any risk of serious consequences to the sick person or of conscientious remorse to himself. However, on a moment's reflection, he remembers that after a succession of some dozen or more of these cases, in which he might have put off the visit to a more convenient time, there was one instance in which he found the patient in his agony, and had barely time to administer extreme unction. So he goes to the church, takes the Blessed Sacrament from the tabernacle, the holy oils from the sacristy, and in the darkness of night walks the silent street till he arrives at the door of the sick man, only to find that the patient has no serious illness.

Nothing is so trying to the patience of city priests as this practice, which prevails among the poor, of summoning them at inconvenient hours without necessity, and of exaggerating the urgency of the case, in order to secure their attendance. Still, there can be no doubt that this anxiety for the presence of the priest at the side of the sick has its foundation in a deep sense of the importance of his ministrations in sickness and at the hour of death. It is also a recognition of the potency and efficacy of those sacraments, on the proper reception of which the salvation of a sinner may depend.

"The Catholic poor," writes Canon Oakely, "look upon the priest as Protestants do upon the physician; and as every reasonable and humane person would call in a physician where there is the slightest chance of illness being serious, even though, in fact, it be not so, I hope the time will never come when we shall pass a severe judgment on our poor for summoning the priest in twenty cases, of which nineteen may have been less urgent than their fears had led them to suppose."*

This continual wear and tear soon tells upon any but a rugged constitution, and if he lives till the age of 50, the priest is practically an old man. It is gratifying, however, to learn that vocations for the holy priesthood are increasing, and that in the division of labor which will follow, the priest will have a better chance for a long life. The dean had passed through the trying ordeal of his early priesthood, retaining an unimpaired constitution and cheerful spirits. After a personal and individual acquaintance with his parishioners, extending now over six years, he became convinced that if he could organize the men and establish a large temperance society, he would be accomplishing for them and for God a great and

* "The Priest on the Mission," p. 151.

meritorious work. He was accustomed to say that drunkenness, amongst Protestants and Catholics alike, "was a pickled rod with which the devil scourged the people;" so, to the eradication of this vice he now bent his energies. He measured the warmth and attachment of his people, young and old, to the traditions of the past—their love for Ireland and its national emblems.

After he had established his temperance society— named after St. Patrick—he imported suitable banners and badges and presented them to the association. In making the presentation he said : " There is a tragedy beneath them—in a melancholy and touching way they tell the latter-day history of Ireland :

> " Under the new skies
> They bring you memories of old village faces,
> Cabins, gone now, old well-sides, dear old places,
> And men who loved the cause that never dies."

He went from house to house enrolling men in the organization, and pleading, even with the total abstainer, to become a member, if only for the sake of example. As the society grew in numbers the condition of its exchequer suggested the establishment of a brass band. Instruments were purchased in New York, a bandmaster engaged, and in a few years it was the boast of the society that it had the best band in the peninsula. Gradually a change took place in the moral and material condition of the people ; the sacraments were frequented more regularly, and on Sundays the church was too small to hold the people. With his customary energy he resolved to enlarge the building, and in the spring of 1870, he called for tenders and let the contract for building the west wing, which cost $6,000.

The dean was an indefatigable collector, never sparing himself when working for his people. In all seasons of the year he went from house to house and man to man soliciting subscriptions for the new wing. Waving all feeling of humiliation, he boarded the boats as they passed through the canal, and as he was as well known as the captains, and respected by the sailors, irrespective of creed, he always received generous donations for the work in which he was engaged. In the meantime his temperance society continued to flourish ; men began to save their money, purchase lots and build houses thereon. Mortgages were lifted, bank accounts opened, and an air of order and prosperity was everywhere noticeable. The influence of the organization extended to the neighboring parishes, and at a joint parade held in St. Catharines, March 17th, 1873, over 1,200 men, bound by a pledge of temperance, walked in procession.

Bartoli, in his "Life of St. Francis Xavier," says that " one single man, full of spirit and vigor like Sampson or Daniel, is, in the army of God, equivalent to ten thousand others who are not thus qualified." This was noticeable in the case of the dean, and his influence not only among his own people, but among his Protestant fellow-citizens became a power for good that remains to this day. He was the Father Matthew of the peninsula, and as the generation that knew him passes away, the succeeding generation will hold his name in benediction and respect. There are in St. Catharines to-day several families who are indebted to Dean Mulligan, not only for the homes which they own, but also for the blessing of peaceful and happy lives. There are walking the streets of that city strong, healthy men, in prosperous circumstances, that to-day would be in their graves if it were not for his benign influence and priestly zeal. His untiring energy knew no rest; one after the other, he built the churches of Port Dalhousie, Jordan, St. Mary's on the Western Hill, St. Patrick's and St. Joseph's. He furnished his parish church with a wealth of vestments and sacred plate fit for a cathedral. In the large brick house on Welland Avenue, which he purchased for a presbytery, he expended several thousand dollars, contending that nothing was too good for the generous Catholics of St. Catharines.

While engaged in church building he received valuable assistance and encouragement from Protestants as well as Catholics. He, on more than one occasion, acknowledged himself indebted to one of his parishioners, Patrick Marren, for the deep interest he manifested in the temporal prosperity of the parish. Mr. Marren was a gentleman of a quiet

22

and unobtrusive nature, well educated and intensely devoted to his religion. He emigrated to Canada in 1837, and a few years subsequently settled in this part of the country. He took a prominent part on the side of peace and order, and the Government of the day, in recognition of his services, appointed him on the Commission of the Peace. In 1871 he was elected Mayor of St. Catharines by acclamation, being the first Catholic to occupy that office. He was for many years chairman of the Relief Committee of the Town Council, and was a man who in his day was greatly esteemed by rich and poor. He died in 1872, and in the resolution of condolence, passed by the Municipal Council of that year, we find the following expression of admiration embodied : " This Council feels that as by his urbane and kindly disposition during the long life, he so endeared himself to all as never to estrange a friend or create an enemy, so regret for his loss will be universal; yet among the poor, whose firm friend and constant supporter he ever was, will that regret be especially poignant."

We owe to the dean's zeal and enterprise St. Joseph's Convent, a monument to the generosity of the people and an ornament to the city itself. After the construction of the new Welland Canal the tide of prosperity which flowed in upon the city began to ebb, and when it subsided whole families were left destitute. The dean now began to publicly plead the cause of the poor; he became a beggar for their sake, and

> "With what he begged, his brethren he relieved,
> And gave the charities himself received."

He visited the poor in their houses, chatted with them on terms of intimate familiarity, and when he left a benediction accompanied his alms. For their relief he threw open the basement of the church, and organized a charitable society of ladies who, every Friday, doled out the provisions which the dean had collected. In addition, he established the St. Vincient de Paul Society, whose members visited the houses of the poor, and reported every Sunday the names of those requiring assistance. This society was bound by its rules to know no discrimination between Protestant and Catholic, but to relieve a fellow-creature whenever and wherever found, leaving the rest to God. In his intercourse with the poor the dean was courteous and friendly. What part he took in consoling them in their sorrow, in encouraging them in their depression, and still more,

> "That best portion of a good man's life—
> His little nameless, unremembered acts
> Of kindness and of love,"

none but the recording angel knows. He was always moving around among his beloved people, so that it was said of him, he carried his library and his office in his pocket. At length his splendid constitution began to weaken under an accumulation of work. The old elasticity and buoyancy were passing away, the shoulders were stooping, and the effacing fingers of decay were ridging his handsome face. Heedless of the warning of his medical adviser, he still continued to rise every morning at five o'clock, and the first one who went to the church for the early mass was sure to find the good priest walking up and down saying his daily office. At last he was compelled to rest, and yielding to the advice of his doctor, went to the seaside. Returning much improved in health, he began again his ceaseless rounds of charitable visitations, but the old vitality was gone; and he was frequently noticed returning home much earlier than in the past. The old spirit was indeed there, the undying zeal and affection for his people still consumed him; but the body was almost worn out. He was now compelled to remain in his room; his legs began to swell, and alarming symptoms manifested themselves. For weeks he was a recluse, and again his physician advised him to visit some watering-place, or, what was still better, take a sea voyage. Crawling to the church the following Sunday he, in a voice broken with emotion, bade his people an affectionate farewell, intimating that he hoped God would spare him to return and, if it were His holy will, die in their midst. The congregation was deeply moved, and the following day a representative delegation waited upon him, and, on behalf of his people, tendered him an address and a purse of $500.

On July 1st, 1884, he was driven to the *Persia*, where a large number of people were waiting to bid him good-bye. At one o'clock that afternoon the *Persia* cast off her lines, moved into the middle of the canal, and, amid the affectionate cheers of his people, the brave and large-hearted priest began his homeward voyage.

The dean never again returned. He lived for a few years after his arrival in Ireland, but never regained his strength ; and, at last, with his head pillowed on the breast of his aged mother, he yielded up his soul to God. He was in the thirty-fifth year of his priesthood, almost nineteen of which were given to the service of the people of St. Catharines. To him, if to any one, may be fittingly applied the words of the epistle in the mass for a confessor: "Behold a great priest, who in his days pleased God and was found righteous, and in the time of wrath he made a propitiation. The blessing of his people was upon him, and the mercy of the Lord encompassed him. He found grace before God, who exalted him among his people, and in the end gave him a crown of glory."

With him appropriately ends our history. We began with the opening of a Neutral grave on the shores of Lake Erie, and we finish with the closing of a grave on Irish soil, where rests the body of an exemplary priest and a faithful servant of God.

> "Green be the turf upon thee,
> Friend of my early days ;
> None knew thee but to love thee,
> Nor name thee but to praise."

APPENDICES.

APPENDIX A.

INDIAN SCOUTS AND TRAILERS.

As soon as the Neutral child began to understand something of his surroundings, he was taught to note and examine every mark on the ground. He was instructed how to walk when in an enemy's country, how to place his feet, and how under all circumstances, whether in peace or war, to hide his trail. Many who read the works of Cooper are inclined to look upon the wonderful feats of trailing recorded by the novelist as inventions of his imagination, or supernatural acts surpassing the possibility of man. A little reflection will convince us that the extraordinary alertness and sharpness of the Indian scout or trailer are simply the result of a lifetime of training and education.

The most remarkable feat of trailing that ever came to the writer's knowledge is from the statement of an eye-witness as to the finding of a lost child in the Holland Marsh, some seventy years ago. Major Gorham, who figured so prominently in the Rebellion of 1837, and who is still living in the vicinity of Buffalo, told the author the following extraordinary incident, of which he was an eye-witness: "A little girl, four years old, wandered away from her home in the village of Holland's Landing, and was not missed for several hours. Apparently no trace of her was left, and the distracted father asked his neighbors to assist in the search for her. Every man in the village turned out, and searched all that day without finding a single trace of the child.   At last it was suggested to ask the assistance of a band of Nipissing Indians, who were camped some miles away.

The Nipissings did not arrive until twenty-four hours after the child disappeared, and then the whole marsh had been so tramped that all hope of a trail was simply lost.   Two of the Indians bent to the work, encouraged by the hope of a liberal reward, and in three hours found the child unhurt, but trembling from fright and exposure. They went about their work in a systematic manner, and covered the ground so thoroughly, that they soon found the direction taken by the child.   Now began an ideal bit of Indian trailing.   Foot by foot they went over the ground, noting a broken twig here, a turned stone there, or a small impression in the damp earth.   Sometimes they would go for a mile without finding anything that would indicate they were on the right scent, and then would find the half-effaced impression of a little bare foot in a muddy spot.   The child was found eight miles from its home, and hid herself so carefully when the Indians approached that they were almost at fault when they were at the end of the trail, and were compelled to double-back several times before they espied her, crouching under a fallen tree."

The story of the man who described the lost camel so accurately that he came near being arrested as the thief, finds its parallel in the Apache country, where an Indian so accurately described a horse and rider that the soldiers who were after the thief took him prisoner, and would have held him but for the fact that he guided them to the real thief.   The horse had been stolen by a deserter, who was trying to make his way out of the country.   A squad of cavalry was sent after him, but missed the trail.   Meeting the Apache boy, they asked him if he had seen a man on a horse go by.   " Was the horse a sorrel, lame in the right hind leg, and ridden by a tall man who belonged to the army?" asked the boy.   Having been answered in the affirmative, he said he had not seen him.

This made the sergeant angry, and he ordered the arrest of the boy for killing the man and stealing the horse. The boy protested his innocence, and told how he knew that the horse was a sorrel and was lame. He showed where the horse had rubbed against a tree and left some sorrel hairs, and the tracks of the animal going over a damp spot indicated that the impression of the right hind foot was lighter than the others. He showed where the man had got down from the horse, making the mark of his army boot in the soil, and also where he had reached up and broken off the limb of a tree, at such a height that only a tall man could reach it. The soldiers were not convinced, and the boy offered to trail the horse, if they agreed to release him and pay him. This they agreed to do, and he led them to the deserter, who was compelled to rest on account of the lameness of the horse.

The Indian, who was a constant and close observer of natural things, became as proficient in the forest and on the plain in reading the signs of nature as did Sherlock Holmes in tracing criminals. To watch the trail he crossed was as instinctive as hiding his own. But it was not alone from the marks left on the ground that he followed the trail of man or beast. His knowledge of the country told him where the fugitive was bound to pass, if not too closely pursued; and instead of following an intricate trail over a wide expanse of country, he made directly for the place he believed the trail would cross a ridge or a pass.

"An expert trailer," writes Col. E. C. Edwards, one of the oldest of the Indian scouts, "can follow a trail where a hound would fail. The Indian hunts first for a sign, then another and another, until he starts the trail. To become a good trailer or scout, it is necessary to have keen eyes, a good knowledge of the country, and a thorough acquaintance with the habits of the animals or men you are trailing. In this branch of field-craft the white man is a failure. Even those captured when boys by Indians, no matter how thoroughly instructed, have never been able to equal their red companions in following a trail."

General Dodge, now in command of the Arizona troops, records the following story of his experience with Pedro Espinosa, the famous Mexican trailer : " I was once sent in pursuit of a party of murdering Comanches, who had been pursued and scattered and their trail abandoned by a party of so-called Texas rangers. On the eighth day after the scattering, Espinosa took the trail after a single shod horse. When we were fairly into the rough, rocky Guadalupe mountains, he stopped, dismounted, and picked up from the foot of a tree the four shoes of the horse ridden by the Indian. With a grim smile he handed them to me and informed me that the Indian intended to hide his trail. For six days we journeyed over the roughest mountains, turning and twisting in apparently the most objectless way, not a man in the whole command being able to discover, sometimes for hours, a single mark by which Espinosa might direct himself. At times I lost patience and demanded that he show me what he was following. '*Poco tiempo*' (in a short time), he would blandly answer, and in a longer or shorter time show me the clear-cut footprints of the horse in the soft banks of a mountain stream, or point with his long, wiping stick to other unmistakable 'signs.' Following the devious windings of this trail for nearly 150 miles, and only once or twice dismounting to examine more closely the ground, he finally brought me to where the Indians had reunited."

Reference is frequently made to the Cheyenne raid in Kansas. This occurred in 1878, and was not a raid in a true sense of the word. Wild Hog, one of the famous war chiefs of the Northern Cheyennes, led his band in an effort to break away from the Reservation in the Indian Territory, and get back to their old home in the north. One hundred and twenty men, with all their women and children, left Fort Reno and fought their way through one line of troops and evaded and outran two other lines. They travelled three hundred miles in ten days, but so expert was their chief that they left scarcely a mark to show where they went over the prairie. They marched in open order, covering a belt from three to eight miles wide, and made a trail so slight on the hard prairie, that the most expert trailers with the troops were unable to trace them. The fourth line of troops turned the Indians after a battle, in which Colonel Lewis was killed, and then Wild Hog turned towards Kansas to get fresh mounts. The raid was made, and the band fled to the sand hills, where they secreted themselves near pools known only to themselves. Among the trailers at the fort was a Pawnee Indian. He followed steadily after the fleeing band, and where the trail was lost he used his knowledge of landmarks, and never hesitated for a minute, but ran the band to earth, while all the white scouts gave up the task.

The extent to which the senses may be developed surpasses belief. The powers of hearing and seeing, which were cultivated and brought to such perfection by the Indians, prove that there are latent in man almost unknown quantities, which conditions and circumstances of life alone make known to him.

APPENDIX B.

THE JESUIT STONE.

The story of the attempted conversion of the Attiwandarons by the Jesuits has been told hundreds of times since the facts were first recorded in the " Relations des Jesuites," and it is impossible to add anything of archæological value pertaining to this historic episode, unless what may be contained in the following reference to the finding of "The Jesuit Stone" within a few miles of Toronto.

It will be remembered that when the Fathers Jean de Brebeuf and Joseph Marie Chaumonot were on their return from the Neutral country to their house in Huronia, their plight was a very sad one, indeed. Blocked by heavy snow, they were compelled to remain at the village of Teotongniaton, or St. William's, as they named it, where an Indian woman, probably of the Aondironnons (a clan of the Neutrals whose territory adjoined the Huron country), took pity upon them and gave them shelter for nearly a month. After leaving this haven, the journey to Ste. Marie occupied eight days. Mr. Coyne says the village of St. William's was "perhaps in the vicinity of Woodstock;" but there are reasons for supposing otherwise. The distance from Woodstock to Ste. Marie (near Midland), on Nottawa-saga Bay, is 120 miles in a straight line, and by trail must have been at least from one-fourth to one-third more, or from 150 to 160 miles in all, a distance which, if accomplished in eight days, would give an average of nearly twenty miles travel daily. This would be good travelling through the forest for even strong men in the most favorable circumstances, but this portion of the journey was made in the middle of March, when the frost was intense at times and the keen winds had the effect of speedily lowering a vitality which, in the case of these travellers, was not high to begin with. It must also be remembered that Father Brebeuf, having broken his shoulder-blade shortly after starting, continued to move only with great difficulty, having to rest frequently. In such a case less than half of twenty miles a day would be a fair rate of speed. The inference, therefore, is that St. William's could not have been in the vicinity of Woodstock.

Dr. Parkman does not appear to have placed Teotongniaton so far to the west when speaking of this event, for he says: "Bidding their generous hostess farewell, they journeyed *northward* through the melting snows of spring and reached Ste. Marie in safety." In refer-ence to this matter I am permitted to quote from a letter of General Clark to Mr. David Boyle:

"I believe that in the journey to the Neutrals, the return journey of Daillon, 1626; Brebeuf and Chaumonot, 1640-41; and of the parties sent for their relief, were all on the same trail. Brebeuf started from Ste. Marie on the Wye, travelled south-east 10 or 15 miles to Tean Austaye, or St. Joseph's, thence around the Bay

at Barrie, thence to Holland River, and portage to the east branch
of the Humber, and thence through the towns a few miles inland.
Going around the west end of Lake Ontario by any feasible route
to Niagara River would be a little over 150 miles. The 'Relations'
say it was five days' journey to Kandoucho, and thence four days'
journey to Niagara River. If the computation was made from Ste.
Marie, of which there is no doubt, it would make the town of
Kandoucho 83⅓ miles from Ste. Marie, and 66⅔ miles from Niagara,
locating on this theory the town not far from Brampton, in Peel
county. Teotongniaton was the next village south of Kandoucho,
and between Kandoucho and Ounontisaston. This estimate gives
16⅔ miles per day, or by allowance for circuitous parts of travel, say
20 miles per day. This was in 1640, and is substantially in accord
with the general estimates of a day's march of 8 to 10 leagues, or 20
to 25 miles on a fair trail.

"The return of Brebeuf and Chaumonot was in winter, when,
wounded and weary, 10 miles would be a large estimate. My
present knowledge of town sites indicates Lake Medad as the
probable site of St. William's. . . . I find no other trail mentioned in any early account, or any one indicated on any map. The
Toronto trail appears as the only one in that immediate neighborhood, and, consequently, that it was the one taken by Daillon and
Brebeuf."

From this it will be seen that while there is still some un-
certainty relative to the location of town sites, General Clark
substantially agrees with the estimate made regarding the rate of
travel, and distance to be travelled by the missionaries from their
wigwam asylum to Ste. Marie, as well as with the belief that the
trail was along the Humber. At any rate, Teotongniaton, wherever
it was, could not have been at a greater distance from Ste. Marie
than 80 or 90 miles. In the township of Vaughan, within a few
miles of the city of Toronto, there are well-marked traces of an
Indian village, and here a few years ago the owner of the land found

in his field a very symmetrically water-worn stone, flattened oval granite cobble, reminding one in form and size of a shoe-maker's lap-stone.   On one side of this stone is rudely cut the date, " 1641." The distance as the crow flies from this locality to Ste. Marie is less than 70 miles, to which, if we add from one-fourth to one-third, as in the former case, we get an average of about 11 miles per day for eight days— fully as much as we might expect weak and disabled men to travel "through the melting snows of spring," as Parkman puts it.   Regarding the genuineness of this find there is hardly a doubt, and as the Jesuits, Brebeuf and Chaumonot, were the only Europeans known to have been in this neighborhood in 1641, the relic in question has been called "The Jesuit Stone."   The chief reason, perhaps, for hesitation in accepting the stone, or rather the carving on it, as the work of the priests, is a negative one, and consists in the fact that there is no cross accompanying the figures.   With the well-known respect entertained by Catholics for this sacred symbol, we might very naturally look for something of the kind, if this date was cut to commemorate the residence of the missionaries in the wigwam of the Aondironnon woman, and their thankfulness for deliverance from what otherwise might have proved extreme privation, if not death itself to one or both of the priests.   On the other hand, the absence of the mark in question is equally a proof of genuineness, for it is almost inevitable that had anyone prepared the stone as a "plant," the work would have been thought incomplete without a cross.

We can scarcely conceive anything more natural than the two priests occupying a little of their enforced leisure in so commemorating the date of their return from a perilous undertaking.   They had travelled several hundreds of miles in all sorts of weather, their lives had many times been endangered, both *en route* and on account of Attiwandaron hostility ; but now all was about over, and they were nearing their home, such as it was.   Here by the Aondironnon fire-side, their recent experiences crowded on their memories—hunger, thirst, fatigue, sickness, filthiness of food, discomforts of all sorts, mockings, rebuffs, ridicule, threats of personal violence, and what, in their estimation, was worse than all, failure to accomplish the object of their mission, and this fruitless return to Ste. Marie.

Here was the first resting-place they had reached that could be regarded as either safe or reasonably comfortable since leaving Huronia the previous November. Their Attiwandaron hostess had provided them with such fare as their religious rules permitted them to partake of—coarse, unclean, and badly cooked, as it no doubt was—rents in their garments had been repaired, their moccasins mended, their frost-bitten members healed ; and they had actually compiled an Attiwandaron vocabulary for the use of others who might once more attempt the work they had been unable to accomplish. Of all men living, they must have felt thankful they had come safely through so much, and really done so much, although not all they intended.

We may surely suppose that on some occasion during their stay— perhaps on the very morning of their departure—they said, one to another, "Here is a very proper stone, let us carve upon it the number of this eventful year."

The reader may truly say, "·This is neither history nor archæology." Granted. But to the writer nothing bears an appearance of greater probability than that in some way the so-called "Jesuit Stone" is connected with the return of Brebeuf and Chaumonot from the country of the Neutrals to that of the Hurons in the spring of 1641.

APPENDIX C.

LA SALLE'S BLOCKHOUSE.

As there appears to be some confusion among local historians touching the number and class of buildings erected by La Salle, I insert the letters of Mr. James Bain, Librarian, Toronto, and Mr. Frank H. Severance, the historical writer, Buffalo :

"PUBLIC LIBRARY,

"TORONTO, *January 24th*, 1895.

"At the time La Salle left for the West there were two houses built, and a fort in contemplation—one house at Lewiston, one at Cayuga Creek, and the fort at the mouth of the river. All the party had been living at Lewiston until the *Griffon* was commenced, when they removed nearer their work, but it was evident that they always had some one at the lower end of the portage. The records say that Watteau was to remain at Niagara with La Salle's men, and the presumption would be that this would be Lewiston, where the older and larger house was, no doubt, and from whence they could do something towards building the fort at the mouth of the river. I can find no positive information as to exact house, but on La Salle's return on foot from Fort Crevecœur, '*they arrived at Niagara the 21st of April, 1680, on Easter Monday. Some of his men, who had wintered in a shanty above the Falls, met him, and communicated to him information of an irritating and annoying nature.*' I don't think that the few men left by La Salle would have split into two parties, so that the presumption is that Niagara and 'above the falls' are the same place, namely, Cayuga Creek. The extract is taken from the 'Relation Officielle de l'Enterprise de Cavelier de La Salle, de 1679 a 1681.'

"Yours faithfully,

"JAMES BAIN, Jr."

"OFFICE 'ILLUSTRATED BUFFALO EXPRESS,'

"BUFFALO, N.Y., *January 26th*, 1895.

"La Salle's Blockhouse.—The testimony which I find most explicit and to the point is this, from O. H. Marshall's 'The Niagara Frontier':

"'The name Niagara was sometimes applied by the early historians not only to the river but to a defensive work and group of Indian cabins which stood at or near the site of the present village of

Lewiston.   La Salle constructed at this point a cabin of palisades, to serve as a magazine or storehouse' ("Hist. Writings " of Orsamus H. Marshall, Albany, 1887, p. 285).   But 'The Marquis de Nouville .   .   fortified the tongue of land which lies between the lake and river and thus founded the present fort' (*i.e.*, Fort Niagara—" Marshall," p. 286).   La Salle, therefore, made two palisaded forts or blockhouses—the one at the point more of a fort than the other (La Salle planned it, La Motte caused it to be built); another at the foot of the portage, just south of Lewiston, more of a storehouse than a fort, yet strongly palisaded.   Of the second one, Marshall further says (p. 287): 'The French having, through the influence of Joncaire,. obtained the consent of the Senecas, rebuilt their storehouse at Lewiston in 1719-20.   It formed a blockhouse 40 feet long by 30 wide, enclosed with palisades, musket proof, and pierced with port holes.   .   .   .   This blockhouse must have soon fallen to decay, for we find Louis XV. proposing to rebuild it in 1727, but the project was abandoned next year.'   Authorities on this are 'Charlevoix' and the 'N.Y. Colonial Documents,' Vol. ix., p. 964.   I have these, also Hennepin and Margry, but have not had time to look up the matter in them.   Mr. Marshall, I believe, had access to much of Margry's material before it was published, and relied largely on it.

" I do not find that there was ever a palisaded fort or blockhouse on Cayuga Creek, where the *Griffon* was built.   Authority on this point, besides Hennepin, is found in the 'Archives of the Ministère de la Mariné,' in Paris, where are three maps of our region of date 1688, 1689 and 1699.   On the first, on the east bank of the river above the Falls, is the design of a cabin   .   .   .   with this inscription, 'Caban where the Sieur de La Salle built his first vessel.'   The other two maps call it ' chantier ' (stocks).   None of them call it fort or palisade, stockade or blockhouse.   Marshall says (following Hennepin): ' After La Salle's departure, Tonty and Hennepin returned to their duties at the shipyard.   Two bark cabins, including a chapel for the special use of Hennepin, were built with the aid of the Indians.'   In

23

order to lighten the vessel and get her up the river, 'the crew had been reduced by leaving Father Melithon and others at the stocks above the Falls.' If they did not rejoin the vessel farther up stream, they must have gone back to the fort at the mouth of the river. I know of nothing in the subsequent history of what is now known as the 'Shipyard of the *Griffon*,' to indicate that there were ever any fortification or palisade there.

"Sincerely yours,

"FRANK H. SEVERANCE."

APPENDIX D.

Colonel Macdonell, the Speaker of the House, entered the army at the commencement of the war as ensign, and was subsequently lieutenant in the 84th or Royal Highland Emigrant Regiment, serving three years and two months. He then exchanged into Butler's Rangers as captain, and in that corps served with great distinction five years and ten months. Upon the raising of the Royal Canadian Volunteer Regiment of Foot in 1796, the headquarters of which were at Fort George, he was appointed lieutenant-colonel, commanding the 2nd Battalion, and served as such six years and four months, until the regiment was disbanded at the Peace of Amiens in 1802. He was colonel commanding the Glengarry Militia, and lieutenant of that county. In 1807 he strongly urged upon Colonel (afterwards General Sir Isaac) Brock the advisability of the formation of a regiment from the Highland settlers in Glengarry, his proposals being approved by Brock in communications to the War Office, but not carried out until the outbreak of the war of 1812, when the Glengarry Light Infantry Regiment was raised, largely through the instrumentality of the Rev. Alexander Macdonell (afterwards Bishop of Upper Canada). This gallant soldier and gentleman, having served his country with singular disinterestedness, to the utter ruin of his private fortune, was at the close of his active life greatly reduced in circumstances, when family influence and his own former services secured for him the honorary position of paymaster of the 10th Royal Veteran Battalion, then stationed at Quebec, where he shortly afterwards died. Dr. Canniff, in his "Settlement of Upper Canada," quotes from a Quebec paper of the time an article which appeared at his death, of which the following is an extract :

"While yet an ensign in the 84th Regiment, he did not fail to distinguish himself by his bravery and good conduct, and on one singular and trying occasion he exhibited the greatest intrepidity and coolness. When advanced to a company in Butler's Rangers, the services required were of the most arduous kind. They were sent out as scouting parties, and employed in picking up intelligence and in harassing the settlements of the enemy. As their marches lay through pathless forests, they were frequently reduced to the greatest necessities. In the many expeditions and contests in which this regiment was engaged during the war, Captain Macdonell bore a distinguished part, but the great hardships which he had to surmount undermined a constitution naturally excellent, and entailed upon him consequences which embittered the remaining part of his life. He had been exceedingly infirm for many years, and perhaps the severe climate of Quebec was too much for his weak constitution. He was not thought dangerously ill till within a short time of his death, but his feeble constitution could not stand, and he expired on the 21st. For some time past his appearance was totally altered, insomuch that those who had not seen him for many years could not recognize a single feature of the swift and intrepid captain of the Rangers."

APPENDIX E.

Captain Hugh Macdonell—who, with his brother, Colonel John Macdonell, the Speaker, was one of the two members for Glengarry in this Parliament—began life during the Revolutionary war as ensign, and was subsequently lieutenant in the 2nd Battalion King's Royal

Regiment of New York, serving seven years. He subsequently served for six years in the Royal Canadian Volunteer Regiment of Foot, being senior captain in the 1st (Lower Canadian) Battalion, under Lieut.-Colonel the Baron de Longueil. He was lieut.-colonel of the Glengarry Militia Regiment, and was appointed to be the first Adjutant-General of Militia of the Province of Upper Canada, and was the founder of the Militia system. After leaving Canada he was appointed by H.R.H. the Duke of Kent, as Assistant Commissary-General at Gibraltar in 1805. In 1810 he was sent with Lord Cochrane, K.B., and Captain Harding, R.E., to Algiers to inspect and report upon La Colle, and in 1811, under the patronage of the Duke of Kent, was sent as Consul-General to Algiers, where he rendered most valuable service to the British Government. Lord Exmouth, in command of the fleet which bombarded Algiers, in order to procure his release from the hands of the infamous Dey of Algiers, having affected his purpose, publicly thanked Mr. Macdonell as follows: "I cannot deny myself the satisfaction of offering you my public thanks for the assistance I have received from your activity and intelligence in my late negotiations with the Regency of Algiers, and more especially for the manly firmness you have displayed throughout all the violence and embarrassments occasioned by the late discussions, of which it will afford me sincere pleasure to bear testimony to His Majesty's Ministers on my return to England." He continued as Consul-General to Algiers until 1820, when he was pensioned by the British Government. Colonel Playfair, in his work, "The Scourge of Christendom," states that "for many years Mr. Macdonell had rendered excellent service to the State. The Duke of Kent always entertained the highest opinion of his character and abilities, and maintained a constant personal correspondence with him." The Duke's secretary, Colonel Harvey, on Mr. Macdonell's death, wrote a highly eulogistic letter, declaring the gratification which his career had afforded to his Royal Highness, who reflected with pleasure upon being the first to bring him forward.

One of his daughters was a nun of the Order of the Sacred Heart, the others contracting distinguished marriages. His widow married the Duke of Talleyrand-Perigord. Of his sons, Sir Alexander Macdonell, K.C.B., who died in 1891, was a general in the army, and Colonel-Commandant of the P.C.O. Rifle Brigade, serving with great distinction in the Crimea, Indian Mutiny and elsewhere. His second son, His Excellency Sir Hugh Guiver Macdonell, C.B., K.C.M.G., is now British Minister Plenipotentiary to the King of Portugal, having served as Her Majesty's Minister to Denmark, Brazil and elsewhere.

APPENDIX F.

PARISH OF NIAGARA.

Niagara Peninsula.—1626, Father de la Roché Daillon, first missionary; 1640, Fathers Brebéuf and Chaumonot, Jesuit missionaries; 1669, Fathers Galineé and Dollier de Casson, Sulpician priests; 1678, Rev. Louis Hennepin, Franciscan priest.

Father	Le Dru ..	1794.
"	Burke ..	1796.
"	Desjardines	1800.
"	Campion	1826 to 1830.
"	Lalor	1830 to 1834.
"	Gordon	1834 to 1846.
"	Carroll ..	1846 to 1849.
"	Forbes ..	1849 to 1850.
"	Lynch	1850 to 1852.
"	Mousard	1852 to 1855.
"	Wardy ..	1856 to 1857.
"	Mulligan	1857 to 1860.
"	Griffa	1860 to 1861.

Father Hobin	..		1861 to 1868.
,, Sullivan		.,	1868 to 1869.
,, Kelly	..	..	1869 to 1871.
,, Laboreau			1871.
,, Bergin	..		1871 to 1875.
,, O'Reilly			1875 to 1876.
,, Kiernan			1876 to 1877.
,, Gallagher	..		1877 to 1878.
,, Murphy	..	..	1878 to 1879.
,, Harold	..	.	1879 to 1889.
,, Shanahan			1889 to 1890.
,, Harold	..		1890 to 1894.
,, Lynch			1895.

NAMES OF PRIESTS STATIONED AT ST. CATHARINES.

(Formed into a Parish in 1832.)

PASTORS.

Father Cullen	..	..	
,, Burke			} 1832 to 1840.
,, Cassidy	..	..	
,, Lee		..	1840 to 1842.
,, McDonagh			1843 to 1851.
Dean Grattan			1852 to 1865.
,, Mulligan	..		1865 to 1884.
,, Harris		..	1884.

ASSISTANTS.

Father Conway	— 1854, to — 1857.
,, Juhl ..	Sept., 1857, to Sept., 1858.
,, Michel	Dec., 1860, to Oct., 1861.
,, O'Connor	Oct., 1861, to Jan., 1862.
,, Laboreau	Feb., 1866, to Aug., 1866.

Father Morris	Sept., 1866, to April, 1867.
,, Lee ..	May, 1867, to June, 1867.
,, McCann	Aug., 1867, to Nov., 1867.
,, Goddard ..	Sept., 1867, to Jan., 1868.
,, Cassidy ..	June, 1869, to June, 1871.
,, Bergin :.	June, 1871, to April, 1872.
,, Hobin	April, 1872, to Dec., 1882.
,, O'Reilly	Feb., 1877, to April, 1880.
,, Cody	Feb., 1877, to April, 1877.
,, Sheridan ..	April, 1877, to Sept., 1877.
,, Gallagher	Sept., 1877, to April, 1878.
,, E. Kiernan ..	April, 1878, to Oct., 1878.
,, McMahon	Oct., 1878, to Nov., 1878.
,, Power	Dec., 1878, to Nov., 1885.
,, Gavin	Jan., 1881, to Aug., 1882.
,, Fell ..	Aug., 1882, to Jan., 1883.
,, Hayden ..	Jan., 1883, to Sept., 1884.
,, Shanahan	Nov., 1885, to April, 1888.
,, O'Hagerty	Nov., 1885, to Nov., 1886.
,, McPhillips ..	April, 1887, to April, 1888.
,, Smyth	April, 1888, to Nov., 1894.
,, O'Malley	Nov., 1894.

PARISH OF NIAGARA FALLS.

Erected into a separate parish 1858. Since then has been served successively by Fathers Juhl, Mulligan, O'Connor, Michel, McSpiritt, and the priests of the Carmelite Order.

PARISH OF FORT ERIE.

This parish was attended from Niagara Falls till 1868, when the Rev. G. A. Voisard was appointed parish priest. It was intermittingly attended by various priests until February 1st, 1891, when the Rev. James Trayling was appointed pastor, who a few years ago was succeeded by the present incumbent, the Rev. Father McColl.

PARISH OF PORT COLBORNE.
(Erected into a Parish, 1859.)

Father Voisard	.. .. ..	1859 to 1865.
„ Keane		1865 to 1868.
„ Voisard		1868 to 1871.
„ Kilcullen		1871 to 1890.
„ McEntee		1890 to 1895.
„ Trayling		1895.

PARISH OF SMITHVILLE.

Constituted a parish in 1866. This parish has been attended since its erection by Fathers Laboreau, Beausang, McMahon, Skelly, Davis, McRae, and Lafontaine.

PARISH OF MERRITTON.

Established in 1883. Beginning that year with the Rev. A. P. Finan, it has had in succession Fathers Allain, Shanahan, McColl, Lynett, and Smyth.

PARISH OF THOROLD.

Erected into a parish 1860, with Rev. Eugene O'Keefe as pastor, who was followed in succession by Fathers Christie, Wardy, Griffin, Michael O'Reilly and Laboreau, who remained until November, 1871, when he was succeeded by Rev. T. J. Sullivan, the present pastor.

PARISH OF ST. MARY'S, ST. CATHARINES.

Formed with Port Dalhousie and Jordan into a separate mission in 1885, having for its first pastor Father McGinley, who was succeed by Rev. Charles O'Hagerty. In 1890 the present incumbent, Rev. L. A. H. Allain, was appointed pastor, and since then has labored with characteristic energy and zeal on behalf of his warm-hearted people. Father Allain was raised to the priesthood September 21st, 1878, in his native city of Chatham, N.B. Soon after his ordination, he happily identified himself with the Diocese of Toronto, and for sixteen years has faithfully and efficiently discharged his sacred duties with honor to himself and great spiritual benefit to the different parishes with which he was associated.